Childhood in a Global Perspective

For David Lawrence McKuur 1960–2006

Childhood in a Global Perspective

KAREN WELLS

polity

The right of Karen Wells to be identified as Author of this Work has been asserted in accordance with the UK Copyright, Designs and Patents Act 1988.

First published in 2009 by Polity Press

Polity Press
65 Bridge Street
Cambridge CB2 1UR, UK

Polity Press
350 Main Street
Malden, MA 02148, USA

ISBN-13: 978-0-7456-3836-2 (hb)
ISBN-13: 978-0-7456-3837-9 (pb)

A catalogue record for this book is available from the British Library.

Typeset in 11.25 / 13pt Dante
by Servis Filmsetting Ltd, Stockport, Cheshire
Printed and bound in Great Britain by
MPG Books Group, UK

The publisher has used its best endeavours to ensure that the URLs for external websites referred to in this book are correct and active at the time of going to press. However, the publisher has no responsibility for the websites and can make no guarantee that a site will remain live or that the content is or will remain appropriate.

Every effort has been made to trace all copyright holders, but if any have been inadvertently overlooked the publishers will be pleased to include any necessary credits in any subsequent reprint or edition.

For further information on Polity, visit our website: www.politybooks.com

Cover images: All images from iStock.com except where indicated. Top row left to right: © Anna Yu; © Peeter Viisimaa; © Elena Kouptsova-Vasic; © Thefinalmiracle@Dreamstime.com; © Rypson@Dreamstime.com; © Pathathai Chungyam. 2nd row left to right: © Gina Smith; © Cliff Parnell; © Andrey Shadrin; © Robert Churchill; © poco_BW; © Pathathai Chungyam. 3rd row left to right: © Daniel Rodriguez; © Rhoberazzi; © SZE FEI WONG; © poco_BW; © Roman Goncharov; Tomasz Markowski. Bottom row left to right: © Editor's own; © Raido Väljamaa; © Igor Balasanov; © Marek Walica; © Duncan Walker; © Aman Khan

Contents

1

Childhood in a global context

Introduction

This book is about children and childhood in a global context. In it I connect children's experiences to concepts of childhood, drawing on research about children's lives across the globe. I show how concepts of childhood shape children's lives and how children, in turn, shape concepts of childhood. These concepts or ideas about what children should and should not do, of where children are safe and where they are at risk, and of where childhood begins and where it ends have been the central theme of the new social studies of childhood (Jenks 1996; Prout and James 1990; James, Jenks and Prout 1998). These studies have been important in advancing our understanding of how childhood is shaped by cultural and social practices and processes. However, with one or two exceptions, existing studies have focused on national contexts and have been dominated by accounts of North American and European childhoods. In an increasingly globalized world, a focus on national contexts has to be supplemented by an understanding of how local practices are impacted on by global processes and that *where* people live affects *how* they live. It is the task of this book to show that where children live affects what kinds of childhood they have and to explore how global processes and structures – especially the increasing influence of international law and international NGOs are reshaping childhood.

Is there a global form of childhood?

Childhood is socially constructed

The new social studies of childhood, whether from a historical, spatial or social perspective, have established that children's lives are shaped by the social and cultural expectations adults and their peers have of them in different times and places; what concept of childhood prevails in any specific

1

time or place is shaped by many factors external to a child. Even in a particular time and place, say the Southern states of America after the Civil War ended in 1865, what it meant to be a child depended, as it does now, on the complicated intersection of age with 'race', gender and class. Childhood is socially constructed, and children's lives are profoundly shaped by constructions of childhood – whether in conformity, resistance or reinvention. This is not to say of course that, if we could take a particular society and identify its model of childhood, all children's lives will measure up to what the model prescribes as a proper childhood.

Childhood has universal characteristics

Although childhood is socially constructed and therefore profoundly different expectations can be had of children depending on the society and culture of any specific time or place, childhood also has universal features because all children, by virtue of their immaturity, have similar needs and limitations. Infants are dependent on others for their physical care: for food, shelter, hygiene and safety. An abandoned infant cannot survive for very long. Children also need emotional attachment and, as with their physical care, how and who forms emotional bonds with the young child can be subject to a great deal of variation but the forming of strong emotional attachments to close caregivers is apparently a universal feature of human society. Of course the need for emotional attachment does not end with the end of childhood, but secure attachment seems to be very important, cross-culturally, for the child's wellbeing. If the infant's biological immaturity makes him dependent on others for his physical care, the child can also be considered as socially and culturally immature. Children may not be born as blank slates, but teaching young humans the whole range of cultural practices from how to eat their food to living ethically or morally is a shared concern of all human societies.

This is a material fact that places limits on how plastic or constructed early childhood can be. Nonetheless the limits that the infant's dependency places on the plasticity of childhood can be very broad. Europeans, for example, tend to think of the newborn child as being a 'tabula rasa'; sometimes the idea of the child as a blank slate might extend back to the unborn child's experiences, but in any case it is the child's sensory awareness (whether before or after she is born) that is the beginning of making marks on the blank slate of the child. This view contrasts very sharply with the widespread view in sub-Saharan Africa that infants remember the world they came from and indeed that, to stay in this world or even in a way to become human, they have to forget this other life (Gottlieb 2004). Similarly, the infant has to be fed, but who feeds the infant will vary from culture to culture. In eighteenth-century Europe wet-nursing was a widespread and acceptable practice, but changing ideas about what the baby ingested with her mother's milk made the practice less acceptable. In Gottlieb's study any lactating woman may feed the child and the child will only be passed back to her mother if she refuses other women's milk.

Childhood is governed by international institutions and international law

A good deal of what is expected of children's primary caregivers and other individuals or institutions that also have responsibility for the child is codified in customary, religious or national law or ritual. In Islamic law, for example, the child is the responsibility of their mother until the age of seven when they become the responsibility of their father. In Jewish law the boy child should be circumcised on the eighth day after his birth. National laws about children are concerned with establishing full entry into adulthood, which is generally preceded by the acquisition of responsibilities or rights (e.g. criminal liability; sexual consent; hours and places of work; compulsory schooling) at different ages. Increasingly the Convention on the Rights of the Child is being incorporated into national law, changing the legal definitions of childhood as well as establishing in law rights and responsibilities that may be at odds with socially or culturally prevalent models of childhood. In tandem with the CRC, international agencies translate international law into local practice.

Childhood is shaped by both the local and the global

In one sense then history and social studies suggest that there cannot be a global form of childhood; on the other hand children and therefore childhood do have universal characteristics. Additionally, there is a presumption that it is the responsibility of adults to care for children, in culturally sanctioned ways. Finally, there is now a body of law and a group of international actors – intergovernmental, non-governmental and private – that is based on the presumption that childhood can be governed at a global level. One way of resolving the question of whether there can be a global form of childhood is by thinking of the global level, including international law and international actors but also global media, economic flows, war and politics, as a structure that shapes childhood at the local level. Thought of in this way the global becomes one of several structures – others would include the family, school and work – that shape the lives of children and concepts of childhood in any specific socio-cultural setting.

The organization of the book

The aim of this book is to examine this intersection between the local and the global by exploring how global processes and structures shape childhood in different domains of children's lives and how in turn children have actively tried, and sometimes succeeded, in remaking ideas about childhood. This book is structured around the argument that a particular model of childhood, one that originates in contemporary Western ideas about what it means to be human and what differentiates children from adults, is being globalized through international instruments. This model of childhood constructs healthy childhood as one that orientates the child towards independence rather than interdependence, towards school-based rather than work-based learning, and separates them from the wider forces of politics, economy and society. I call this model of childhood the 'neo-liberal model' because of the compatibility between liberal ideas that value independence, rational choice and autonomy, and the concept of childhood inscribed in this model.

In the rest of this chapter I introduce the models that are being used to theorize the experience of children and the concept of childhood in the broad field of social studies. I then summarize the key international legal instruments that are central to how dominant ideas about childhood get circulated globally. In the final section I explore how the insistence of social studies that children's lives and concepts of childhood are practised in different ways in different times and spaces can be reconciled with the attempts of international law and NGOs to produce a universal child.

The new social studies of childhood

The new social studies of childhood are a catch-all term for research from different disciplines in the social sciences and humanities that has put children and childhood at the centre of its concerns. These new social studies are united by their interest in children's social agency, and their recognition that children are active participants in society and not passive subjects of social processes. In the following sections I discuss the most important contributions to the new social studies of childhood in three disciplines: history, geography and sociology. I have framed the discussion around the topic of 'What is a child?' This may seem like a very simple question, but where societies set the boundaries of the beginning and end of childhood, how children are raised, and what children themselves think about their place in society, are complex questions that have been answered in many different ways in different times and places shaped by wider changes in society. This chapter looks at what studies in history, sociology and geography have contributed to our understanding of how the question 'What is a child?' has been answered by societies, historically and in the contemporary world.

History of childhood

In 1960 Philippe Aries published his seminal study *L'Enfant et la vie familiale sous l'ancien régime*. This book, first published in English in 1962 as *Centuries of Childhood: a Social History of Family Life*, has been the reference point for the debate on whether the concept of childhood is an invention of the modern period. Aries' argument was essentially that as soon as children left the dependent state of early childhood there was no concept of children as a separate category of people requiring special or distinctive treatment from adults. Children in the Middle Ages in Europe, he argues, were treated like small adults and were immersed in all aspects of social and working life and were not accorded any special protection, rights or responsibilities. Aries' work has been staunchly criticized by historians for the inferences that he drew from his sources (Pollock 1983). Those sources, mostly analysis of images of children in medieval portraiture, depicted children as small versions of adults. In these pictures, Aries claims, children are invariably wearing the same clothes as adults, without any of the stylized features – chubbiness, large eyes, body–head ratios, smiling faces, small hands – that later artists used to depict children as different kinds of people from adults. Aries infers from this difference in how children are depicted that in the earlier period there was no such thing as childhood.

Historians have taken issue both with the limited sources that Aries relies on and the inferences that he draws from these sources (Vann 1982). Portraiture was expensive and the people who commissioned portraits of their families or themselves were a small elite whose attitudes to childhood and, for the children, experience of childhood were likely to be very different from that of the general population. Portraits are also highly stylized and use special conventions, so that how children are portrayed in these paintings cannot necessarily be taken as an indication of their experience of everyday life.

Despite the lively debate about Aries' work the central contention of *Centuries of Childhood* that the attitudes, sensibilities and experiences that we now think of as immanent to childhood are an invention of the modern period is widely accepted by historians and social scientists. In their introduction to the important collection of papers on historical research into American childhood, Hawes and Hiner comment that 'Aries has been justly criticised for his selective and sometimes uncritical use of evidence, but no one has successfully challenged his essential point that childhood is not an immutable stage of life, free from the influence of historical change' (Hawes and Hiner 1985: 3). Since Aries a steady flow of historical accounts of childhood has been produced in North America and Europe, and there has been renewed interest in the history of childhood by historians of Africa, Asia and Latin America. It is these regional studies that I will now discuss.

Historical studies of American childhood

Although Aries' *Centuries of Childhood* was first published in English in 1962, it was not for another twenty years that the history of childhood became a major theme of historical studies of American society. Despite the relative paucity of historical work on childhood in the 1960s and 1970s some key texts were published including Robert Bremmer's three-volume collection of sources, *Children and Youth in America* (1971), and Joseph F. Kett's *Rites of Passage: Adolescence in America, 1790 to the present* (1977). Since the mid 1980s the new interest in children's studies across the social sciences and the humanities has stimulated the publication of books exploring the experience of childhood at different points in history, as well as the experiences of groups of children. Joseph Hawes and Ray Hiner published their edited collection on the history of American childhood in 1985. This collection is an invaluable source that brings together in one volume chapters that review the historiography of childhood and provide an outline of the conditions of childhood in colonial North America and the United States from the seventeenth through to the third quarter of the twentieth century. Taken together the chapters in this book tell a now familiar story in which children's lives become less harsh, more sheltered and possibly more cherished as the centuries unfold. However, this picture is complicated by the acknowledgement of how race, class, gender and geography impacted on children's lives and on expectations of childhood held by both children and adults.

A decade after the publication of *American Childhood* Hawes and Hiner edited the Twayne's History of American Childhood series, which has published books on child-rearing in the period from the Revolution to the Civil War (Reinier 1996), on how the Civil War and industrialization shaped the experience of childhood (Clement 1997), on the impact of Progressive Era reforms on children (Macleod 1998), and on how children experienced the interwar years (Hawes 1997).

Reinier uses archival sources to trace what she argues is a shift in child-rearing from authoritarian, patriarchal discipline to the management and guidance of 'malleable' children. This shift in ideals of child-rearing was uneven in its impact, and Reinier shows that poor and enslaved children's labour provided the capital accumulation on which middle-class children's education and consumption depended. Clement's study also picks up this theme of the differentiation of childhood. Her main argument is that industrialization and civil war sharpened differences between the experience of working-class and middle-class children and between African American and European American children. Macleod's study continues the chronology of American childhood, covering the period 1890–1920. Macleod's claim is that the hardening of class differences in experiences of childhood did not diminish in the Progressive Reform era. Indeed he contends that the ideal of a protected childhood stigmatized parents who were unable to protect their children as well as those children who resisted increased protection because it diminished their freedom. Hawes's study of the interwar years is good on the role that the new sciences of childhood played in the formation of our idea of modern childhood. Sallee's *The Whiteness of Child Labor Reform in the New South* (2004) also points to how the emerging concept of protected childhood was used to deepen racialized exclusion in campaigns that mobilized support for the abolition of child labour around the idea that it undermined white power and childhood for white children to be working.

The unevenness of the shift to protected or sheltered childhoods draws attention to the need for multiple histories that describe and illuminate how the experience of childhood has been shaped by race, class, gender and region. There is a small body of work on the history of African American, immigrant and working-class childhoods, as well as references to their experiences in general histories. Wilma King's *African American Childhoods* (2005) is a useful collection of essays on different aspects of African American childhood from slavery through to the civil rights era. It explores different aspects of children's lives in this period including slavery, education and violence. Many of the chapters focus on minority experiences of African American childhood – there are chapters on African American slave-owners and on African American families categorized as Native American for school attendance. While this is very interesting there is yet to be a comprehensive history of the experience of the majority of African American children in any era of American history. Steven Mintz has a chapter in his *Huck's Raft* on growing up in bondage. In *Growing up Jim Crow: How Black and White Southern Children Learned Race* Jennifer Ritterhouse (2006) examines how the determination of most white adults to maintain racial inequality after the Civil War shaped the childhood experiences and sensibilities of black and white children.

Ritterhouse's book makes extensive use of archival interviews and biographies of adults looking back on their childhood. This illustrates some of the problems with constructing histories of childhood: children leave few written records, and those that do tend to be children of elite groups. Despite the limitations of the sources and the focus on relations between black and white children, *Growing up Jim Crow* rounds out the experience of African American childhood after emancipation. A growing literature on children's involvement in the desegregation of schools and civil rights movement has also added to our understanding of childhood and the agency that children bring to bear on their lives in very difficult circumstances (King 2005: 155–68; de Schweinitz 2004).

Latin American childhood

In his introduction to *Minor Omissions*, an edited collection of essays on the history of Latin American childhood spanning the seventeenth to the twentieth century, Tobias Hecht cites del Priore's *Historia das criancas no Brasil* (1999) as 'the most ambitious – and successful – attempt to deal with children as part of a national history in Latin America' (2002: 9). Other than del Priore's volume, which is only available in Portuguese, the history of Latin American childhood is less developed than that of North American childhoods (Hecht 1999: 3; Kuznesof 2005: 859). The central focus of Latin American history has been on family structures, with Freyre's 1933 (1963) account of family life on a sixteenth-century Brazilian sugar plantation remaining a keystone of the literature. His 'vivid portrait made it clear the Portuguese family was the dominant institution in Brazil for colonization, government, education, maintenance of order and economic investment' (Kuznesof 2005: 862). The North American history of childhood forms part of a narrative of general progress and improvement, tempered by increased differentiation by 'race' and class of children's experiences. This is not the case for Latin American history where the themes that preoccupy historians of childhood continue to be the focus of the contemporary sociology of Latin American childhood. *Minor Omissions*, for example, has chapters on abandoned children and the structure of the family, criminal children, children and urban disorder, the child-saving movement, the impact of war on children, the practice of informal fostering, or 'child-circulation', amongst poor families, and street children. Each of these, especially street children (Guy 2002), child-circulation, family structure, and conflict (Peterson and Read 2002), remain core themes of the Latin American sociology of childhood.

Histories of African childhood

What we know of children's experiences and society's concepts of childhood in the history of Africa is very limited. In *The Encyclopedia of Children and Childhood: In History and Society* (Fass 2003) there is only one entry on the continent, the entry for South Africa. There are no general surveys that form part of a coherent narrative of children's worlds in Africa as there is for North American and European history. With the exception of *East African Childhood: Three Versions* (Fox 1967), there are no readily available sources that attempt to recover the voice of the African child. The contributors to *East African Childhood* give a vivid picture of early childhood in colonial East Africa. The emphasis here is on the child's feelings about the child's world and, although they are written by adults in a rather stylized narrative, this is an invaluable collection of memoirs. More recently the biography of his boyhood in turn-of-the-century Ghana by the Asante social scientist T. E. Kyei (2001) has made an important contribution to our understanding of colonial African childhood. These memoirs, and other more literary memoirs by both African and European adults remembering their African childhoods, aside, most of the rather small historiography of African childhood is focused on child labour.

The emerging literature on African child labour (Swai 1979; Chirwa 1993; Hansen 1990) shows how important African child labour was to the processes of capital accumulation for white farmers and the (colonial) state in East and Southern Africa. Beverley Grier's 2006 *Invisible Hands: Child Labor and the State in Colonial Zimbabwe* is the first book-length study of the history of child labour in an African country. Grier's seminal contribution to the historiography of African childhood shows how African children 'struggled to shape the circumstances of their own lives and . . ., in the process, helped to shape the history of the colony' (2006: 2).

An organizing theme of Grier's book is that childhood in Zimbabwe was a racialized concept that meant that the lives of black children and white children and expectations placed on them by the colonial state, white farmers, and their families were entirely shaped by racist ideology. In the areas of significant white settlement childhood was 'racially based, with the childhood of settlers being organized in radically different ways from the childhood of Africans' (Grier 2006: 18). This theme is also at the heart of

Owen White's study of the children of African–European parents, *Children of the French Empire: Miscegenation and Colonial Society in French West Africa 1895–1960*. This is also one of the few histories of African childhood that does not take either school or work as its main focus (although it discusses both). It explores instead how the French state responded to African–European children or what they called ' the Métis problem' through strategies of separating in school, work and family métissage children from both African and European populations. Surprisingly, given the obsession during Apartheid rule with establishing degrees of Europeanness/Africanness, there is no comparable history for South Africa.

The meaning of childhood and children's experiences are inseparable from the ways that colonial rule was established over African territory. The colonial state and white settler capital utilized '[t]he belief that children should contribute to the material reproduction of their households [which] was a core aspect of the construction of childhood among the Shona and Ndebele people' (Grier 2006: 29) at the end of the nineteenth century. This belief has to be situated in a context of labour-intensive agricultural production which meant that all household members had to contribute their labour to the maintenance of the household. Children were no exception, and whilst boys and girls mostly took on different tasks, all children had to work. Colonization changed the organization of agricultural production and with it African concepts of childhood, particularly in relation to work and school (Grier 2006: 33–68). Ironically, as Africans started to seek out school education for their children in the belief that this might erode the material and status differences between themselves and the white settlers, the colonial state banned white children from work and made school compulsory for them but not for African children.

European childhood
Comprehensive surveys of European childhood can be found in Colin Heywood's (2001) *A History of Childhood: Children and Childhood in the West from Medieval to Modern Times*, Linda Pollock's (1983) *Forgotten Children* and Hugh Cunningham's (1995) *Children and Childhood in Western Society Since 1500*. Cunningham's interest is in what he describes as middle-class childhood and the ways that this particular concept of childhood was generalized to the wider, working-class populations of industrial Europe. From about 1750 Cunningham argues that there was a great increase in state intervention in children's lives, beginning with the gradual regulation of child labour in the nineteenth century and the introduction of compulsory schooling making school a common experience of childhood by the end of

the nineteenth century. Heywood's book uses a wide range of historical sources about children's lives in North America and Europe and contends that childhood (or the 'concept of childhood') is not a modern invention but that what people expect of children ('conceptions of childhood') has changed in response to wider changes in society, especially in the shift from agricultural to industrial economies. Heywood refutes the view, advanced most famously by de Mause (1988), that parents were abusive or neglectful of their children in the past. He argues that parental practices such as swaddling that might seem, from a contemporary viewpoint, abusive were motivated by care and concern. Linda Pollock's *Forgotten Children* also finds evidence from diary sources that a concept of childhood is not a modern invention and that harsh treatment of children was not normative in the four centuries of her study (from 1500 to 1900).

These histories of European childhood are much more circumspect than the North American histories about a general narrative of progress. Heywood charts the fall in child mortality and the improvements in children's health, the expansion of schooling and increases in state intervention, but stresses the persistence of inequalities between classes, regions and ethnic groups so as 'to avoid an air of triumphalism' (Heywood 2001: 145).

Histories of Asian childhood
Presenting a coherent historiography of childhood for Asia is more difficult than for the Americas or Europe and Africa because of the extraordinary diversity of this region. I have decided therefore to focus on China, both because of its demographic and spatial predominance in Asia, and its economic significance in the international political economy. The historiography of childhood in China has a wealth of written texts, mostly of course from elites, to draw on literally over centuries. Little of this is available, however, either synthesized or translated into English. Jon Saari's (1990) *Legacies of Childhood: Growing up Chinese in a Time of Crisis, 1890–1920* is a study of how Chinese concepts of becoming human inflected concepts of childhood and attitudes towards children and parenting practices. He weaves Chinese ideas about becoming human together with a history of the lives of privileged young men in turn-of-the-century China. A much broader picture of Chinese childhood is to be found in Ping-Chen Hsiung's *A Tender Voyage* (2005). Hsiung draws on twelfth-century sources to show that paediatric health care was well developed in China from a very early period and locates this as an indicator of the high cultural value attached to children. In an apparent, and rather surprising, echo of a Western binary between Romantic and Puritan concepts of childhood, Hsiung identifies

within the Confucian tradition a neo-Confucian model that emphasized control, discipline and punishment and the Wang-ming school of awakening the child through education and self-reflection.

Histories of childhood: an overview
I began this section on the history of childhood with a brief discussion of Aries' contention that childhood is a modern invention. My reviews of the historiography of childhood in four continents show that this claim is clearly wrong. In each of these diverse regions societies recognized childhood as a distinct phase in the life cycle, and children as different kinds of people to adults. A historical narrative of general improvement in children's lives secured through a combination of state intervention, philanthropic concern and economic growth is evident in North America and, less decisively, in Europe. In both these regions, however, this story of progress went hand-in-hand with an increased differentiation of children's lives by class, ethnicity and region. In Africa and Latin America there is no comparable narrative about the constant improvement of children's lives and increasingly benign experience of childhood. The differentiation of childhood experience evident in North American and European histories is deeper, and a protected, nurturing childhood has been available only to a minority of elite and white settler children. In the absence of a narrative of progress there is considerable continuity between the history of childhood in these two regions and the sociology of African and Asian childhood, small though that literature is. In both history and sociology we find a preoccupation with children's social problems – in particular in relation to work and family life.

Sociology of childhood

The influence of Aries' *Centuries of Childhood* was not only felt in the historiography of childhood, it also provoked a rethinking of the concept of childhood in sociology (Prout and James 1990; James et al. 1998; James and James 2004: 13). Aries' thesis was the starting point for establishing childhood as a social construction formed by 'the complex interweaving of social structures, political and economic institutions, beliefs, cultural mores, laws, policies and the everyday actions of both adults and children' (James and James 2004: 13).

The new sociology of childhood generally situates its starting point as the publication of Prout and James' 1990 edited collection *Constructing and Reconstructing Childhood: Contemporary Issues in the Sociology of Childhood* and the subsequent publication with Chris Jenks of *Theorising Childhood* (1998).

Their work was prefigured by Jenks' much earlier edited reader of key texts on the *Sociology of Childhood* (1982) and his later *Childhood* (1996).

It is interesting to note that few of the contemporary texts on the sociology of childhood refer to an earlier development of a new sociology of childhood (to which Aries' book was one contribution). Holloway and Valentine, for example, note that 'the new social studies of childhood claim an epistemological break from previous sociological work, in that they study children as social actors, as beings in their own right rather than as pre-adult becomings' (2000: 5). They cite, in support of this contention, the work of Brannen and O'Brien on children and families (1996), James et al. 1998, Qvortrup et al. 1994 and Waksler's 1991 reader on the sociology of childhood. However, there is another body of work of the late 1970s, which in many ways was more explicitly politically engaged than the sociology of childhood of the 1990s. This earlier body of work was concerned with restoring to children an agency and parity with adults that the authors claimed had characterized the lives of young humans in the medieval period in Europe. It was informed by a concept of child liberation self-consciously fashioned on the model of (second wave) feminism or women's and gay liberation that flourished in Europe and North America in the late 1960s. Influenced by the work of Foucault on the invention of sexuality (1978 (1990)), it argued that children had a right to sexual expression that was repressed by the concept of childhood as a state of innocence and vulnerability. Foucault's radio dialogue with Guy Hocquenghem and Jean Danet, broadcast in 1978, was published in English in 1980 in *Semiotext(e) Magazine* as part of a 'Special Intervention Series 2: Loving Boys/Loving Children'. It was reprinted in 1988 as 'Sexuality, morality and the law' (Foucault 1988). In it Foucault claims that 'to assume that a child is incapable of explaining what happened and was incapable of giving his consent [to sex with adults] are two abuses [i.e. the refusal to believe a child had the capacity to consent and the ability to understand what he was consenting to] that are intolerable, quite unacceptable'.

The radio conversation was a response to proposals to reform the French Penal Code. In 1977 a letter was sent to *Le Monde* signed by prominent French intellectuals, including Jean-Paul Sartre, Simone de Beauvoir, Giles Deleuze and Roland Barthes, defending three men who were being tried for having sex with twelve- and thirteen-year-old boys and girls. Whilst neither of these interventions was specifically within the field of sociology, the idea of children as competent social actors informs both the sociology of childhood and this defence of adult sexual relations with children (on the grounds that children are capable of giving consent). The Paedophile

Information Exchange, a network of paedophiles who argued that consensual sexual relations between children and adults were both possible and desirable, consciously used the language of child liberation in support of its claims and activities. In the wake of feminist activists' work on sexual violence and child sexual abuse in the 1980s this interest of the sociology of childhood in children's sexuality and their 'right' to sexual relations with adults (Jackson 1982) was consigned to obscurity. I recover it here in order to highlight the ethical problems of overstating the similarities between children and adults and with underplaying the extent to which childhood *is* biologically conditioned. The dialectic of childhood is not only the play between social structures and children's agency; it also involves the movement between the materiality of the child's body (its immaturity, size, vulnerability) and the sociality of the child's lifeworld (Prout 2000). This also means attending to age as an important element impacting both on how children experience the world and what the social world expects of children. A young child, for example, will have a very different experience of the physical and the social world than a young teenager, and yet both might be discussed in the category of 'child' (Holloway and Valentine 2000: 7).

The new sociology of childhood established a field of inquiry about children (the lived experiences of children) and childhood (the concept that informs expectations and attitudes towards children) that sought to understand children's lifeworlds as they were lived. This focus on children as they are, rather than how their childhood experiences might shape the adults they may become, differentiates the sociology of childhood from other social science disciplines, particularly education and developmental psychology, that have been most engaged with the academic study of children and childhood. James and James contend that '"childhood" is the structural site that is occupied by "children" as a *collectivity*. And it is within this collective and institutional space of "childhood", as a member of the category "children" that any individual "child" comes to exercise his or her unique agency' (James and James 2004: 15). They argue that the term 'child', which is often used, especially in policy discourse, in place of 'children', as if all children's experience could be collapsed into a singular, uniform experience, dismisses children's uniqueness. The use of the term 'the child', as for example in the UN Convention on the Rights of *the Child*, makes us think of the child as an individual lacking *collective* agency.

In *Constructing Childhood* James and James claim that only the sociology of childhood recognizes children's active agency in contrast to 'the more structurally determined accounts of childhood change offered by historians of childhood and the family, by developmental psychologists, social policy specialists, socialisation theorists and others' (2004: 17); but perhaps this is overstating disciplinary differences. Histories of childhood and children are not only 'structurally determined', they also attempt to record and account for the interplay between children's agency and the social structures that organize and constrain their lives. Similarly, the sociology of childhood has to consider how social structures constrain or at least shape the lives of contemporary children. One attempt to do so is William Corsaro's concept of 'interpretive reproduction' (Corsaro 2005).

James and James also note that childhood, whilst a specific moment in the life course with common experiences, is also embedded with differences that fracture or cut across the shared experiences of children and shared concepts of childhood in any particular time or space (2004: 22). Whilst this is clearly the case, the challenge of depicting and analysing how childhood is shaped by other social identities, including 'race', class and gender, has not been actively taken up within the contemporary sociology of child-hood; the childhoods of white and middle-class children have remained the central subject of the sociology of childhood. An early exception to this is Newson's classic text (1968) *Four Years Old in an Urban Community*. Although this study is based primarily on interviews with the mothers of young children it offers a wealth of detail and insight into how class shaped the interplay between parental attitudes and children's responses (and how children's responses acted in turn on parents' attitudes) in urban England.

One of the goals of the new paradigm of childhood has been to stress the agency of children and to incorporate the voice of children into child-hood studies. Berry Mayall (2002) in her book on the lives of London children over a ten-year period argues for a 'child standpoint'. Standpoint theory, an approach developed by some feminist scholars, claims that a subaltern social group, say women, or children, have a deep understand-ing of the structures of feeling developed through the experience of living within a patriarchal or age-patriarchal (Hood-Williams 1990) society. This experiential understanding enables a social group to theorize society more robustly precisely because they approach it from a particular standpoint. Feminist standpoint theory has been criticized for its implicit assumption that women's life experiences are not radically fractured or cut across by other social locations, particularly 'race' and class. The same critique can be made against the child standpoint theory – that it emphasizes the common, age-based and generational experience of being a child over the way that experience is shaped by children's raced and classed identities and locations. Furthermore, child standpoint theory shares with participatory methods of child-research the problem that the researchers working with children are not themselves children, a fact that stretches the coherence of both stand-point theory and participatory methods almost to breaking point.

The new sociology of childhood also emphasizes that childhood is a relational category that cannot be understood, in any time or place, without an understanding of the expectations of adulthood. Mayall identifies this as a 'structural sociology of childhood', contrasting it to 'a deconstructive sociology of childhood' and also to a 'sociology of children'. It is within the 'structural sociology of childhood' that Mayall places her own work and that of Jens Qvortrup, both of whom deploy Mannheim's concept of generation to understand how childhood is conceptualized and lived by cohorts of children (Mayall 2002: 27; see also Alanen 2001). It emphasizes the shared experiences of children. A deconstructive sociology of child-hood, by contrast, attends to local constructions of childhood whilst the sociology of children stresses 'children's relations with adults in their daily lives' (Mayall 2002: 22). These distinctions seem to me to be overdrawn. Qvortrup does argue for the use of the singular 'childhood' rather than the multiple 'childhoods', but his work is confined to the European context, in which there is a normative childhood against which the actual lived experi-ences of children are understood as being 'normal' or 'pathological'. Within any particular historical and social context there will be a normative and hegemonic concept of childhood against which children themselves are compared as individuals and collectives. Finally, although Mayall places her own work in the 'structural sociology of childhood' (2002: 23), elsewhere in the same book she argues for the importance of understanding children not only as actors but also as agents (2002: 21). In brief, the sociology of child-hood shares with other sociological perspectives an interest in structure *and* agency and the iterative relationship between the two (what Giddens refers to as structuration and Marx as dialectical materialism) and in how binary concepts (in this case adult/child) are relational to one another.

Berry Mayall raises the interesting question of 'how far it is appropriate to understand children as contributors to the division of labour' (Mayall 2002: 21). Many sociologists of childhood have been influenced by feminism, politically and methodologically (Mayall 2000: 24). It is from feminism, for example, that the sociology of childhood derives its interest in participa-tory research methods and research towards empowering children, as well as its relational understanding of childhood, and its problematizing of the division between the spheres of the public and the private. Useful as these insights have been in developing a sociology of childhood, they have also tended to overemphasize the similarities between the interests and experi-ences of women and those of children, especially girls.

Social and cultural geography

The study of childhood within geography can be traced to the 1970s when a small but significant literature on children's environments was being written (Holloway and Valentine 2000: 7). Enduring contributions to our understanding of how the built environment shapes children's lifeworlds and how children's perceptual capacities shape their engagement with their physical environment were made by James Blaut and David Stea (Blaut and Stea 1971; Blaut et al. 1970) in their 'Place Perception Project'. Roger Hart's work spanning the period from the publication in 1971 (with Gary Moore) of a research report for the Place Perception Project to his current work on children's participation in the design of the built environment, particularly his 'ladder of participation' (1992), has influenced the design of participatory research and NGO-led action research with children. The geographer Kevin Lynch published an edited collection, *Growing up in Cities*, that reported the findings of a UNESCO-funded project on 'children in the city'. It remains an important source for researchers interested in how place impacts on children's everyday experiences. Although this work was rather isolated in the 1970s and 1980s, a renewed interest in children's geographies, perhaps stimulated by the resurgence of the sociology of childhood, emerged in the 1990s. Some of this work continues in the tradition of children's environmental cognition and spatial awareness mentioned above (Chawla 2002; Driskell 2002), but there is also a new interest in this work on the interplay between society and space and in giving children 'voice'.

One of the central concerns of childhood geographers has been to examine children's use of public space. Much of this work contends that children subvert the intended use of designed play space and make play and leisure spaces out of the interstices of public space – hidden spaces and wasteland. Colin Ward's lovingly photographed *The Child in the City* (1978) is probably the classic text here. Other geographers working in this area include Stuart Aitken (2001a) and Owain Jones (2000). On a slightly different but perhaps related track, other geographers have written on how children in public spaces are often considered to be 'out of place' and therefore unruly and threatening. This is an interesting area of inquiry in that it allows for comparative analysis of the experiences of street children in the south and that of teenagers caught in the liminal space between childhood and adulthood in the north (see Valentine 2004; Beazley 2000; Matthews et al. 2000).

Holloway and Valentine in their introduction to a very interesting collection of papers on *Children's Geographies* claim that 'geographical studies can add texture and detail to the currently rather broadbrush analysis of the social construction of childhood' (2000: 9). Whether the claim that the sociology of childhood has a 'broadbrush' approach is justified, social geography has made it very clear that, just as childhood changes over time or in history (see above), it is also shaped by place or geography. Literally, where children live will shape their experience of the world and the expectations placed on them (Holloway and Valentine 2000: 9–11). The split that James et al. (1998) identify between global processes that shape children's lives and local cultural lifeworlds can be transcended by a spatial appreciation of the connections between the local and the global. Cindi Katz's excellent comparative study of the lives of children and youth in Howa, a Sudanese village and in a district of New York, *Growing up Global*, shows how global economic restructuring has reshaped experiences and expectations of childhood and youth; and how children and their parents are responding to the new demands that new economic processes have placed on them (Holloway and Valentine 2000: 11; Katz 2004). In the following section I delineate some of the international processes that govern childhood in a global era.

Governing childhood internationally

The field of child law is not new; debates about the legal competence of young people and the necessity of separate legal procedures for dealing with minors date back to at least the sixteenth century. Alongside this concern about when children could be held responsible for breaking the law runs a connected anxiety about how to keep children from causing injury or harm to themselves or others. It is this anxiety that fuelled the child-saving movements of the nineteenth century in North America and Europe, but the concern about the ability of children to distinguish right from wrong and the moral instruction of children are there in the writings of Locke and in the records left by the Puritans in sixteenth-century colonial America.

What is new is the emergence of a field of international law that seeks to regulate childhood at a global scale. This body of law is primarily framed as legal instruments to regulate the protection of children in the participating nation-states. Its most important instrument is the UN Convention on the Rights of the Child (hereafter the UNCRC or the Convention). Although the special circumstances of children were noted in earlier legislation, for example in the UN Declaration of the Rights of the Child and even earlier in the 1924 Declaration of the Rights of the Child by the League of Nations (Sheppard 2000: 40), the adoption of the UNCRC coincided, and perhaps stimulated, a growth in the field of child rights monitoring.

UN Convention on the Rights of the Child

When a special human rights instrument for children was proposed in 1979 by the Polish government to mark the International Year of the Child, children's rights were very low on the political agenda. C. P. Cohen, who was involved in drafting the Convention, has commented:

> Throughout the drafting process, there were strong indications that the Convention on the Rights of the Child might be just a sentimental, symbolic gesture on behalf of children – one that would be quickly disregarded and ignored. Originally, there appeared to be little interest in the Convention. Participation in its drafting was very poor during the first few years. Some critics strongly opposed the creation of a special treaty protecting children's rights, arguing that children's rights were already protected under the two human rights Covenants. Other commentators were concerned about poor participation by underdeveloped countries, urging that these countries might consider the Convention to be insensitive to their needs and customs.
>
> (Cohen et al. 1996: 471)

In the event, developing countries were willing to ratify the Convention; all but one of the first twenty countries to ratify were developing countries (Cohen et al. 1996). Nonetheless, the concept of a global model of childhood that the Convention implicitly expounds was far from accepted by the signatories. Many states entered blanket reservations to the Convention of the kind entered by Djibouti, an Islamic state, which affirmed that '[t]he Government of Djibouti shall not consider itself bound by any provisions or articles that are incompatible with its religion and traditional values' (Harris-Short 2003: 135). Several states, including Singapore, entered reservations that subordinated the Convention to national law.

Given that the model of childhood encoded in the Convention follows a well-established Western discourse on childhood as a time of play, innocence and learning, it might be expected that 'the West' was happy to ratify the Convention without reservations. In fact this was not the case. The United States has not ratified the Convention; it is the only state other than Somalia not to have done so. The UK entered reservations in respect of immigration law.

The final draft of the Convention was adopted by the UN Commission on Human Rights in 1989 and came into force on 25 September 1990, just over six months after the signing ceremony and nearly one month before the World Summit for Children in New York. The Summit had originally been planned as an effort to keep children's rights on the international

agenda 'because no one had anticipated that this would happen spontane-
ously' (Cohen et al. 1996: 441).

Despite the reservations entered by many participating states, and notwithstanding the low level of interest in children's rights and even opposition to the very idea of a separate human rights instrument for children,
since the Convention came into force the field of international children's
rights law has proliferated. There are now over 100 instruments of international child law (Angel 1995; Van Bueren 1998; Saulle and Kojanec 1995),
many of them legally binding.

International NGOs

Globalization has not only occurred at the level of increased international cooperation between states and increased financial flows. It has
also involved a parallel shift below in both the movements of people and
increased communication across national borders and the emergence of
an incipient international civil society. The phenomenal growth in non-
governmental organizations (NGOs) operating at the international level,
or INGOs, is part of this emergent international civil society. International
human rights law and particularly the Convention have played an important part in creating a role for INGOs and therefore stimulating their
expansion.

In the UN Charter there is provision for consultation with NGOs. It
has been claimed that this provision 'has produced much of the international practice concerning NGOs, and the "rights" given to them' (Breen
2003: 455). NGOs participated in the drafting of the Convention through
their involvement with the Ad Hoc NGO Group on the Drafting of the
Convention on the Rights of the Child (now the NGO Group for the
Convention on the Rights of the Child). It was through this group that
'NGOs had a direct and indirect impact on this Convention that is without
parallel in the history of drafting international instruments' (Breen 2003:
457, citing Cantwell 1992). The Convention is also the only international
human rights treaty that expressly gives NGOs a role in monitoring its
implementation (Breen 2003: 457).

The Optional Protocol on the involvement of children in armed conflict

Despite the substantial role of NGOs in drafting the UNCRC and their
success in getting a provision on the protection of children in armed conflict included (Cantwell 1992), they were unable to get the age in Article

38, on the prohibition of children in armed conflict, raised from fourteen to eighteen.

The failure of the Working Group charged with drafting the UNCRC to extend children's protection beyond that already made available in law (by the Protocols of the Geneva Convention) suggests that the UNCRC was not quite as unremittingly global as it is often portrayed. Signatories were not prepared to extend protection to children if it might undermine *national* defence. The reluctance on the part of some government representatives to extend protection to all under-eighteens was, as the representative from the United Kingdom demonstrated, due to reasons of military strategy since it would be 'difficult in times of hostilities' (cited in Sheppard 2000: 44). As Geraldine van Bueren, who was involved in the drafting of the Convention, has rightly commented, 'the alarm bells ought to begin to ring when the majority of states negotiating a treaty on children's rights are willing to risk giving children's lives a lower priority than military feasibility' (Sheppard 2000: 4).

The protection of children in armed conflict was raised at the first session of the Committee on the Rights of the Child, where it was the main point of discussion. This discussion led to the adoption by the Commission on Human Rights of a Resolution to establish a Working Group to elaborate a draft optional protocol to the Convention (Breen 2003: 465). The meetings of this working group were attended by observers from NGOs including Defence for Children International, Friends World Committee for Consultation, and International Save the Children Alliance. The Quakers took an active role in the drafting process, 'on an equal footing with state representatives and other international organizations, such as the ICRC' (Breen 2003: 466). In 1998 the Coalition to Stop the Use of Child Soldiers was formed. The Coalition has a Steering Committee of seven international human rights NGOs including International Save the Children Alliance and links with UNICEF, the International Committee of the Red Cross, and the International Labour Organization. It was instrumental in the drafting of the Optional Protocol to the UNCRC on the Involvement of Children in Armed Conflict. The Optional Protocol was intended to prohibit the use of people below eighteen years in armed conflict. This was not achieved, however, and the Optional Protocol, which came into force in 2002, prohibits the direct involvement of children (under eighteen) in armed conflict, but it does not prevent states from recruiting under-sixteens into the armed forces (non-state organizations are not allowed to recruit under-eighteens).

The Optional Protocol has improved the protection of children in armed conflict in relation to earlier international law – including the Protocols to the Geneva Convention that distinguished different levels of protection for different age groups and allowed the direct participation of children older than fifteen years in hostilities. However, the discussions in the drafting of the Optional Protocol show that there is far from global agreement on the age when childhood ends. The question 'What is a child?' is as pertinent for the drafters of international law, it would seem, as it is for social scientists.

International Criminal Court – the protection of children against war crimes

If the Optional Protocol has improved the legal provisions for the protection of children in war, that has been no guarantee that even the signatories to the Optional Protocol have upheld it in practice. In 2002 the Rome Statute of the International Criminal Court (ICC) came into force. The Statue is legally binding on the 102 states who have agreed to be bound by it. It has jurisdiction over the crime of genocide, crimes against humanity, and war crimes. It is a court of 'last resort', which means that it does not try crimes that are being dealt with at the national level. Many of its provisions explicitly relate to crimes against children, including preventing the conception or birth for a group of people as representing an act of genocide (Art. 6 (d)); forcibly transferring children of one group to another group (Art. 6 (e)); conscripting or enlisting children under the age of fifteen into the national armed forces or using them to participate actively in hostilities (Art. 8 (2) (b) (xxvi), Art. 8 (2) (e) (vii)). The ICC obviously acts after the event and cannot therefore be said to protect children directly. However, in defining the recruitment of under-fifteens into armed forces as a war crime, and in extending the definition of child soldiers from direct participation in hostilities to include support services, it may lessen the risks for children of being recruited into the armed forces in future conflicts.

International Labour Organization – ending child labour

The International Labour Organization (the ILO) is a tripartite organization of state representatives, workers and employers. It was established by the Treaty of Versailles at the end of the First World War. The ILO quickly adopted several Conventions on children working. These early Conventions were not against all child labour, viewing some work, particularly apprenticeships, as a part of a child's education. The ILO also excluded work within the family or in agriculture so long as this work did not prevent a child from attending school. In 1936 the ILO raised the minimum working age to fifteen. In 1973 Convention No. 138 Minimum

Age was adopted. This applied to all young people, and it was the first time that the ILO committed itself to 'achieving the total abolition of child labour' (Hanson and Vandaele 2003: 99). A general Minimum Age of fifteen is qualified in the Convention for light work (thirteen years) and hazardous work (sixteen or eighteen years) or where the compulsory school leaving age is above fifteen, in which case the minimum age at which the child can legally work is also increased. Convention No. 138 is the least ratified of the ILO's seven core Conventions. In 2001 less than two thirds (107 / 175) of the ILO Member States had ratified the Convention, and none of the African and Asian Member States had done so (Hanson and Vandaele 2003: 113). The ILO adopted the Convention on the Eradication of the Worst Forms of Child Labour in 1999. It includes slavery, sex work, trafficking, and any other work that endangers a child's health or morals.

UNICEF

UNICEF – the United Nations Children's Fund – was formed in 1946 to manage post-war reconstruction in Europe for children. Originally set up as an emergency fund (from which the still used acronym derives its name), in 1953 it became a permanent part of the UN. In 2002 the United Nations Special Session on Children adopted a resolution on 'A World Fit for Children', which included a Plan of Action on health, education, armed conflict, child labour, trafficking and sexual exploitation, and combating HIV / AIDS. UNICEF is funded by governments and through corporate sponsorship and fund-raising by national agencies (NGOs). Since 1988 it has had its own research arm, the Innocenti Research Centre.

Summary on international law

Historically international law was intended to codify agreements between states about mutually agreed rules of conduct on international matters. International law has a long history. The Treaty of Westphalia, which is considered to be the beginning of the formation of a community of states, was signed in 1648, at the end of the Thirty Years War in Europe. It is only in the twentieth century that another body of law was formulated, and international actors were instrumental in drafting, implementing and monitoring this law. This body of law, called Humanitarian and Human Rights Law, is a product of globalization. It attempts to govern not only relations between states, as international law had previously done, but also relations between states and societies. The expansion of this field of law to children has been sporadic. I have noted that the first World Summit for Children in 1990 was organized to mark the adoption in 1989 of the Convention on the Rights of the Child because it was feared that the Convention would otherwise attract little interest and be merely symbolic, even sentimental. Human Rights and Humanitarian Law in general, and in respect of children's protection in particular, has been remarkable for the extent to which it has involved, and sometimes been initiated by, non-governmental organizations.

The proliferation of international children's rights legal instruments and the close involvement of NGOs are not, however, entirely without their problems. A key problem, for the purposes of this book, is that to construct a body of law to deal with 'the child' presupposes that there is universal agreement on what a child is and what children need to flourish. My review of the historical and social studies of childhood in this chapter demonstrates that an agreement across cultural and national borders about what children's capacities and vulnerabilities are, and what states and societies should be morally or legally obliged to do for children, is far from assured.

In the following chapters I explore in more depth the tensions and contradictions between a global idea of childhood and the practices and concepts of childhood in diverse settings.

Recommended further reading

Gottlieb, A. 2004. *The Afterlife is Where we Come from: The Culture of Infancy in West Africa*. Chicago: University of Chicago Press.
An exemplary ethnography of early childhood that illustrates in a compelling way that childhood is a local cultural practice that is relatively impervious to global norms.

Grier, B. C. 2006. *Invisible Hands: Child Labor and the State in Colonial Zimbabwe*. Portsmouth, NH: Heinemann.
A decisive contribution to the history of African childhoods and the history of child labour.

Katz, C. 2004. *Growing up Global: Economic Restructuring and Children's Everyday Lives*. Minneapolis, MN: University of Minnesota Press.
A ground-breaking ethnography of the comparative impact of globalization on the lives of young people in a Sudanese village and a New York neighbourhood.

Mintz, S. 2004. *Huck's Raft: A History of American Childhood*. Cambridge, MA: Harvard University Press.

If you were to read only one volume on the history of American childhood, this should be it.

Pollock, L. 1983. *Forgotten Children: Parent–Child Relations from 1500 to 1900.* Cambridge: Cambridge University Press.
A nice corrective to the view that childhood is a modern invention.

Prout, A. and A. James. 1990. *Constructing and Reconstructing Childhood.* London: Falmer.
One of the founding texts of the new sociology of childhood.

2

Policy and practice

Introduction

This chapter is about how charitable institutions, philanthropists and government have responded to the problem of child poverty on a national and international scale. It shows how a wave of reform energy targeted on children in the nineteenth century in North America and Europe gradually moved the responsibility for children's welfare from charities to governments. While the entry of government into the fields of child welfare and juvenile justice did not eradicate charities from the landscape, it did reframe concern for children within a new political paradigm of rights and justice. This gradual shift from child-saving to child rights is evident in the emergence of national and international law intended to protect the rights of the child and found its fullest expression in the UN Convention on the Rights of the Child. However, a simple evolutionary narrative of a concern for child welfare that moves from child-saving to child rights does not tell the whole story. In practice the field of child welfare constantly shifts around these two poles rather than moving decisively from one to the other. The contention that child-saving and a politics of pity are still relevant to understanding the field of child welfare is illustrated through a study of representations of children by a major international child welfare organization and in news reporting.

Rescuing children: the history of child-saving

The nineteenth century was a century of change on an unprecedented scale: industrialization stimulated a dramatic growth in the scale and density of urban life and parallel shifts in rural life. The nineteenth century witnessed dramatic population movements that criss-crossed the globe. If industrialization and urbanization did not necessarily increase poverty they did make it more visible and, in an era of democratic reform, inequality could no longer be legitimated by divine right or natural law. The long nineteenth century is said to have opened with the French Revolution of 1789 and closed with the 1917 Bolshevik Revolution. In between these epoch-shaping events there were revolutionary outbreaks in Haiti in 1791; Europe in 1848 and again in 1879; and Mexico in 1910. It is in this context of a landscape of revolutionary change of society, politics and economy that the era of social reform that begins in the nineteenth century should be situated.

The upheavals of the nineteenth century produced new problems of government, and the management of childhood poverty became, and has remained, a central problem of modern government. Many themes from this era of social reform can still be traced in how children are depicted by contemporary social reformers working with or on children.

The end of the nineteenth century ushered in what has been referred to as the 'century of the child'. It is in the late 1800s that most of London's most influential child charities were launched: Barnardo's in 1867; the London Society for the Prevention of Cruelty to Children in 1884; the Liverpool Society in 1883; the National Society for the Prevention of Cruelty to Children in 1889 (Murdoch 2006: 3). England was not unusual in Europe in expanding child welfare institutions in this period; Germany saw the establishment and significant expansion of child welfare charities between 1830 and 1868 (Dickinson 1996: 11). In the case of Germany most of this activity was organized by private philanthropy; state action on child welfare was limited before 1870, although after that date it expanded considerably. In 1878 the German Legal Guardianship Code gave the state responsibility for 'neglected children' (Dickinson 1996: 18). In France there was a gradual shift in child welfare from private religious charities in the seventeenth century to the state in the late eighteenth century, and in the early nineteenth the state assumed complete legal responsibility for the care of 'unwanted children' (Fuchs 1984: 26). Following the agitation of private, philanthropic child protection agencies from the 1860s through to the 1880s (Fuchs 1984: 59) the state's powers over families were expanded in a late nineteenth-century law for the protection of the *moralement aban-donnés* which gave the state the right to separate children from 'immoral' parents; by the turn of the century judges had the power to remove children from their families and place them in public guardianship.

The concern with child welfare in the nineteenth century was also evident in the United States. What is referred to in America as the 'Progressive Era' (1890–1920) concentrated its 'reform energy on children' (Katz 1986: 414). Levine and Levine begin their history of *Helping Children* (1992) by noting that nearly all modern professional community-based services for children were established between 1890 and 1916.

State welfare policies in the nineteenth century addressed poverty by attacking the rights of poor parents (Murdoch 2006: 4). In England the New Poor Law 1834 (the previous law to which it was an amendment – hence it was a 'new' law – was enacted in 1601) meant that the workhouse was the only state-administered form of poverty relief. Workhouses separated parents from their children. Initially public opinion was sympathetic to the families separated by the Poor Law, but this diminished by the end of the nineteenth century alongside a 'growing geographical as well as discursive separation between poor parents and children' (Murdoch 2006: 6) and reformers 'continued to assert that poor children needed to be separated from their impoverished parents in order to be fashioned into citizens' (2006: 7). What Murdoch means by 'discursive separation' is the idea that children were targeted as the 'deserving poor', the innocent victims of circumstances beyond their control, whilst their parents were typically depicted as neglectful, abusive, and addicted to drink and sex. Child-savers were preoccupied with prostitution, nakedness and sexual danger (Murdoch 2006: 20–4). In order to be saved children had to be taken from the close proximity of their parents and neighbourhoods and 'transplanted to a new kind of domestic space' (Murdoch 2006: 48). Institutions for children, particularly once the 'family system' for children in care was well established, were depicted by reformers as the best place for children to grow up and learn the habits of domesticity and work (Murdoch 2006: 64). George K. Behlmer in his study of the SPCC, Child Abuse and Moral Reform in England, 1870–1908 makes the rather unlikely claim that the SPCC did split families up but did so without regard to class. If this was the case in Britain, and Murdoch's study would suggest otherwise, it was not the case in America. The American SPCCS, as Katz remarks, 'reflected a major strand in social policy from the 1870s through the mid- or late-1890s. The only way to eradicate pauperism, argued many reformers and officials, was to break up the families of the very poor; inability to support one's children had become evidence of parental incompetence' (Katz 1986: 417).

If the depiction of poor children as geographically or discursively separated from their parents, and the obsessive attention to sexual danger, are familiar from the contemporary landscape of child-rescue, another focus of nineteenth-century reformers is not: the importance placed on 'discipline and work as the key values that would enable poor youths to escape the fates of their parents' (Murdoch 2006: 121). This emphasis on the virtues of work for children seems odd to our modern conceptions of childhood. The importance of discipline and learning the habits of work shifted location in the later part of the nineteenth century from the factory to the school.

The Education Act 1870 established ten as the minimum school leaving age; exactly ten years later another Education Act made full-time school compulsory for under-elevens (excluding agricultural workers), and this was raised again in 1899 and again in 1914 (to age fourteen).

The use of education as a tool of child welfare was partly motivated by the decreasing opportunities for work for children, under the combined impact of successful labour reform campaigns limiting the hours of children's work and changes in production methods that made children's labour less attractive to employers. The increases in the urban population, the inadequacy of working-class housing and the decrease in children's employment contributed to a growing visibility of poor children and young people on the streets of the major cities of Europe and North America. Indeed, part of the motivation driving child welfare reforms and interventions was to address a middle-class fear of the criminality of working-class youth (Dickinson 1996: 38). It was this fear of working-class youth, Anthony Platt argues in his now classic text *The Child Savers* (1969), that stimulated reforms in the administering of juvenile justice. Contrary to a narrative of juvenile legal reform that claims that the separation of adults and children in the legal system protects the child from harm, Platt argues that it created new categories of wrong-doing, status offences that would not be liable if committed by an adult and denied children their liberty without the protection of due process. Donzelot (1980) presents a similar case for the pernicious effects of juvenile reform in nineteenth-century France. One of the effects of attempting to decriminalize juvenile justice was that juvenile 'offenders' were no longer afforded the protection of due process including representation or legal counsel.

The main focus of Platt's study, Illinois, was where the first juvenile court in America opened in 1899. The early juvenile reformers advocated that the state should act as a good parent would to an unruly child. In the USA, as in Europe, the conviction that juvenile justice could change the child's future was based on an optimistic conviction that the application of scientific practice could eliminate or solve social problems. This movement 'stressed the importance of individualized case-by-case diagnosis and treatment, much as a doctor might do with medical problems' (Mears et al. 2007: 225).

From child-saving to child rights

Individual philanthropists and the organizations they established are often referred to as 'child-savers' and referred to themselves in similar terms

(Katz 1986: 413; Levine and Levine 1992: 191); but what were they saving children from – poverty, disease, their families, their neighbourhoods, immorality? In fact 'child-savers' collapsed together poverty and immorality, physical hygiene and moral hygiene, and cast their work as a religious duty. The central strategy of nineteenth-century child-savers was to save the child by rescuing them from their families whose moral degeneracy, in the view of social reformers, was the cause of their impoverishment. Discourses of child-saving were animated by a sense of moral duty which began to be substituted after 1910 by a discourse of social rights (Dickinson 1996: 68). Reformers argued for 'an expansion of the *powers* and prerogatives of the state precisely in the interests of securing the *rights* of the child' (Dickinson 1996: 77; emphasis in the original).

The shift from child-saving to child rights as discourses of public responsibility may be traceable to the failure of the strategies of early child-saving movements to rescue children. Separation of children from their parents and their placement in institutional care did not rescue children but placed them in frequently more dangerous, exploitative conditions; at the same time their parents lost the benefits of the 'civilizing influence' of their children. If children were to be left with their parents this was not because reformers and public officials trusted working-class parents with the care of their children. Instead, 'the strategy of family preservation led inexorably to increased public responsibility and intervention' (Katz 1986: 423).

The era of social reform moved from the provision of private charity to public support and intervention and, in moving child welfare from the private to the public, it changed the status of the child from a subject to a citizen, from a dependent to a semi-legal person. The language of philanthropy and helping children is a language of moral duty and concern or 'moral economy' (Ansell 2005: 226); the language of state intervention and provision is a political language of civic rights and civic responsibilities.

Children's rights: participation or protection?

In the previous chapter I noted that the history of international law governing childhood can be dated to the League of Nations 1924 Declaration of the Rights of the Child. The full text of the Declaration is:

> By the present Declaration of the Rights of the Child, commonly known as 'Declaration of Geneva', men and women of all nations, recognizing that mankind owes to the Child the best that it has to give, declare and accept it as their duty that, beyond and above all considerations of race, nationality or creed:

1 The child must be given the means requisite for its normal development, both materially and spiritually;
2 The child that is hungry must be fed; the child that is sick must be nursed; the child that is backward must be helped; the delinquent child must be reclaimed; and the orphan and the waif must be sheltered and succoured;
3 The child must be the first to receive relief in times of distress;
4 The child must be put in a position to earn a livelihood, and must be protected against every form of exploitation;
5 The child must be brought up in the consciousness that its talents must be devoted to the service of fellow men.

Clearly, this is a long way from identifying the child as a rights-bearing individual. The language is more akin to the nineteenth-century discourse of child-saving than to the contemporary inscription of the child as rights-bearing in the UN Convention on the Rights of the Child. It speaks more to the duties of adults to protect children than it does to the child's right to be involved in determining his or her own life. An expanded version of the League of Nations Declaration was adopted by the UN in 1959. This introduces the principle of 'best interests', which is an important element in the UNCRC. It also removes the child's right to work from the earlier Declaration (see point (4) above), replacing it with the entitlement to free and compulsory elementary education. While the 1959 Declaration was the precursor to the UNCRC, it still defines the child as principally in need of protection and special consideration rather than as a rights-bearing individual. The UNCRC is the first document of international law that speaks of the child as a rights-holder.

The first draft of what became the UNCRC was submitted to the Human Rights Commission of the UN by the Polish government. This draft was more or less the 1959 Declaration of the Rights of the Child with an additional inclusion mechanism added. This was rejected by the Commission, and Poland submitted a second model convention that 'provided the first indicators of the emergence of children as rights-bearing individuals' (Cohen 2006: 189). It gave the child 'who is capable of forming his own views the right to express his opinion in matters concerning his own person' (Cohen 2006: 189) and was incorporated in a slightly revised form into the final text as Article 12. Cynthia Price Cohen, who participated in the drafting of the Convention, claims that this clause 'would soon centrally contribute to changing the status of children worldwide' (Cohen 2006: 189) by reclassifying children as rights-bearing individuals. The view that the Convention established the child as a rights-holder is widely held. Deirdre Fottrell in her contribution to an assessment of the Convention 'ten years on' (Fottrell 2000) notes that the director of UNICEF regarded it as a 'Magna Carta for children' (2000: 1).

For Cohen, ironically in view of the fact that the USA is one of only two states who have not ratified the Convention, the US delegation to the working party was instrumental in ensuring that the Convention shifted the understanding of children's rights towards participation. She notes that it was the USA who proposed the inclusion of articles on freedom of expression (Article 13), freedom of religion (Article 14), freedom of association and assembly (Article 15), and the right to privacy (Article 16).

The drafting of the Convention was done by consensus so that if any delegation objected to the inclusion of a text then it could not be adopted. It was on this basis that the US delegation was able to prevent a change in the age of combat from fifteen to eighteen. In the second reading of Article 14 the Islamic delegations objected to the inclusion of freedom of religion on the grounds that the Qur'an says that children must follow their father's religion and that they cannot make a choice of their own. Article 14 was retained by inserting a paragraph on parental guidance. This weakened the presumption of the child as a rights-bearing individual in the final text.

Cohen clearly views the UNCRC as bestowing on children the status of rights-holding individuals with a right to participation in decisions over themselves. While Cohen shares this view with many other commentators, and especially children's rights NGOs, it is by no means an uncontested view. Pupavac for example, although she recognizes that the 'novelty of the international children's rights regime is that children are considered not just as recipients of rights' protection, but as rights-holders in their own right' (Pupavac 2001: 99), says that the separation of the rights-holder from the moral agent (the person/body capable of acting to ensure the delivery of rights) undermines the claim that children are the bearers of rights. She points out that 'inherent in children's rights is the need for advocacy on the behalf of the child' (Pupavac 2001: 100).

Pupavac maintains that the advocate for the child, within a regime of international children's rights, is neither the child nor her parents or guardians but professionals. This shift in responsibility from the parents to the state, she claims, is used to undermine the moral agency of adults in developing countries, and the sovereignty of developing nation-states. While there may be some truth in her claims (for example, the rights of children to protection from tyrannical regimes were cited in defence of the invasion of Iraq and Afghanistan), the Convention does not justify this shift in responsibility from the parent to the state. Indeed nearly half of the articles of the Convention stipulate the rights of parents over their children or the right of children to family life.

In any case, as Lyon points out, since the UNCRC is unenforceable unless it has been adopted into domestic law, the right to participation apparently made available by Article 12 is far from guaranteed. In addition to this, when children's participation is sought it is generally an institution that initiates the opportunity for children to participate. Children who do participate in institutionally driven agendas often find the process token- istic and in any case cannot claim any representation for a wider group of children (Lyon 2007).

It would seem then that the shift from discourses of child-saving to child rights is far from complete. In the UNCRC and in the international declarations that foreshadowed it the child remains a special category of person who is entitled to protection from harm by virtue of their specific vulnerabilities.

Responding to images of children

One way to test the proposition that concerns about children's welfare have shifted from a child-saving to a child rights agenda is to look at how children are represented in the work of NGOs and in the media. In the following section I discuss how representations of suffering connect to political questions about how to alleviate suffering and what responsibili- ties the spectator has towards the suffering other. I then look specifically at how images of children are used to mobilize pity and connect feelings of sympathy to political action. I do this in two case studies – one of the repre- sentations of children used in Save the Children appeals and one of the press reporting of a major disaster. I begin by outlining the scholarly literature on looking at images of suffering. The central question that this literature addresses is: what is an ethical response to looking at images of suffering others? I then turn to a brief discussion of the specific ethical demands made on the spectator by looking at images of suffering children before turning to the two case studies.

Looking at suffering

There is a growing literature on how to respond to images of suffering (Boltanski 1999; Moeller 1999; Sontag 2003; Chouliaraki 2006; Donham 2006). The central problem that most of these works attend to is: what action is an appropriate response to being a spectator of suffering? Luc Boltanski's *Distant Suffering* is an exploration of how the spectator should respond to images of suffering circulating in the media. His central argument is that a spectator feels a moral obligation to act in the face of distant suffering. Our spectatorship of the suffering of distant others generates what he calls a 'politics of pity'. The idea of a politics of pity is developed from Hannah Arendt, who articulates it in *On Revolution*. The politics of pity involves the spectacle of suffering: '[the] observation of the *unfortunate* by those who do not share their suffering, who do not experience it directly and who, as such, may be regarded as fortunate or lucky people' (Boltanski 1999: 3). Boltanski makes the point that pity must be singular and generalized: singular in that we see an individual's suffering and it is this that arouses our pity, and generalized in that we know that this individual is replaceable by any number of other individuals who are experiencing the same suffering (1999: 12). It is the generalized quality of the response that moves it from 'pity' to a 'politics of pity', in which a response is demanded. We feel, he claims, compelled to act in response to this suffering and this action is of two kinds: 'paying and speaking'. No one, he points out, 'ever suggests, for example, that the spectator should drop everything and take himself to the unfortunate's side' (1999: 15). What interests Boltanski is how the spectator's imagination is mobilized in ways that enable him or her to contemplate what the suffering of another might feel like. He says: 'By describing the different ways of transmitting the spectacle of suffering to another person, of sharing the emotional experiences it has aroused, and of making perceptible how one is both *affected* and *concerned*, we would like to suggest that the persistence of these ways trace [*sic*] relatively stable facilitating paths. They pick out common *sensibilities* on which prereflexive agreements – of the order, if one likes, of prejudice if not prejudgement – can be sustained between persons who recognise if not the same ethical values then at least a community of reactions' (1999: 54). What Boltanski means by this is that there are only a few ways in which suffering can be depicted that will result in a response of concern from the spectator. These ways of depicting suffering depend on the use of shared symbols that we know how to respond to. This is particularly pertinent to understanding how and why images of children are routinely used in fund-raising campaigns by charities.

Susan Sontag's meditation on *Regarding the Pain of Others* points to the literalist quality of the photographic image – its being-there quality which is often regarded as the special force of the still image (Barthes 1981). Sontag maintains that the depiction of suffering is likely to be more vivid, less veiled, the further we are from the protagonist. For her images of suffering are provocations to ask: 'Who caused what the picture shows? Who is responsible? Is it excusable? Was it inevitable? Is there some state of affairs which we have accepted up to now that ought to be challenged? All this, with the understanding that moral indignation, like compassion, cannot dictate a course of action' (Sontag 2003: 105). The course of action compelled by different ways of presenting suffering in the news is the topic of Chouliaraki's study of *The Spectatorship of Suffering*. Chouliaraki's study returns us to Boltanski in so much as she takes up his use of Arendt's concept of a politics of pity to argue that certain ways of presenting the suffering of distant others can be responded to within a concept of a cosmopolitan politics.

If most of the writers discussed here (Boltanski 1999; Sontag 2003; Chouliaraki 2006) are concerned with how images of suffering move the spectator to action, Moeller, in her study of *Compassion Fatigue*, approaches the problem from the opposite point of view: why do images of suffering fail to move the spectator to action? However, like Boltanski she suggests that there are relatively few ways in which suffering is depicted and that each image is intended to call forth an appropriate response. 'Images of crisis', she says, 'rely on a repertoire of stereotypes: the heroic doctor; the brutal tyrant . . . the innocent orphans . . . If the images that document a crisis are of starving orphans, the remedy is humanitarian assistance. If the images are of the brutal tyrant, the remedy is military force' (Moeller 1999: 43). Moeller's argument about the iconic force of images and the common symbolic meanings they share is strikingly similar to Boltanski's and yet Moeller maintains that iconic images dull the spectator's response whereas Boltanski suggests they mobilize the spectator's concern.

Looking at images of children

The research on images of suffering can be distilled into one question: what is the moral response to this knowledge of the suffering of distant others? Each of the sources that I discussed in the previous section suggests that images of suffering in NGO and news media deploy well-established cultural symbols that are intended to evoke some kind of conventional reaction. Images of children are in themselves cultural symbols whose impact slides across thought, provoking an emotive response which forecloses political or financial calculation. Patricia Holland's *What is a Child?* (1992) and her more recent study *Picturing Childhood* (2004b) have both made seminal contributions to our understanding of how images of children that circulate in different media produce and reflect a society's concepts of childhood. Holland is also concerned to point to how images of suffering children pull at the sympathies of adult spectators by foreclosing questions of blame, culpability and responsibility that might arise with images of adults. Boltanski claims that the images of suffering within a politics of pity demand that we do something, and specifically that we attempt to remedy suffering through either speech or payment. He claims that suffering at a distance demands action at a distance: recall that he says that no one 'ever suggests, for example, that the spectator should drop everything and take himself to the unfortunate's side' (Boltanski 1999: 15: see above). In the case of the suffering of children this claim that distance is maintained has not been upheld. The figure of what Lisa Cartwright calls the 'global social orphan' has in fact been responded to by the spectator taking 'himself to the unfortunate's side'. Cartwright asks: 'If in a politics of pity distance is traversed by words and money, what happens when that distance collapses and the exchange is no longer mediated by distance?' (Cartwright 2005: 189). Her argument is that the circulation of images of suffering children in institutional care mobilizes not only action at a distance but the collapsing of distance as the spectator refashions himself or herself as parent or prospective parent to the suffering child. However, this image of the ragged, abandoned child as a figure that demands more of the spectator than words and payment has a longer lineage than Cartwright acknowledges. In her analysis transnational adoption of 'social orphans' is facilitated by the possibilities of the global circulation of images and the shrinking of physical distance that she takes to be characteristic of globalization. However, the use of images of abandoned children and the transnational (dis)placement of these children can be traced to the nineteenth-century philanthropic child-saving movements that I discussed earlier (Koven 1997).

In the next section I closely analyse the use of images of children in contemporary NGO fund-raising campaigns. My specific focus in analysing these images is to what extent representations of suffering children evoke the figure of the child as an object of pity connected to a politics of pity or a subject of rights connected to a politics of justice.

The depiction of children in fund-raising campaigns

> The authorization of action through an appeal for foreign aid, even foreign intervention, begins with an evocation of indigenous absence, an erasure of local voices and acts. Suffering is presented as if it existed free of local people and local worlds. The child is alone. This, of course, is not the

way that disasters, illnesses, and deaths are usually dealt with in African or other non-Western societies, or, for that matter, in the West.

(Kleinman and Kleinman 1996: 7)

Typically the picture used in child-saving campaigns is of the child alone. The closely framed shot of a young child's face stares out at us from countless NGO appeals. With certain exceptions, the child alone is a forlorn image. Key themes of the discourse of childhood, including the family as the ideal site of childhood and play as its ideal activity, converge to make an image of the lone child symbolize the abandonment of the child. Cutting out of the frame the adults and other children who surround the child places the viewer of the image in the role of these missing carers. The child alone is abstracted from politics, culture and society. This stripping away of the wider context means that difficult questions about the destructive impact of structural inequalities on the child's life can be evaded. His or her suffering becomes a consequence of the human condition, rather than an effect of specific political and military interventions (Burman 1994: 243). The abandoned child, the child alone, cannot lose in being 'rescued' the security and comfort of existing networks and affective ties because, the image suggests, these are already absent from the child's life. Rather, if the child is not rescued, then he or she will be abandoned to their fate.

The image of the lone child signifies not a momentary loneliness but a permanent abandonment. Such images hail the spectator as a parent, inviting her or him to take the place of the absent parent. Often in fund-raising campaigns, particularly those that are intended to support the ongoing work of a charity rather than a specific campaign, this hailing will be quite explicit, asking 'you' to 'adopt a child'. In some cases it will be made very explicit, the sponsored child being spoken of as 'your child' (Wells 2008a). These representations form part of a familiar narrative: abandoned (or neglected, or inadequately cared for) child needs to be rescued from misery and abjection by a substitute parent. This misery is not depicted as simple poverty, the relationship between the child and his or her would-be rescuer is cast in emotional terms: you give something to the child as a token of love and in return the child gives you the possibility of loving a child.

In the following section I describe and analyse representations of children used in Save the Children appeals. My argument is that Save the Children appeals mobilize two apparently contradictory or conflicting discourses of childhood: child-saving and child rights. This analysis demonstrates not only the continuing salience of child-saving in contemporary discourses about children's welfare but also the contradictory impacts of child rights discourses, some of which, I argue, contribute towards a view of the child as a site of investment (financial and emotional) that follows from a neo-liberal view of the self and its responsibilities towards others. The campaigns that I analyse are the child sponsorship appeal, Child Link, and a disaster appeal that followed the Kashmiri earthquake.

Child Link

The International Save the Children Alliance is an alliance of twenty-five member country organizations. The majority of these member organizations do not use any form of direct child sponsorship as a fund-raising strategy. Australia, Britain, Italy and New Zealand each have appeals that link the donor to a child-country representative in a selected country in Africa, Asia or Latin America. There is no individual contact between the child and the donor and nor is the donation given directly to the child. In these kinds of child sponsorship campaigns what the NGO is attempting to do is to use the strategy of child sponsorship while avoiding the paternalistic (actually, maternalistic) framing of the relationship between the donor and the recipients. The reason why NGOs might want to continue using child sponsorship even while they repudiate the implications of it is that it is a highly successful fund-raising strategy precisely because it makes an individual and very personal link between the donor and the recipient, between 'you' and 'your child'. Only two of the Save the Children member organizations use a standard model of child sponsorship appeals: Italy (in addition to its Child Link appeal) and the USA.

The front of the Save the Children UK Child Link leaflet is divided into three folded sections. The front of the leaflet (when folded) is a large photograph with the Save the Children logo beneath it. The main image is of an Asian boy holding a battered exercise book. The book is closed. He is sitting on the floor of his house at the threshold of the door. He is looking out of the picture towards the right of the frame. He is neatly dressed with short, tidy hair. The boy is in focus but in the background of the picture, out of focus and wearing muted colours, is a woman sitting on the floor with a small child next to her. The woman is looking down at her lap, possibly sorting through a bowl of dry rice. The small child is next to her with her head leaning on the woman's leg. The placing of the child on the right of the frame might suggest, using the given–new/left–right grammar of images proposed by Kress and van Leeuwen (1996), that this representation of a young boy in a developing country is unusual, even aspiring. His gaze is outside of the frame. We are both looking at something, but only he can see what 'we' are looking at. This distant look can be used to convey an attitude that is 'forward-looking, future-oriented, and determined' (Lutz and Collins 1993: 202). There are only five words anchoring this image: 'Child Link' and 'Save the Children'. This sparse presentation tells us what to do: make a connection (a link) with this child to save children. The third part of the leaflet is detachable. On one side is a direct debit instruction and on the other side the address of Save the Children and a photograph of two children in school uniforms, one of whom is writing with a biro. The aspirations of the boy on the front of the leaflet, looking towards the future, holding a closed exercise book, is transformed by the action of completing the direct debit instruction to the realization of the boy's aspirations in the image of children studying in school.

The inside or reverse of the leaflet is in two parts. One third is the direct debit instruction; the other two thirds have a central image of children playing on a large open, muddy area with houses in the background. To the left of this picture are two small images and to the right one smaller image. These images are all of children on their own, but in each they are actively engaged in a task (writing on a blackboard, feeding grass to a cow, cooking) rather than, as is more common in charity appeals using images of children, looking directly at the camera/spectator. The text that surrounds the images stresses the personal relationship between the donor ('you') and a particular child ('help a Child Link representative', 'you will hear from the child', 'you will be introduced to the child', 'you'll receive regular updates from the child'). A line of text, separated out from this, says: 'Be part of something amazing'. In each of these statements the individual relationship between the donor and the child is emphasized. The bonds of reciprocity implied by the claims that 'you will hear from the child', or 'you will be introduced to the child' and the close association between this campaign and the familiar genre of 'sponsor a child' or 'adopt a child' campaigns places the individual donor and the individual child in a quasi-familial relationship, with all the bonds of reciprocity and longevity that such a relationship implies. The hailing of the spectator as a parent is more muted in this campaign than in some other child sponsorship campaigns that describe the sponsored child as 'your child'. Clearly, while Save the Children are attempting to distance the campaign from appeals to sponsor or adopt a child that are a familiar part of the fund-raising landscape, they are nonetheless reluctant to jettison the familiar (in both senses) rhetoric of those campaigns, precisely because of the long-term relationship that the donor will (they hope) form with Save the Children. The campaign straddles uneasily the hailing of the donor as a surrogate parent and her or his interpellation as a supervisor or investor. The leaflet avoids appeals to sentiment, love or caring, and avoids a depiction in the words or the text of children as vulnerable. This positioning is exemplary of the shift in welfare discourse and practice over the last twenty years or so from regarding human beings as subjects of care to regarding human beings as subjects of rights (Rose 1996: 36). In these images and text the absence of an adult is not used to signal the vulnerability of the child but rather their resourcefulness and determination. However, the shift to a discourse of rights has not entirely erased an earlier discourse of care.

Save the Children's Kashmir earthquake campaign
The following analysis is of Save the Children International's home page on the days following an earthquake in Kashmir that killed an estimated 21,000 people in Pakistan, and 1,200 in India. On this day the picture reproduced below covered about two thirds of the page horizontally and about one third vertically.

The gaze   'The gaze' or 'the look' is a term used in film theory especially since Laura Mulvey's seminal essay 'Visual pleasure and narrative cinema' (1975) to analyse how film addresses the spectator. Analysis of the gaze attends to what look the photographic image or film invites (or demands – see Kress and van Leeuwen 1996: 122) from the spectator and how the depicted person is positioned in relation to the interior of the photograph, the camera angle,

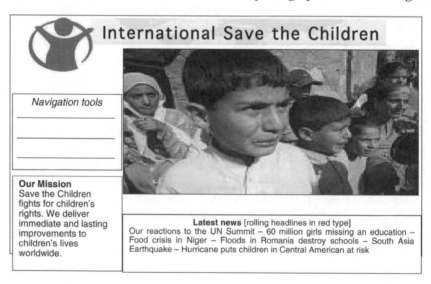

Figure 1: Representation of SCF home page: © Reuters/Danish Ishmail

and the viewer. Lutz and Collins (1993) read the photograph as an intersection of gazes offering a typology of seven kinds of gaze (the photographer's; the magazine's; the reader's; the subject's; western gaze; the refracted gaze; and the academic gaze (1993: 187–216). The analysis of the gaze often draws on psychoanalytic theory, particularly Lacan's mirror stage (Metz 1975) and the Foucauldian concept of surveillance (Foucault 1979). The empirical analysis of the gaze in specific images and films is informed by general cultural conventions about the meaning of looking: of the meaning of a direct look and an averted look, for example (Kress and van Leeuwen 1996: 122). The facing, 'demand' look in images is often considered confrontational and aggressive, but it is a very familiar look from fund-raising campaigns that use images of children. Children, being less powerful than the putative spectator, empty the direct look of its confrontational connotations, combining demand (you must respond) with appeal (please respond).

In the Save the Children campaigns in general the gaze is very different from that usually deployed in campaigns that use images of children. Aid campaigns that use images of children depend in general on the direct appeal of the gaze of the child appearing to look directly at the viewer. In contrast, all of the figures in this picture are looking with evident distress and horror and perhaps even disbelief at something that we, the viewers, cannot see. We do not know what has caught their gaze but we can assume it is something we too would find distressing and horrifying. The direction of their gaze positions the viewer of the photograph as being asked to 'look' at, or at least attend to, something we cannot see, and to look past the distress of these children towards what they are looking at. The invitation to look is an invitation to look at or respond to what is *not* depicted and to not look at what is depicted. This has the effect, which is compounded by the presence of a woman in the photograph, of resisting the classic interpellation of the viewer of pictures of children as a feeling, caring (feminine) adult. We are not hailed as surrogate mothers/parents to these children. They do not attend to us at all. The positioning of the children in the image does not invite us to care for them. Their gaze is not the imploring gaze so familiar from countless aid campaigns. Despite her marginal place at the edge of the photograph the woman depicted here is an important figure in framing our reading of the image; her familial role refuses our interpellation as the absent carer. Since the viewer is not invited to look at the children who are, in any case, already in the care of an adult, what are we invited to look at and what action are we asked to take following this looking? The direction of their gaze rests on an object, people or situation that, although they cannot be seen by us, are intended to be the subject of our attention. The children's tears, their distress and horror (and here again perhaps the adult serves to signify that this is real horror that would distress adults and children alike) serves to mark the gravity of the problem they face, not their need for comfort or maternal care.

This almost painterly tableau of human suffering draws on the genre of the painting that Chouliaraki (2006: 38) identifies, citing Boltanski, as one of the three genres of a 'historical typology of suffering' – the others are the novel and the manifesto. For Boltanski the *tableau vivant* 'directs the spectator away from specific emotional states and towards a distantiated contemplation of the aesthetics of suffering in the medium of the painting' (1999: 114–30). Aesthetic contemplation is an unusual mode to deploy in a fund-raising campaign. It separates the viewer from the activity of the campaigning organization. Nonetheless it is an image of suffering in which, according to the authors cited earlier, some response has to be made even if it is simply to voice concern or pity for the children depicted here. The appeal made in it cannot, I would suggest, be interpreted through the frame of child rights/politics of justice, but is more easily understood through the frame of child-saving/politics of pity. Arguably the difference between this appeal and the Child Link campaign discussed earlier is that the former is a response to an immediate disaster whereas the latter is an attempt to build longer-term funding for Save the Children's development work.

The mise-en-scène of the image   Mise-en-scène is also a term borrowed from film theory. It involves the analysis of the arrangement of people and objects in a scene to evoke an appropriate response in the audience. Analysing the mise-en-scène of images of children, particularly in fund-raising campaigns, is a useful device for exploring the theatrical presentation of suffering. Chouliaraki claims that two kinds of presentation of suffering predominate in news media: the agora and the theatre. The public space of debate and argument of the former is replaced in the latter by identification and immediacy: 'dispassionate observers are invited to feel for and identify with characters already active in the suffering' (Chouliaraki 2006: 45). We can think of aid campaigns as little dramas, or morality plays, in which the two genres of the novel and the film/theatre are brought together to evoke identification.

In another page linked to the Kashmir earthquake appeal on the website is a photograph of a girl's face almost entirely filling the frame of the image. Her gaze is absent – her face screwed up, her left finger pressed against her eyelid. Our gaze is divided between her and a boy who is sitting behind her. He is looking directly at the camera/the viewer. We are drawn to look at her grief but also at his more composed response. He is very neatly dressed. His white shirt is buttoned up to the neck, his tie is knotted close to his shirt collar, and his hair is short and neat. He is sitting behind her, positioned in a way that suggests they are sitting in rows in a classroom. In short, his demeanour is that of a schoolboy. This demeanour anchors her image as that of a schoolgirl. In this picture we are perhaps more likely to notice that she is also wearing a white school shirt and tie and that her hair is neatly plaited and tied with two large white bows. This picture was used by several other agencies in their fund-raising appeals. In those images (e.g. the one used by the British Red Cross Asian Earthquake Appeal) the photograph was cropped to exclude the boy from the frame. The cropping of the image changes the mise-en-scène. The school type setting of the Save the Children framing offers a different reading than the 'distressed girl alone' image of the other appeals, despite their use of the same photograph. Schools imply, amongst other things, discipline, regulation, improvement, and progress. Including the classroom in the photograph serves to disrupt the possible (and indeed prevailing) Western reading of India and Pakistan as underdeveloped, backward and (at least for Pakistan) Muslim. The familiarity of the image of the schoolchild encourages identification and recognition, affects connected with empathy rather than with pity.

These images of children in immediate need are familiar images from disaster campaigns in some respects. They are familiar in as much as they do not attempt to hail the viewer as arbiter of who might or might not deserve assistance. They take for granted that the 'naturalness' of the disaster obviates the need for calculation and that the empathetic, the human response is simply to give. However, in other respects they are more unusual. Firstly, the children are not represented as alone or abandoned. In both of the images analysed here the child is contained within his or her 'natural' domain of either the family (figure 1) or the school. Secondly, the gaze of the figures in the image is interior to their own social worlds: they look outside of the frame of the photograph but they do not meet the gaze of the viewer. The viewer can observe them but only as an outsider; there is no attempt to invite the viewer to intervene, or to overstate the role he or she can play. It is as if the passivity that has marked so many aid campaigns has shifted from the recipient of aid to the donor. This outsider status of the viewer is also evident in other Save the Children campaigns that are intended to encourage longer-term commitments to SCF. However, there is a discernible difference between the representation of children in the immediate and the longer-term campaigns. In the former, as I have suggested, the donor is not invited to calculate the legitimacy or credibility of the recipient's need. In the latter such an invitation to calculate is implicitly made. The children are presented alone, but rather than being alone and vulnerable they are competent and active.

From child-saving to child rights: helping those who help themselves

In 2004 a Tsunami devastated south-east Asia killing thousands, wrecking the fragile infrastructure of coastal villages, and leaving hundreds of children orphaned. Media coverage of the event in the UK, as elsewhere, was extensive. It dominated the front pages of all the major newspapers for several days, and campaigns to raise money for disaster relief were extraordinarily successful. Within two weeks £50 million had been raised from individual donations and fund-raising events. The British government increased its initial offer of aid from £5 to £50 million. The US government also misjudged popular feeling and increased its commitments to $350 million within days. Unusually large as these sums were they were completely dwarfed by the figures which both the US and the British government had then spent on invading and 'securing' Iraq: the United States had spent $148 billion and the UK £6 billion (Monbiot 2005).

The *Guardian* picture gallery showed dozens of images from India, Malaysia, Sri Lanka, Thailand and Indonesia of the devastation wrought by the Tsunami (*The Guardian* 2004). Children appeared in eight of these pictures. They are striking for their unflinching exposure of parents' grief. Three of the eight pictures show parents' grieving inconsolably. Four of them show parents and other adults holding onto their dead children or burying them. In one ('woman laments') a mother lies across a fallen tree, her face crumpled with the pain of loss. Her eyes are closed. It seems unlikely that she knew this picture was being taken, and it is a hard picture to look at. The sense of intrusion onto the awful solitude of loss is shocking. Another picture, from Cuddalore, India. A child's mother puts her head against her dead child's chest and wails; the sound penetrates the silence of the photograph. The father squats next to his child raising his child's arm gently upwards, as if this movement might make the child move. There are only the three of them; like the woman in 'woman laments', they are alone, isolated in their grief. Perhaps there are others, most likely there are others, who stand outside the frame of the picture, but they have been cut out. In two other pictures there is the crowd of people that one would expect to see at these moments. In one a group of men lay down bodies, including the body of a child, into a mass grave. From the edge of the pit a much larger group of people watch them. Another photograph: in Madras, several men walking purposefully through the water; one of them is carrying the body of a girl over his shoulder. Another: a father places his hand on his dead child's head as another man comforts him. The child's father covers his own eyes, his face screwed up with grief.

These images: what do they say to their global audience? Surely, that what has happened is terrible, almost impossible to contemplate; that the grief of these parents is deep and painful; that their loss is almost unimaginable. And also: that people will support each other, that they have families and neighbours, that someone will help them bury their child, will pray for them, will get them somewhere to live. That this is a place with social networks, not an abstract space waiting to be filled with a new history. These images interpellate the viewer as a compassionate outsider. Clearly, as evidenced by the significant sums raised through public donation, they invoked in people a desire to 'do something' to contribute to the restoring of this sudden reversal of fortune. The images evoke the worst fears of parents: the premature death of their child. They speak, perhaps to a shared human anxiety, about the fragility of life. For Christians, whether secular or religious, the fact of this event happening on the day after Christmas Day, a day which evokes the iconic figure of the child and people's shared humanity, added to its terrible poignancy. The apparent 'naturalness' of the disaster emptied it of its political calculation. This, it seemed, was an act of God. The people struck down by this disaster were not the 'undeserving poor'; they were hard-working capable people. It has been suggested that the scale of public donations was a marker of how closely people across the world identified with these tragic events, with a feeling that 'there but for the grace of God go I'. The images that circulated in the press of the Tsunami represented south Asians as ordinary people struck down by fate; images of parents grieving over the bodies of their dead children emphasized the shared humanity of the viewer and the viewed. The subtext that these were the 'deserving poor' who struggled to help themselves is reflected in how the anniversary of the Tsunami was reported.

Charitable fund-raising has long been imbued with a sentiment of helping those who help themselves. Philanthropy has been marked by a resistance to the idea that aid should depend on need. Rather, it has been shaped by a sentiment more amenable to puritan capitalism: that charity should prepare the ground for the poor to cultivate (to use a metaphor familiar from child-saving campaigns) (Chen 2003). Debates about making people dependent on aid or welfare have historically been more concerned with the adult, rather than child, recipients of aid. The dependency of the child on adult care makes a distinction between the deserving and the undeserving poor child difficult, or at least problematic, to sustain.

In the images used in reporting the impact of the Tsunami the appeal to the spectator is to respond within the frame of a politics of pity rather than a politics of justice. The emphasis of both fund-raising appeals and news reporting was on the randomness of the tragedy and the blamelessness of the people it struck down. No attempt was made to construct a narrative about the Tsunami within a politics of justice. Such a narrative would have asked (at the very least) about the differential impact of this disaster on different classes.

Summary

In this chapter I have shown that in the nineteenth century in Europe and North America a concern for child welfare framed in terms of rescuing children, often by separating them from their parents, shaped policy and practice in terms of 'child-saving'. In the twentieth century this discourse of child-saving was gradually inflected with a competing discourse of child rights. Increasingly, since the adoption of the UNCRC into international law action on behalf of children is spoken of within this newer paradigm of child rights, in which the child is invested with rights and capacity to exercise those rights. However, I have also suggested, following an analysis of how children are represented in INGO appeals and in broadcast media, that 'child-saving' has not been entirely displaced by 'child rights' but rather that the two co-exist in an uneasy tension with one another.

Recommended further reading

Chen, X. 2005. *Tending the Gardens of Citizenship: Child Saving in Toronto, 1880s–1920s*. Toronto: University of Toronto Press.
This is an excellent study of child-saving using a Foucauldian approach.

Chouliaraki, L. 2006. *The Spectatorship of Suffering*. London: Sage.
A useful theoretical and empirical study of how people respond to images of suffering.

de Block, E. and D. Buckingham. 2007. *Global Children, Global Media*. Basingstoke: Palgrave Macmillan.
A good overview of the literature on migration as it relates to children and an extended multi-country case study of video productions made by young refugees in Europe.

Holland, P. 2004. *Picturing Childhood: The Myth of the Child in Popular Imagery.* London: I. B. Tauris.
A revised second edition of her now classic study of images of children, *What is a Child?*

Murdoch, L. 2006. *Imagined Orphans: Poor Families, Child Welfare, and Contested Citizenship in London.* New Brunswick, NJ and London: Rutgers University Press.
A compelling study of the development of child-saving institutions in nine-teenth-century London.

3

Race, class and gender

Introduction

This chapter is about how race and gender shape children's lives, and how class is experienced through the prism of race and gender. The aim of the chapter is to show that childhood cannot be understood without an appreciation of how it is lived through gendered and raced identities and experiences. This aim is achieved by showing how children learn gendered roles and racial identities and how their identifications shape their life chances and their experiences. In the first part of the chapter I show that the child's work of learning that she or he has a gender does not begin and end with the simple announcement that 'it's a girl' or 'it's a boy'; the child has to learn what these statements mean: what it is that is involved in being a boy or a girl. The second part of the chapter is a contemporary history of race and racism in the USA. It takes four moments in the history of race in the USA to show the constant work that goes into the maintenance of white racial privilege and how this work is played out in the lives of American children. The final part of the chapter argues that class is not experienced by children as an independent identity but is articulated or experienced through race and gender.

Gender

There are two major currents of thinking in theories of gender: socialization and performativity. In the following section I first discuss gender socialization and, in particular, the research on the role of parents in teaching their children gender roles. I then set out two theories that I have grouped together because of the similarities between them: 'doing gender' and performativity. In the final part of this section on gender I show how gendered expectations of children impact on their use of time and their activities.

Gender socialization

Theories of gender socialization are derived from general theories of social-ization that propose that the child is taught or trained in how to be a compe-tent member of society. Talcott Parsons is probably the best-known figure in functionalist models of socialization. Through formal training and learn-ing how to deal with problems as they arise the child moves from the family to the outside world, gradually learning and internalizing the behaviours necessary to function in society (Corsaro 2005: 8). An alternative model of socialization criticized functionalism for its conservative perspective, arguing that it was only functional to some members of society and that a smooth transition of existing norms reproduced inequalities. Bourdieu, a French socialist, proposed the concept of the *habitus* to describe how children, through the constant repetition of small everyday actions, like eating and talking, come to feel at home in some spaces and not others, and claimed that this effectively reproduced class-based inequalities (Bourdieu 1990). Basil Bernstein, a British educationalist, argued that working-class children were disadvantaged in education because they learned to speak in restricted codes whereas middle-class children spoke in the elaborated codes that are used in schools (Bernstein 1971).

Whereas these theories of socialization are about how children learn a whole range of roles and practices, the idea of gender socialization uses the same models but only focuses on one aspect: socialization into appropriate gender roles. Gender role socialization assumes that 'individuals observe, imitate, and eventually internalize the specific attitudes and behaviors that the culture defines as gender appropriate by using other males and females as role models' (Hill 2002: 494, citing Ickes 1993: 79).

Parents' responses to their children are regarded as one of the most important, and certainly earliest, sites where this gets done. The presump-tion is that parents teach their children gender roles partly through inter-acting differently with boys than with girls. A review of studies published between 1936 and 1973 on differences in parents' behaviours towards girls and boys found that they were treated with 'a surprising degree of similar-ity' (Maccoby and Jacklin 1974: 362). The reviewed work was almost exclu-sively concerned with parents' interactional styles, and compared them between families; later studies that looked more at activities and beliefs and compared parents' interaction of boys and girls within families did not come to the same conclusions. A review of published studies from the 1970s and 1980s on parents' differential treatment of boys and girls found that 'the only area in which fathers and mothers in North American samples showed

significant differences in their treatment of girls and boys was encourage-
ment of sex-typed activities' (McHale et al. 2003: 129).

One of parents' roles in relation to their children's gender socialization
is in providing opportunities for their development and expression. In this
role studies show that parents treat their sons and daughters differently in
a range of activities (McHale et al. 2003: 133), including the way that their
bedrooms are decorated (Rheingold and Cook 1975), the toys children are
given (Fisher-Thompson 1993; Seiter 1995) and the allocation of household
chores (White and Brinkerhoff 1981). When families have limited budgets
'parents are more likely to invest in developmentally enhancing activities
for sons than for daughters' (McHale et al. 2003: 133).

There is a good deal of empirical evidence that children have different
experiences with their fathers than with their mothers and that these differences are significant for children's gendered socialization. Leaper et al.
(1998) found that mothers talk more to their children but are also more
negative in their talk than fathers are. Some studies have found that the
differences in how fathers and mothers interact with their children are
reduced if mothers work longer hours and fathers are pulled more into
daily family life. However, an ethnography of how the migration of Filipino
women has impacted on gender roles in the family as fathers are left to care
for their children found that gender norms were not undermined and in fact
were strengthened (Salazar Parreñas 2005).

Doing gender

Gender socialization theories have been criticized by feminist researchers
for their tendency to see socialization as a smooth transmission of ideas
from adults to children that reproduce gender-based inequalities. Within
the sociology of childhood there is a general dislike of socialization theories
because of their tendency to represent children as empty vessels into which
appropriate behaviours are poured. Barrie Thorne in her ethnography of
girls and boys at school, *Gender Play*, notes: 'Adults are said to socialize
children, teachers socialize students, the more powerful socialize, and the
less powerful get socialized' (Thorne 1993: 3). Leena Alanen (1994) notes
that treating children as in an 'immature and socially unfinished condition'
renders them problems and victims (1994: 28), making them the concern
of welfare and social policy rather than sociology. Socialization theories
have taken on these criticisms and more recent work on gender socialization does increasingly recognize that children are active agents in their own
socialization. William Corsaro's concept of 'interpretive reproduction'

captures this notion that socialization is not a transmission from adult to child but that the child is involved in an active process of interpretation and reworking of gender, race and class (Corsaro 2005: 18–27).

Another way of thinking about gender is as unavoidable social practices or what West and Zimmerman (1987) called in their seminal paper of the same title 'Doing gender'. They cite Spencer Cahill's work on gender development to illustrate their point that although gender is a performance it is not one we can refuse: 'little boys appropriate the gender ideal of "efficaciousness" that is, being able to affect the physical and social environment through the exercise of physical strength or appropriate skills. In contrast little girls learn to value "appearance" that is, managing themselves as ornamental objects. Both classes of children learn that the recognition and use of sex categorization in interaction are *not optional, but mandatory*' (West and Zimmerman 1987: 141; emphasis added). Despite West and Zimmerman's claims of a radical break with gender socialization theories their contribution to gender theory is more about the importance of naturally occurring data to understanding gender than it is a radical reworking of the concept of gender itself.

Judith Butler's concept of performativity, despite having a superficial resemblance to West and Zimmerman's theory, does pose a radical challenge to our understanding of the concept of gender and to the sex–biology/gender–culture binary that underpins most theories of gender. Like West and Zimmerman in their ethnomethodology of gender she emphasizes its performative character. They challenge the idea of gender roles on the grounds that '[g]ender is not merely something that happens in the nooks and crannies of interaction, fitted in here and there and not interfering with the serious business of life' (West and Zimmerman 1987: 130), and this closely resembles Butler's contention that gender is inescapable. The resemblance between the two theories is nonetheless superficial because the power of Butler's theory lies in its notion that there is 'no doer behind the deed' (Butler 1990: 142); that is to say that there is no ungendered or universal human subject who decides to 'do gender'. The core of Butler's thinking about gender and other subject positions like race and sexuality is that subjectification is necessary in order to become a part of human culture (Butler 1997) – at least as human culture is currently configured. Her second major contribution to the theory of gender is that gender identification is inseparable from the normalization of heterosexual desire. There has been some interesting small-scale empirical research done using Butler's theory on how children's gender performativities are bound up with heterosexual discourse at a very early age (Boldt 1996; 2002), and on how parents' anxieties about homosexuality impact negatively on their prior commitment to gender-neutral child-rearing (Martin 2005).

Early theories of gender socialization were rather superficial; their strength was in the way that it challenged the idea that observable differences in the behaviour of girls and boys, and women and men, were somehow natural or biological. It therefore opened up the possibilities of changing gender-based inequalities. Theories of how children come to learn to 'do' or perform gender retain this advantage of gender socialization theories and in addition they enable us to think of children as active participants in shaping their social worlds. Empirically perhaps there is not so much distance between them; whether we learn, practise or perform gender, the crucial point is that we cannot avoid gendered positions and practices, so long as gender is accepted as a meaningful distinction between humans.

It is to the empirical data that I now turn in the following section, where I describe across two sites, caring and labour, how gender affects children's lifeworlds. In demonstrating how gender affects children's lives these are not the only sites I could have chosen. Play, school and sexuality are at least as important in understanding gender in childhood. I chose to focus on care and labour because play and school are two sites that have had a lot of attention in childhood studies whereas, probably because they are considered unchildlike, care and labour have not.

Gendered care and gendered labour

The allocation of tasks, the organization of time and space: these are all done in gendered ways. It is through these kinds of practices that children come to understand what their gender means for how they spend their time, where they can go and what they can do. It is also through these social practices that children invest in themselves as gendered people; that they desire to be not just a particular kind of person or child but that they want to be a particular kind of girl or boy.

Most children in the world work (see chapter 5). The age at which children start work depends on the particular context that they live in. In South Africa in migrant hostels it might be as late as nine years old (Jones 1993: 131), in the Caribbean work might begin at five or six years (Chevannes 2001: 206; Liebel 2004: 77). When children start work that does not mean that they have to stop playing; Cindi Katz points out in *Growing up Global* (2004) that clear divisions between play and work are more prevalent in industrial and post-industrial than in agricultural societies, and amongst adults than children. She says that in the Sudanese village where she did her fieldwork '[a]n element of play was always fused with the work of children – they worked at play and played at work' (Katz 2004: 60). She describes boy shepherds, for example, playing while protecting their herds: 'The animals eat their way about one hundred meters to the east and every once in a while one of the boys casts an eye toward them. Their mala [a game like jacks] is spirited, full of pinching cheeks and hitting vanquished opponents' (Katz 2004: 61). Manfred Liebel also comments on the pre-industrial integration of work and play noting that '[s]eparating play, work and life would appear to the people of the Andes as if nature had been transformed into a resource to be exploited' (Liebel 2004: 182). In a perhaps slightly romantic description of boys tending cattle in Ethiopia he notes that they 'play the most varied games, put on races and tell each other stories' (Liebel 2004: 183). He cites an ethnography of Australian Aborigines that describes children 'helping the adults or imitating them while they worked . . . Girls go with the mothers, grandmothers and aunts on the daily search for food, roots and tubers, leaves, fruits, small animals . . . Boys practise hunting, aiming at birds, lizards and other small animals' (Liebel 2004: 183, citing Thomson and White 1993: 373ff.).

Even in these brief descriptions of children at work and play it comes across clearly that boys and girls do different work: it is boys who are tending cattle and shining shoes, and girls who are looking after their younger siblings and doing domestic chores. In her ground-breaking ethnography of children's work in Kerala, South India, Olga Nieuwenhuys (1994) describes how most of the work that girls do involves the care of their siblings and of the house. When they do help their mothers in weaving coir they do not describe it as work but as helping out. When boys do the same tasks they do think of it as work and they expect to receive some payment for helping their mothers.

In many respects then girls' work is not very different from women's work. Like women's work it is rarely recognized as work but is more thought of as care. In a later chapter in this book on children and work I discuss the ways that thinking of the work that girls do as not really work distorts our understanding of what girls do with their time. The UN in their *State of the World's Children* reports defines child labour as the involvement of a person aged five to eleven in at least one hour of economic activity or *twenty-eight hours* of domestic work in one week; or a child aged twelve to fourteen who did at least fourteen hours of economic activity or *forty-two hours* of economic activity and domestic work combined. Clearly the UN does not think that domestic chores are work!

Although all contemporary societies have a sexual division of labour this does not mean that only girls do 'girls' work' or only boys do 'boys' work'. Mothers living in migrant workers' hostels in South Africa feared for their boys' safety because they could not find work to occupy them in the city and so their sons were left to their own devices. They did not worry about their daughters because even in the city there were still younger children to be looked after, food to be prepared, and housework to be done. However, if there were no girls in the family to do this work, then a boy might be called on to do it instead. One of the researchers' boy informants said: 'I do not think there is a difference between boys' duties and girls' duties. I have a friend, Sabela, and he does all the things that girls do because his sister does not live here' (Jones 1993: 123). In *East African Childhood* (Fox 1967), for example, Joseph Lijembe describes how in the 1940s, when he was himself four years old, he was given the role of 'nursing', that is feeding, toilet-training and playing with his baby sister. This role fell to him even though boys were not supposed to take care of their siblings because 'there was no older sister in the family, and my mother had to go off to work in the shamba every day' (Fox 1967: 4).

Despite a kind of pragmatic reworking of roles when there are not enough girls to do 'girls' work' or boys to do 'boys' work' this does not mean that the idea that there is such a thing as girls' work and boys' work does not persist. Even when there is a general shift in law and policy towards gender equality, it seems that gendered expectations of work still hold. Hewitt and Wells (n.d.), for example, in their qualitative study of white working-class families in London found that girls' and boys' expectations of their life course were highly gendered, with girls wanting to work in hairdressing or beauty salons until they had children, when they intended to leave work to look after their children, as their mothers had done, and boys generally expected to work in the building trade or as motor mechanics. Linda McDowell's research on white working-class school leavers also suggests a persistence of gendered expectations of work. She comments that her respondents held 'depressingly traditional views about gender-specific skills and abilities', going on to quote a respondent who says 'I think there is more jobs mainly for boys really. There are mainly motor places and stuff like that and places where you have got to do heavy lifting and they're for boys', and another respondent who says 'Industry and engineering, they don't usually take girls on, do they? Most girls aren't interested in that anyway, they usually go for office work or journalism or something like that' (McDowell 2000: 409, 410; 2002; see also Nayak 2003).

The impact of globalization on gendered childhoods

Family life is one of the most important sets of relationships within which children learn the significance of gender in all its dimensions from the psychological to the political and economic. For some children globalization has profoundly changed the structure of family life, through the expansion of global circuits of labour. These global circuits often depend on 'regimes of labour intimacy' (Chang and Ling 2000; Hochschild 2002) that involve women leaving their children in one country to do paid care for families in another country.

Rachel Salazar Parreñas set out to examine what impact the migration of Filipino women had on the gendered relations between fathers and their children who stayed behind. She reasoned that if gender is a social construction then, when society changes because, as in this instance, men become the primary carers of their children, gender is also likely to change. Migrant parents in the Philippines work in a whole range of jobs from professional to semi-skilled and unskilled. Most migrant mothers are working as nurses or domestic-care workers. She notes that increasing numbers of women in the USA and Europe make their own participation in the labour market possible by hiring the labour of other women from the global south to care for their children. Although both men and women migrate and 9 million Filipino children have a parent abroad, absent fathers are considered less of a problem than absent mothers because, whilst mothers can nurture and discipline their children, the prevalent view is that fathers only know how to discipline their children. Although both mothers and fathers migrate, 'mothers are not automatically assumed to migrate for the sake of the collective mobility of the family. Therefore, mothers must perform greater work to show their children that despite the distance they do really still care for the family. This burden raises the bar in the transnational family work of migrant mothers, who find themselves responsible for both the emotional and the material well-being of their children in the Philippines' (Salazar Parreñas 2005: 66).

Salazar Parreñas' hypothesis that gender roles would change since many fathers now had, at least in theory, primary responsibility for their children was not valid for most of her respondents. Mothers were still expected to do the emotional care for their children, and other women – neighbours and relatives – took on their physical care. One of her respondents, a seventeen-year-old girl, said: 'I try to carry the burden of solving my problems on my own, because I cannot help but think that she [i.e. her mother] is already so far and I should not be there to only give her more problems' (Salazar

Parreñas 2005: 99). A few men did 'sometimes find themselves with no choice but to adjust accordingly to their new household arrangements' (Salazar Parreñas 2005: 103).

Commenting on the findings of research on immigrant children in Los Angeles that girls carry far more responsibility than boys in the maintenance of immigrant families, Salazar Parreñas says that this is also the case when the girls are at home and only the parent migrates. Girls translate; they do advocacy work in financial, medical and legal transactions; and they look after younger siblings. The eldest child helps younger siblings with schoolwork, helps them to get ready for school and feeds them. Daughters do more of this work than sons. Some resent it but 'most daughters report finding they gain skills from their added responsibilities' (Salazar Parreñas 2005: 111).

Race and racism in the USA

The impact of Jim Crow on children's lives

In *Growing Up Jim Crow: How Black and White Southern Children Learned Race* (2006) Jennifer Ritterhouse emphasizes the importance of experience and the recollection of experience as 'fundamental to the interior process by which individuals came to think of themselves and others in distinctly racial terms' (Ritterhouse 2006: 5). This emphasis on experience and memory is central to Ritterhouse's method, which uses published autobiographies and (existing) oral history interviews. What she shows in *Growing Up Jim Crow* is that adults remember events from their childhood as formative to the production of a racial identity; race structured children's lives, regardless of whether or not they experienced themselves as racialized people. Of course how race structured children's lives was different for white children than it was for black, but in both instances race and racism erased any possibility of children living within the idealized protected spaces of childhood. It is important to recognize that it is not that in this period there was no vision of an ideal childhood as a space of protection and innocence; the point is that this vision was restricted by white racism to white children (Sallee 2004), and that this limitation on the rights of childhood was encoded in law. While the 'ideal of an innocent and sheltered childhood took hold in the South in the early twentieth century . . . a surprising number of [white] families seem to have felt no need to shield their children from the most brutal acts of racism, as the many white children who appear in lynching photographs attest' (Ritterhouse 2006: 19). In this section I focus on how racism under Jim Crow – the period from the end of the Civil War to the 1964 Voting Rights Act – shaped family life, and on black children's exposure to and white children's involvement in racist violence.

Family life
It was in the home and from the instruction of their mothers that white children learned what Ritterhouse calls 'racial etiquette' – the overly polite term that she uses to describe the spoken and unspoken rules that governed relations between white and black Americans in the Jim Crow South. The gradual acceptance of a new ideal of childhood innocence and dependency was not extended by most whites to black children, 'even those white Southerners who devoted the most attention and material and emotional resources to their own children rarely saw any but the very youngest black children as innocents or extended the ideal of the sheltered childhood to blacks' (Ritterhouse 2006: 63). Many white children were taught not to use terms of respect for black people, including 'Lady' or 'Sir', 'Miss', 'Mr' or 'Mrs'. Clifton Johnson in his *Highways and Byways of the South* (1904) recorded an exchange between a white girl and her grandmother whose home he was lodging at in Florida. 'There's a colored lady out on the porch wants to speak to you', the girl told her grandmother. "Colored lady! Colored lady! Say "that nigger"' (Ritterhouse 2006: 55).

It is one of the contradictions of social inequalities that those with social power both despise those without power and are dependent on their labour. In Southern households domestic labour and the care of children was often done by black servants. The intimacy of the contact between white people and their black servants is illustrated by countless stories of white children's emotional attachments to black servants; this intimacy did not in most cases erode white racism. (A fact that should give pause to those who argue that contact across the boundaries of social difference undoes prejudice and discrimination.) Indeed, stories of white children being reprimanded by their parents when they ignored the rules of contact across the 'colour line' are very common in white narratives of growing up in the American South (Ritterhouse 2006: 78–80; Quinn 1954) and in settler colonies. (Nor was this insistence on refusing polite forms of address to black adults a private matter. In the 1940s white sociologist Arthur Raper was called before a grand jury for using courtesy titles for black people: Ritterhouse 2006: 81.)

Not all white Southerners were wealthy, and neither were all African Americans poor (although most were), but being middle class for African Americans was no protection against racism; middle-class African Americans were subject to the same public or social mores and legal regulations of segregation as working-class African Americans. It is true that middle-class African Americans had the financial resources to allow them to not engage with or to get around some aspects of segregation. One of Ritterhouse's sources recalls how her father would never travel by bus so that he could avoid the humiliation of having to sit at the back.

If the class privilege of middle-class African Americans could not insulate them from racism, conversely the class oppression of working-class whites did not prevent them from being included in the politics of white supremacy. Sara Brooks in her autobiography comments that their white neighbours were as poor as her own family but they still 'musta thought they was more than we were because when we'd go to the spring to get water, Mr Garrett [the white neighbour] had to drink the water first . . . he'd drink and his kids would drink and then we'd drink' (cited in Ritterhouse 2006: 127).

One of the roles of a parent is to protect their children. This is a difficult role for black parents in a racist society. In the National Association for the Advancement of Colored People (NAACP) newsletter there was constant debate about how parents could counter their children's exposure to racist violence and disrespect. Strategies to counter the influence of white racism on the child's sense of self ranged from the politics of respectability to a refusal to discuss white racism while insisting that, in the interests of their safety, their children should accept the limits that racism placed on their freedom (Ritterhouse 2006: 98–102).

Public violence

One of the most stark instances of how even those children who were supposed to be living a sheltered childhood, that is to say white children, were not sheltered from racist violence, indeed were encouraged to participate, as actors or spectators, in acts of racist violence is found in accounts (written and photographic) of the lynching of black men by white mobs (Ritterhouse 2006: 64, 71–8). Lynchings and race riots (attacks by whites on black neighbourhoods) were a common experience in the South, and children were as exposed to the possibility and reality of violence as adults were. Walter White, the future executive of the NAACP, describes his experience of being caught up, at the age of thirteen, in a race riot. The riot taught him, he says, 'that there is no escape from life' (Ritterhouse 2006: 109). This telling phrase grasps exactly why children's lives cannot be considered as if they live in a separate space from adult society and politics: there is only one life and children are as much a part of it as adults are.

Social psychology and theories of racial identification

Jim Crow is shorthand in the USA for the legal and social structures and processes that white Southerners constructed after the end of the Civil War to reverse the gains in the civil rights of black Americans that Union victory should have guaranteed. Slavery could not be reinstated but all kinds of other legal, political, economic and social obstacles were erected to prevent African Americans from attaining social, economic or political equality with white Americans. One of these obstacles was that children were educated in segregated schools. The Fourteenth Amendment of the Constitution makes it unconstitutional for Americans to be treated unequally before the law. White Southerners got round this by arguing that black and white children were getting an education that was separate but equal. This was a blatant lie. In Clarendon County, South Carolina in 1950, they spent $179 on public schools for each white child and less than a quarter of that sum, $43, on every black child. There were sixty-one schools for black children, 'more than half of them ramshackle or plain falling-down shanties that accommodated one or two teachers and their charges, and twelve schools for whites' (Kluger 2004: 8). The total value of the black schools, attended by over six and a half thousand black students, was less than $200,000; the total value of the white schools, attended by less than two and a half thousand students, was $673,850, over three times as much as the black schools (Kluger 2004: 8). White children had thirty publicly funded school buses to get them to school; there was not one school bus for black students.

The NAACP chose school segregation as its major legal case to argue that segregation and unequal treatment of African Americans was unconstitutional. Schools were an excellent starting point for the campaign to use the law to force the ending of Jim Crow in the South because by 1950 there was not a dual ideology of childhood; all children were regarded as innocent, dependent and vulnerable. Who could regard it as right to prevent respectable children, eager to learn, from having an equal right to learn? Who in the North would not be shocked by the sight of white adults screaming at black children and trying to prevent them from doing something as ordinary and worthwhile as going to school?

To pursue their case the NAACP wanted to demonstrate in court that segregation caused damage to the self-esteem of black students. They asked Kenneth Clark to give expert evidence to the court using his 'doll tests' in the 1951 case of *Briggs v. Elliott*, one of five suits that collectively were known as *Brown v. Board of Education* (Patterson 2001: 25).

Kenneth Clark and Mamie Clark had developed a series of psychological tests using pink and brown dolls to investigate the impact on African American children's racial identity and self-esteem of their awareness of racism. The NAACP's Legal Defense Fund's attorney, Thurgood Marshall, wanted to prove that segregation caused injury to black children (Kluger 2004: 316). The NAACP's case rested on the theory that school segregation did psychic damage to black children and this was essentially what the Clarks had found in their 'doll studies'.

The Clarks had been publishing their work on the impact of racism on the self-identity of black children since 1939. The doll tests involved showing black children ages four to seven two brown and two white dolls and asking them to 'give me the white doll', 'give me the colored doll' and 'give me the Negro doll', and then they were asked which doll was nice, which they would like to play with, which doll looked bad and which doll had a nice colour. They found that wherever they did these tests the children showed 'an unmistakeable preference for the white doll and a rejection of the brown doll' (Kluger 2004: 317). Another series of tests, using outline drawings of different objects and of a boy and a girl which the subject child was asked to colour in selecting a colour or colours from a choice of black, brown, white, yellow, pink and tan, found that black children displayed a preference for white and yellow colours and random mixtures of colours when colouring in the outlines of the boy and girl. The Clarks interpreted their data to mean that black children suffered from self-rejection (Kluger 2004: 318). In 1955 Kenneth Clark was commissioned to write a report on their findings for the White House Midcentury Conference on Youth. It cited other studies, including those done by Marian J. Radke and Helen G. Trager, who had run similar tests in Philadelphia. They used cut-out brown and white dolls; both black and white children were asked to say which they preferred. They found that 57 per cent of the black children and 89 per cent of the white children preferred the white cut-out doll.

To prepare his evidence for the *Briggs* case Clark did the doll test on sixteen randomly selected children at a black segregated school in Clarendon County. The children, all between six and nine years old, were asked to choose the doll which most looked like them: seven of them chose the white doll. The findings were consistent with the other studies that the Clarks had conducted (Kluger 2004: 331).

The Clarks were not the only experts to give evidence in the case of *Briggs* v. *Elliott*. Although the three judges hearing the case were convinced that education in South Carolina was highly unequal, they found against the NAACP's plea that schools should be desegregated, with one dissenting opinion, that of Judge J. Waites Waring. The NAACP had not expected a ruling in their favour, their intention in bringing *Briggs* and the other four cases was that by the time they appealed to the Supreme Court they could present 'a record of pervasive and undeniable injustice' (Kluger 2004: 368).

Social psychology and childhood innocence

The early studies of the Clarks were substantiated over and over by subsequent studies. They showed consistently that children were aware of race and that racism impacted negatively on black children's self-esteem. These findings contradicted a commonsense view that children were too young to understand race or to understand when they were being discriminated against on the basis of race. In 1952 Mary Goodman published her research on race awareness in young children. She used psychological tests together with observation, school records and interviews with parents of a sample, balanced for race and gender, of 103 children at nursery schools to research the extent of race awareness amongst young children. She found that very young children are aware of 'race' but that they are not necessarily antagonistic towards people of other races. Her study replicated the findings of the Clarks that a large majority of the African American children (74 per cent) showed a preference for the company of white children; only 8 per cent of white children showed a preference for the company of African American children. She also found that mothers found it difficult to explain race to their children and tried to put it off until they thought the children might be able to understand it; this was truer of African American mothers than of white mothers. She referred to children's 'precocious raciality' against parents' conviction that their children were unaware of race. Although the cumulative evidence that young children have some understanding of race is pretty convincing, we still have no empirical evidence about this for children younger than three years old (Katz 1976).

In-group; out-group

When the Clarks devised their doll studies their interest was in the impact of racism on the self-esteem and racial identification of black students. Their work set the stage for much of the subsequent thinking in social psychology on the impact of racism on black children's psyches. The other major strand in social psychology on race and racism in childhood draws on Henri Tajfel's (1981) concept of social identity and intergroup relations. Tajfel's theory is a general theory that postulates that all human societies establish group identities and that prejudice operates to maintain the boundaries of the in-group against the out-group. The basis on which this sorting into groups happens can be entirely random. The most famous test of this is the experiment in which a school teacher on the day after Martin Luther King Jr was assassinated divided her all-white class of school children into blue-eyed and brown-eyed groups and treated one group as a superior group to the other on an arbitrary basis (http://www.pbs.org/wgbh/pages/front-line/shows/divided). Like Clark's doll test, Jane Elliot's classroom experiment also showed that children who are treated as if they are expected to do well tend to do well and children who are expected to do badly tend to do badly.

Frances Aboud (1988) argues that children start to recognize the existence of racially based social or group identities at about the age of three years and that between the ages of four and eight years the child aligns themselves with a racial group based on perceived similarities between themselves and the group. Katz (1987) claims that young children have a tendency to over-generalize and an inability to manage contradictory information and that 'their greater receptivity to global and affect-laden statements may make them particularly prone to prejudicial thinking' (Katz 1987: 95).

Learning the first R: school studies of race and racism

Most of the studies of race and racism in childhood have been done in schools by ethnographers, social psychologists and educationalists. This is partly for the simple reason that children in schools are relatively easy to access and most children in the population will be attending school. It is easy to draw a random sample of schools and a random sample within schools; claims can therefore be made about the likelihood that the findings of the study can be extended to the general child population. The interest in race and racism in schools also reflects the concerns of educationalists that African American children underachieve in public (state) schools and the suspicion that this is because fifty years after *Brown* v. *Board of Education* black students are still getting a lower standard of education than their white peers and that black students have to contend with racist attitudes in schools.

Amanda Lewis's *Race in the Schoolyard* (2003) is an ethnography of three schools in California: a mainly white school in a suburban neighbourhood, a mixed Latino and African American urban school, and an elective school with a mainly Latino student body. Her main contention is that schools are 'central places where race is made and remade in the everyday' (Lewis 2003: 11). *Learning the First R: How Children Learn Race and Racism* (Van Ausdale and Feagin 2001) has a similar premise that educational institutions are one of the key sites in the learning of race. Van Ausdale and Feagin's study is an ethnography of an urban pre-school in the USA in which they argue that young children are aware of racial privilege and that white children use racist statements as ways of demonstrating their racial privilege. Whilst I found some of their interpretations overdone, their argument that the children in their study were aware of racial categories was convincingly demonstrated. Since these children are very young (ages three and four) Van Ausdale and Feagin also argue that their study undermines Piagetian claims that moral and abstract reasoning is absent in young children.

Learning the First R is one of a handful of ethnographic studies of young children in school that focus on race and racism. The other major studies are Paul Connolly's *Racism, Gender Identities and Young Children* (1998) and Barry Troyna and Richard Hatcher's *Racism in Children's Lives: A Study of Mainly White Primary Schools* (1992). Both of these were done in English primary schools. The subjects that Connolly's study focused on were mainly black and South Asian boys and girls in an urban primary school. He does not discuss the attitude of white children in the school towards race and racism. Barry Troyna and Richard Hatcher's study was designed to fill the gap in empirical research on primary schools into relations between black and white children. Despite the claims of Van Ausdale and Feagin that their findings are novel, Troyna and Hatcher, writing ten years earlier, albeit in the UK, agreed that 'young people are "racialised" by the time they experience primary school education' (Troyna and Hatcher 1992: 21). Their own study focused on the use of racist language by white children in school and the extent to which efforts at using the curriculum, for example the study of slavery, to undermine racist attitudes were seen by many white students as another opportunity to display racial privilege. They report that many black children interpreted the teaching of the history of racial oppression as a *racist* (*sic*) discourse.

Racial classification, racial identification and mixed-parentage children

Like all social identities race is based on a fiction that has real effects. The fiction is that race is biological and visible; that when we look at one another we know by looking how to classify one another into one racial category or another. The fact is that the ascribing of people into racial categories has real effects on their life chances and their access to resources. The fact that race is a fiction means that a lot of work has to be done to classify people into racial categories and to maintain the boundaries between one classification and another.

A lot of this work on racial classification gets done by state bureaucracies in collecting statistics, by census reports, equal opportunity monitoring reports, identity cards, and so on. Throughout the history of racial classification, people that cross the boundaries of racial classifications have generated anxiety in those whose world-view and privilege depends on the maintenance of racial boundaries. The ongoing debate in the USA about how to ask about multiracial individuals on the census form is a reflection of this anxiety (Brunsma 2005: 1132, 1136). In this context, how do bi-racial children negotiate the meanings of race and racism?

Colonial power and racial boundaries

The European Empire legitimated its rule through a new way of classifying humans: race. All of the European powers and the settler states in the Americas, Southern Africa, East Africa, Asia and Australia set great store by their ability to classify people into races and to maintain the boundaries between these by outlawing sexual contact between people of different races and persecuting their children. The forced removal of the children of white fathers and aboriginal mothers from their mothers in Australia did not end until 1967 (van Krieken 1999). In the United States interracial relationships were illegal in many Southern states until 1967 when the case of *Loving* v. *Virginia* found that anti-miscegenation laws contravened the Fourteenth Amendment and were therefore unconstitutional (Pascoe 1996).

In the United States the children of mixed relationships were classified as black under the so-called 'one-drop rule'; elsewhere in the colonies mixed-race children were more likely to be classified as mixed (métissage, mestizo) or coloured. In French West Africa (White 1999), in Indonesia (Stoler 1995) and in Australia (Manne 2001; Moses 2004) the state and the church encouraged or enforced the separation of these children from their African, Asian or Aboriginal mothers so as to assimilate them into whiteness or to form a racialized middle class.

Contemporary studies of racial identity and classification

Black social workers have argued that placing black children in white families for adoption has a detrimental impact on the racial identity of the children. In their research on the racial identifications of teenagers in Britain, *Black, White or Mixed-Race*, Barbara Tizard and Ann Phoenix (1993) tried to test empirically this claim in a study of whether bi-racial or mixed-parentage children living with their white mothers 'misidentified' as white. They found that they did not and argued that the racial identification of young people was shaped by multiple forces including their family, their school, their friendships and the neighbourhood that they lived in. Frances Winndance Twine has published research on the identifications of 'brown-skinned white girls' in the USA (1996) and on interracial families in England (2004). 'Brown-skinned white girls' is the term Twine uses to describe how bi-racial undergraduates with African American fathers and white or Asian mothers were 'raised white' through 'their immersion in a family and social network which embraced a racially unmarked, middle class identity' (Twine 1996: 207). When they entered college in their late teens many of them responded to demands made on them by their fellow students to classify themselves as black or African American by adopting a bi-racial or black identity, suggesting that racial identification is fluid and contextual. Twine's research in England took up some of the issues that Tizard and Phoenix's study had addressed about whether white parents can raise black or mixed-parentage children in ways that respect their multiracial/cultural heritage, invest them with a clear sense of racial identity and help them respond to the traumas and hurts of racism. She concludes that the white parents of African-descent children engage in 'specific practices designed to discourage biracial identities and encourage the social production of "black" children' through 'the intergenerational transfer of racial literacy' (Twine 2004: 901). Suki Ali's ethnography of children's racial identities in England found that children's identities, whilst not entirely fluid, shift from context to context (Ali 2003). In contrast to Twine's celebration of the anti-racist project of white mothers who encourage their 'mixed' children to take on an unambiguously 'black' identity, Ali is arguing for the possibility of 'mixed-race' children to dissolve racial categories altogether in a project towards the construction of a post-race identity.

Complementing these ethnographic studies of mixed-race identity and identification is an analysis by David Brunsma (2005) of the Early Childhood Longitudinal Study (ECLS-K). This data set of over 17,000 children was representative of the US kindergarten population in 1998. The racial iden-tification questions on the survey included a 'more than one race' option; 2.6 per cent of parents designated their children in this multiracial category, although an analysis of the birth mother and birth father's own racial identification showed that 10.4 per cent of parents could have checked this category for their child. Brunsma found that families with a white or multiracial parent were much more likely than other multiracial families to check a multiracial identification; families with one Hispanic parent were least likely to check multiracial – they mostly opted for the 'Hispanic' designation (Brunsma 2005: 1142). Hispanic-white families in the Southern states are more likely to designate their child 'white'. In his conclusion Brunsma suggests that parents are choosing racial identifications for their multiracial children that are a response to 'a shifting racial order, one more in line with Latin American racial structures' (Brunsma 2005: 1150).

The intersections of class, race, gender and age

Class has become an increasingly marginalized explanation for inequality. Social policy increasingly uses concepts like 'social exclusion' in preference to 'class' to describe the persistence of intergenerational poverty. Social exclusion implies that inequality is not structural and persistent, woven into the very fabric of society, but personal and redeemable. Social exclusion can be overcome by increasing social networks or getting back to work (no matter how poorly paid and tedious); governments can do things to encourage social inclusion – like forcing people to go to work by cutting welfare benefits – but ultimately it is the personal responsibility of excluded individuals to take the initiative and become socially included, or so the argument goes.

In this post-class discourse, class is reduced to an economic category and is talked about in terms of 'poverty' or 'income levels', both terms that elide the structures that produce class.

Disaggregated data by household income are the closest proxies available for any attempt to assess how class shapes children's access to material resources. UNICEF's *State of the World's Children* 2006 report says: 'In every developing country where disaggregated data by household income are available, children living in the poorest 20 per cent of households are significantly more likely to die before the age of five than those living in the richest 20 per cent' (UNICEF 2006: 8). In Peru children living in the poorest quintile are five times more likely to die before their fifth birthday than children from the wealthiest quintile (UNICEF 2006: 18). In general, being born in the poorest quintile of a developing country means a child is two to three times more likely to die than a child born into the richest quintile. Low income is also correlated with low rates of primary school attendance. Over three quarters (77 per cent) of children out of primary school are from the poorest 60 per cent of households in developing countries. Within Latin America and the Caribbean (84 per cent) and in Eastern and Southern Africa (80 per cent) the disparity is even greater. While rural areas tend to have more households living in poverty and without access to services than urban areas, in the slums, tenements and shantytowns of the world's cities levels of exclusion are comparable to those of the rural areas. More than 900 million people live in slums in cramped conditions and most lack access to safe drinking water and decent sanitation facilities.

In *Women without Class: Girls, Race and Identity*, her ethnographic study of Mexican American and white girls at high school in rural North America, Julie Bettie argues that class is always inflected through race and gender. In claiming this she is not arguing that what appears as racial or gender oppression is simply a veil thrown over class inequality, but rather for 'the inextricability of race and class signifiers' (2003: 180). Class clearly structures life chances as the statistics cited above show, but explanations for class inequality and the effects of class inequality are lived out in the lives of racialized and gendered subjects. Clearly class does not always map onto race, and certainly it does not map onto gender: to put it simply, not all working-class people are black and not all whites are middle class. Nonetheless, the exclusion of a racialized or ethnicized group from access to material and symbolic resources has the effect of making all struggles over resources racialized struggles.

Race is not understood here as having a reality outside the social; it is not that races exist and then they are mobilized in order to naturalize class divisions. It is rather the case that race as a social fact is brought into existence through the praxis of capitalism.

How race–class signifiers are experienced is also shaped by gender: the experience of being a white middle-class girl/woman is different to being a white middle-class boy/man. However, this difference of gendered experiences within a race–class nexus does not mean that shared gender identities make the lifeworlds of, say, black boys/men and white boys/men interchangeable. While people might make political alliances across race–class lines on the basis of gender – as with feminism – these alliances cannot erase the material inequalities and symbolic differences between black people and white people or between working classes and middle classes.

These points about the social construction of race, about the ways that racialized inequality and class inequality reinforce one another and are expressed through racialized and gendered identities, are perhaps uncontroversial, at least within a particular tradition of social theory, when we are speaking of adults. However, when we speak about children's race–class and gendered identities, the picture is different. The classed experience of children is hidden from view. This is partly because class is widely understood as being related to waged labour – particularly manual and factory work. Even those analyses that accept that bureaucratic, mental or intellectual labour is also work often attribute the class position derived from work only to the worker and not to his or her dependants. In other words, if a man works for a wage and his family are dependent on that wage he is recognized as having a class position but they are not. Nor is it only being in work that identifies a working man's class but not his dependants'. It is also to do with a presumption that men derive identity from work in a way that women do not; that women's identity is defined in relation to family, children and neighbourhood. If women's relation to class is perceived as derivative and tenuous, so much more is this the case for children.

Conclusion

Analysing the effects and affects on childhood of race, gender and class as both cultural categories and material structures in ways that allow meaningful statements to be made about childhood in its global context is fraught with difficulty. To say that class affects children's life chances on a global scale seems uncontentious enough; and yet even UNICEF's 2006 report on *Excluded and Invisible Children* does not use the language of class to describe economic inequality and its manifestation in inequalities in health and education. Similarly, in the same report, although ethnicity and gender are both mentioned as lines of social difference that affect life chances, we find no talk of racism or sexism but are told that 'the root causes of exclusion are poverty, weak governance, armed conflict and HIV/AIDS' (UNICEF 2006: 11). If these are the root causes of exclusion, then how can we explain their tendency to be unequally distributed by race, gender and class?

I have argued in this chapter that race and gender remain salient to the formation of cultural identity and access to resources, both material and symbolic. The tendency of governments and international bodies to discursively deny the continuing salience of these social categories is congruent with the emptying out by neo-liberal states and the international system (manifested through international bodies and regulations) of the political sphere and its replacement by economic criteria. In short, we are left with individual answers to social questions: poverty becomes a matter of individual failure or success, while 'race' is reduced to cultural expression (hence its substitution by ethnicity), and both ethnic and gender discrimination are blamed on outmoded ideas left over from semi-feudal pasts. If such a view of inequality as being essentially outside of modernity is accepted then, of course, there would be no need to speak of childhood in the plural. However, what I have tried to show in this chapter is that class does structure children's lives; its effects are not simply haphazard or unpredictable. Furthermore, class is experienced by raced and gendered subjects so that not only are these social categories not outside of modernity, they are constitutive of modernity (Goldberg 2001), understood here as (global) capitalism. Indeed race, gender and class overdetermine childhood. That is to say, the model of childhood that is usually described as being a 'Western' model or a Western/contemporary model is not only specific to a particular space and time, it is also specific to a particular class, race and gender. In other words, the model child is in some respects more accurately the model bourgeois white boy. However, even this recognition of the specificity of the ideal of contemporary global childhood does not quite capture the ways that race, gender and class overdetermine childhood because, in fact, the childhood envisaged in this model, above all its innocence of political calculation and economic interest, can no more be true of a white middle-class boy than it can be true of a black working-class girl (to make the point in its most Manichean form). Indeed, once childhood is seen as a racialized, gendered and classed position, the notion of childhood as having the possibility of being innocent, in the sense of existing outside of the symbolic and material nexus of political economy, has to be abandoned entirely.

Recommended further reading

Butler, J. 1990. *Gender Trouble: Feminism and the Subversion of Identity.* New York and London: Routledge.
The seminal text of queer theory and the best starting point for anyone who wants to understand what it means to think of identities – including those of the life course – as performative and contextual.

Nieuwenhuys, O. 1994. *Children's Lifeworlds: Gender, Welfare and Labour in the Developing World.* London: Routledge.
A key contribution to the still small number of ethnographies of childhood.

Ritterhouse, J. 2006. *Growing up Jim Crow: How Black and White Southern Children Learned Race.* Chapel Hill: University of North Carolina Press.
An important contribution to the historiography of North American childhood.

Salazar Parreñas, R. 2005. *Children of Global Migration: Transnational Families and Gendered Woes.* Stanford: Stanford University Press.
One of the few attempts to apply Judith Butler's theories to an empirical context: the impact of mothers' migration on the gender roles in the Philippines.

Thorne, B. 1993. *Gender Play: Girls and Boys in School.* New Brunswick, NJ: Rutgers University Press.
An early and influential text on how children learn to 'do' gender.

Volkman, T. A. (ed.). 2005. *Cultures of Transnational Adoption.* Durham and London: Duke University Press.
An important collection of papers on transnational adoption with contributions by all the key figures in what is still an emergent body of work.

4

Children and families

Introduction

We use the term 'family' to describe a small group of adults and children across the whole of human history, but after only a moment's reflection it seems obvious that who is in a family and what their responsibilities are to one another and to society will be different at different points in history and in different cultures. Once we start thinking about it in any depth the concept 'family', just like the concept 'child', looks rather more complicated than it does at first glance. How do we decide if one person is related to another person? There are rules for making these decisions; some of the rules are laws and others are social conventions. In either case new social phenomena change the rules – the emergence of gay and lesbian families would be a good example of this. How people in a family are related to one another and what legal, social and biological ties have to exist between them for them to be acknowledged as a family by society or culture or law is also subject to change (Burr and Montgomery 2003). Seismic shifts in the society and economy produce equally deep changes in the form and function of families.

We think of children as belonging to families. The UNCRC says in its Preamble that it recognizes 'that the child, for the full and harmonious development of his or her personality, should grow up in a family environment'. The family is idealized as a loving, nurturing environment that can encourage and shape the child's development in appropriate ways. The knowingly ironic statement 'I blame the parents' is a joking recognition that we think of children as the product of their family life. In the social sciences this has been reflected in the importance given to the study of family relations in understanding children's emotional and cognitive development (in development psychology: Amato and Booth 1997) and in explaining underachievement (in education: Henderson and Berla 1994). When children commit violent crimes or simply behave badly, psychologists, educationalists and even criminologists look for explanations in the child's family life, attributing their difficulties to some dysfunction in their family relations or the absence of particular role models.

Despite this central role given to the family in raising children to be good people who can take their place in society, we also think of the family as a very private space where people are free to do what they like without regard to laws or social norms. It is a foundational principle of liberal law that government should not intrude on family life (Chen 1997). The family has also been depicted as 'a haven from a harsh world' (Lasch 1977); a place where we are free to be ourselves and where we can recuperate from the demands of work and life in public. This view of the family as somehow outside of politics and separate from the public sphere has been challenged by feminist scholars who have pointed to the ways that the family produces and reproduces gendered inequalities (Kimmel 2004; Leeder 2004; Uhlmann 2006).

The new social studies of childhood have not so far been particularly interested in family life. In asserting the importance of the child's perspective and identifying an area of inquiry that distinguishes the social studies of childhood from education and psychology the new social studies have focused more on the child than on the family. The aim of this chapter is to bring the family back into childhood studies. Its focus is not, however, on relations within the family but on how the family is governed. The chapter is in two sections. The first section, on the governance of the family, looks at the different ways that law, welfare, work and policies on biological and social reproduction are deployed by governments to organize family life. The second section is about what governments do when this regulating of family life fails – when families cannot or will not do what government thinks they should do – and another level of intervention is put in place. The focus of the second section is on children on the street and transnational adoption.

The governance of the family

The public and the private

The practices of contemporary Western governments and the international bodies that they have been instrumental in forming cannot be understood without some appreciation of the foundational principles of liberal political theory. Liberal democratic political theory is at the core of how contemporary government justifies its rule. Democratic politics legitimates the power and authority of the state by claiming that, by voting, a majority of citizens have agreed to delegate their sovereignty (their right to rule over themselves) to the collective body of the government (Held 2006). Liberal theory places a limit on the rule of government that restricts it to the management of public life. In liberal theory individuals are entitled to a private life that the state should not intrude on (Pateman 1987; Coole 2000). The family is part of this private life and therefore government has no automatic right to interfere in how parents raise their children (Chen 1997). The presumption is that parents act in their children's best interests and that they are entitled to relative freedom in deciding what is best for their child. The state should only intrude on family life in exceptional circumstances, when the family is failing to attend to the moral or physical welfare of the child and this failure is evidenced by e.g. school truancy and violent or criminal behaviour (Archard 2004: 110–27).

How the law shapes family life
Despite the strong presumption that the state does not involve itself in family life, the law is instrumental in defining the family and its responsibilities towards children. It is the law that gives content to otherwise empty concepts like 'best interests'. It sets out the duties of parents towards children and emphasizes the family's role as the duty-holder in relation to children's rights (in this way it supports the liberal aim to govern at a distance and to minimize the state's responsibilities towards its citizens). It is the law that gives parents rights over children's bodies and their time – for example hitting children is illegal in Sweden, is legal to some degree in the UK and is legal in the USA. Who counts as a family is established by law. This is what is at stake in the ongoing debate about whether gay men and lesbians should be able to use the term 'marriage' to describe their committed relationships with their partners. Children born outside of marriage continue to have fewer entitlements than children born in marriage. In England and Wales, for example, unmarried fathers have no rights of custody or access to their children. Registering marriages and births is a way of regulating family life and establishing and legitimating paternity.

All of this is done in the normal course of events: registering marriages and births seems unremarkable because it is done so routinely; the shifts in parents' legal rights over their children as they grow up are accepted as an ordinary part of the loosening of children's dependency on their parents. From time to time new laws and regulations are enacted and this is often in response to extraordinary events and particularly, in relation to children in families, to do with their safety. Inquiries following what are often extreme and unusual cases generate new guidelines, laws and discourses that extend the state surveillance of families in the name of the 'best interest of the child'. In Britain, for example, the conviction of Marie-Therese Kouao for the murder of her niece Victoria Climbie led to an inquiry into how social workers, doctors and teachers all missed the signs of her abuse by her aunt that eventually culminated in her death (Laming 2003). This inquiry recommended that in order to prevent children slipping through the net of different jurisdictions all children in Britain should have their names entered into a national database that is then accessible to all government agencies and details the child's contacts with schools, hospitals, doctors and social workers and the contact that anybody else in the family has with these agencies. This database, the Information Sharing Index, was piloted in 2007 and is planned for January 2009. This represents an extraordinary extension of government powers and a limitation of the right to privacy. Such an encroachment of the state on the private sphere is possible because it is done in the name of the safety of children. Civil liberty groups have found it very difficult to mobilize opposition to encroachments on civil liberties that are done in the name of the child (Penna 2005).

The idea of the family as a private space set apart from public life, like its parallel concept of childhood as a time separated from adult life, is closely related to the emergence of modern capitalist society and bourgeois social norms. This at least is the contention of Jacques Donzelot, whose seminal book *The Policing of Families* (1980) showed how the transition in France from feudalism to capitalism was acted out on the family.

The central argument of Donzelot's book is that in the nineteenth century the urban working-class family was newly subjected to the surveillance of social workers, psychiatrists, family courts and philanthropists who sought to correct what they saw as the indolence and immorality of working-class families. These ideas might seem rather removed from our contemporary experience of family life and its relationship to the state but, although the language that legitimates state intervention in family life has changed, social policy, private philanthropy and criminal justice remain the most important tools through which states govern the family.

Nikolas Rose in *Governing the Soul* describes childhood as 'the most intensively governed sector of personal existence' (1999a: 124). He claims that the state, philanthropists, probation officers, courts and social workers no longer have to be constantly vigilant about 'the policing of families' because the self-regulation of family life has now been fully accomplished. He calls this a strategy of family privacy in which the family is apparently left to govern itself and appears to be separated from both the authority of the state and the scope of market relations. He says:

The strategy of family privacy might appear to stand in opposition to all those attempts to police and regulate the family mechanism over the past 150 years. But the reverse is the case – it stands rather as a testament to the success of those attempts to construct a family that will take upon itself the responsibility for the duties of socialization and will live them as its own desires. No longer does the socializing project have to be implanted by philanthropy or imposed under threat by courts and social workers. At least in its ideal form, it inheres in each of us, maintained and reactivated constantly by the images that surround us . . . No longer do experts have to reach the family by way of the law or the coercive intrusion of social work. They interpellate us through the radio call-in, through the weekly magazine column, through the gentle advice of the health visitor, teacher, or neighbour, and through the unceasing reflexive gaze of our own psychologically educated self-scrutiny.

(Rose 1999a: 213)

Rose's argument is that the coercion and threat by external forces described by Donzelot for nineteenth-century France have been replaced in the contemporary family by the self-surveillance that arises from the desire to be a good family made up of good people. His point is that this has been so successfully accomplished that the external gaze of the state and society has been internalized into the everyday practices of the family. The family, in other words, no longer needs to be closely managed by government because it shares with government the same vision of what it means to be a good parent and a good child.

Governing the family through welfare and health policy
Clearly there is much in Rose's argument as suggested by the proliferation of 'reality' television programmes about how to raise children and of parenting magazines. Nonetheless, even in the case of Britain he underestimates the extent to which families, particularly those in social housing and claiming welfare benefits, are subject to control and regulation by government. When families are claiming welfare or living in social housing the government can and does use the threat of withdrawing welfare and housing to force parents to behave differently towards their children (Dwyer 2004).

In the middle-class family welfare and social housing cannot generally be tools for governing. In this case children's (mis)behaviour is medicalized and the unruly child is more likely to be subjected to diagnosis (any number of changing 'psy' labels – Attention Deficit Hyperactivity Disorder, Autism, Aspergers) and the intensification of surveillance by health visitors and psy-professionals or of medical intervention (such as prescribing Ritalin).

This schema of middle-class families being more or less trusted with the self-surveillance of their members in the ways that Rose describes and working-class families being under a fairly constant state of 'tutoring' (to use Donzelot's term) that they will either engage with voluntarily or be forced to accept by various technologies (social housing, welfare benefits, curfews and so on) is a plausible enough account of relations between state, society and family in established liberal democracies. It is less certain to what extent it can apply at a global level.

There is sufficient evidence to suggest that we are witnessing the diffusion of a bourgeois or middle-class model of family life across different country contexts (Hecht 1998). The elite, at least in the newly industrializing countries, and despite widely different local cultural forms (from, say, Catholicism in Brazil to Buddhism in Thailand and Hinduism in India), is increasingly networked into a shared global culture (Castells 1997). There is increasing continuity in the structures and practices of the middle-class or bourgeois family on a global level, particularly in Asia and Latin America. As for the urban poor, although there are some similarities between families in developing and underdeveloped countries, particularly in the state's aspirations to 'tutor' the family, there are also key differences.

Governments in the south lack the resources, the will and the legitimacy to intervene directly in the private life of the family. Even if the government is aware that the health and welfare of children are compromised because they are living in difficult circumstances – such as in the favelas in Brazil or slums in India – unless the problems spill out from the neighbourhood they tend to be ignored by government. In the absence of a welfare state (in particular social housing and social security benefits) or state control over the allocation of employment the developing state has no disciplinary mechanisms through which it can organize family life. The state wants to be insulated from demands by the families of the urban poor (for adequate housing, access to clean water, access to electricity, a minimum wage, etc.). Yet its inability to meet such demands also removes from it the capacity to regulate, discipline and govern the urban poor except, when necessary, by the very blunt instrument of a violent and arbitrary police force. The protection in liberal theory of the private space of the family, the state's refusal to meet the economic needs of the urban poor, and the well-established pastoral role of religious bodies mean that families are more or less left to their own devices unless their problems spill out into the public sphere. The state concentrates on disciplining, regulating and controlling the family from the outside; at those points where children are already in the public sphere – in school, at work, and on the street.

Family planning

One of the ways that the state organizes, or attempts to organize, family life is through interventions in family planning. Fear and disgust of the fecundity of the poor, particularly the urban poor, has been a key trope of family planning that, for much of the twentieth century, was closely allied to the eugenics movement. Nowadays governments' attempts to regulate the size of families by encouraging some kinds of family to have more and others to have fewer children are more likely to be justified through discourses of economic development. High fertility rates, especially amongst the rural poor, are claimed to trap people and countries in cycles of poverty (Merrick 2002).

There are three main ways in which governments try to control family size: methods to limit family size (abortion, contraception and sterilization); methods aimed at increasing the number of children in the family (financial incentives, tax breaks); discursive practices such as policy reports and news items that produce discourses about what constitutes a good family or a good-size family. Each of these methods uses a combination of law and welfare and of voluntary and forced practices to obtain the governments' desired outcome; and of course these interventions are targeted at specific populations: the expansion of middle-class families and the contraction of working-class families. In Singapore in the mid 1980s working-class families were given financial incentives to have fewer children. A grant of 10,000 Singapore dollars (about US $6,650) would be given to women below thirty years who had no more than two children, earned less than 750 Singapore dollars per month and who had no school leaving qualifications if they were sterilized. Women with more than five O level passes were encouraged to have more children by the incentive of tax breaks (Wee 1995: 199–201). In India during the 'Emergency' in the 1970s the government forced lower-class men to have vasectomies (Chatterjee and Riley 2001: 18). Similar techniques have been used to encourage the expansion of one ethnic group and the contraction of another. The use of population control as a technology of racial governance is well documented, especially in the colonial period (Schoen 1997; Ahluwalia 2001; Klausen 2004).

In governments' attempts to regulate the size of families we can see very sharply that practices that are regarded as private intimate decisions are in fact shaped by public policy and sometimes in very coercive ways.

Work

Notwithstanding the prevailing commonsense view that it is an intensely private place, the family is shaped above all by the demands placed on it by political economy. The (gendered and generational) members of the family are pulled into production in multiple and varied ways, partly by brute economic compulsion, partly through social policy and the agents of the state (welfare officers, social workers, schools), and partly through emotional investments in the relation between personhood, labour and money. Women in poor families have long performed the work of the social reproduction of the families of ruling classes, from wet-nursing to child-raising, cleaning, cooking and shopping for the upper-class household. Increasingly this work is done across national borders with women working as nannies and cleaners in one country and the work of social reproduction being left undone or redistributed amongst children (Katz 2004: 182), other women and sometimes men in their home country. Global migration of women reforms the material practices of everyday family life (Ehrenreich and Hochschild 2002; Salazar Parreñas 2005). The loss of alternatives to waged labour (whether due to the unravelling of the welfare state or increased urbanization and decreased opportunities for subsistence farming), together with the hyperexploitative conditions of labour such that the wage of one job is not sufficient to meet the costs of social reproduction, forces parents to work two jobs, to do shift work, and to deploy all of the family's members in waged labour (see chapter 5). Of critical importance here for understanding the fragility and resilience of families is the concept of social reproduction and how the work of social reproduction is distributed across the fields of society, politics and the economy.

Social reproduction

Social reproduction is 'a critical arena, as yet undertheorized, within which many of the problems associated with the globalization of capitalist production can be confronted' (Katz 2001a: 709). Social reproduction is a concept that refers to the material and discursive practices which enable the reproduction of a social formation and its members. It can also be conceptualized as a 'social wage' – the cost of paying for the material goods necessary for the maintenance and reproduction of life: food, shelter, clothing, health, education and so on. The cost of social reproduction may be borne by the state, by capital or – as is increasingly the case – by families. Cindi Katz argues that

> [g]lobalized capitalism has changed the face of social reproduction world-
> wide over the past three decades, enabling intensification of capital accu-
> mulation and exacerbating differences in wealth and poverty. The demise
> of the social contract as a result of neoliberalism, privatisation, and the

fraying of the welfare state is a crucial aspect of this shift. Children, among others, suffer from these changes, as all manner of public disinvestments take place – including in education, social welfare, housing, health care, and public environments – as part of and in concert with a relative lack of corporate commitment to particular places. The flip side of the withdrawal of public and corporate support for the social wage is a reliance on private means of securing and sustaining social reproduction . . .'

(Katz 2001a: 709; see also Mitchell, Marston and Katz 2003)

The social contract or welfare settlement that Katz refers to was not a global phenomenon in the 1970s, the decade that she marks as beginning a new phase in social reproduction. It was restricted to the advanced capitalist countries with more or less comprehensive social welfare settlements in Western Europe, Scandinavia, the former Soviet Union, Australia, Canada and the USA. Capital always seeks to throw off the costs of social reproduction. The particular settlement of the struggle between workers and capital that has resulted in the state bearing some of the costs of social reproduction has been a recent and partial phenomenon when looked at in a historical perspective. Immigration law, for example, almost always attempts to restrict immigration to adult workers, leaving the costs of social reproduction to the home country (Ciscel et al. 2003: 339). Nonetheless the point is well made by Katz that in the contemporary era the burdens of social reproduction are increasingly borne by families.

The global prevalence of neo-liberal norms makes the family the site where the labour of social reproduction gets done whilst simultaneously making available fewer and fewer resources to make that labour possible. In the rest of this chapter I argue that this has produced a crisis in social reproduction where people who the family cannot care for and the state will not care for get pushed into public arenas and taken up as objects to be removed and even killed (children on the street) or saved ('orphans'). Children on the street and orphans are reminders of the limits to the social reproductive capacities of the family in specific contexts and of the circumscribed possibilities for families to be a 'haven from a harsh world'.

Children in public

Street children

If the concept of the family is quintessentially aligned with the idea of the private sphere, the 'street' as a concept is its complete opposite. The street is a metaphor for the public sphere and for the openness of city life. The transgression of street children is not only that they are not where they belong – at home, in the family (Ennew 1995; Sondhi-Garg 2004) – but also that they are using public space for private activities like eating and sleeping. If the private space of the home stands for the caring, nurturing closeness of the family then the public space of the street stands in opposition to these qualities. It is in our social imaginary a place of strangers (Wells 2005). The depiction of street children as isolated, cut off from social networks, alone in the world is generated more by the idea of the street and its oppositional relation to home than by their everyday lives (Burr 2006: 120; Kilbride et al. 2000: 83). Not only is it impossible to live in the world (and perhaps especially in the exposed environment of the street) without social ties, without interdependencies, it is precisely these ties that make us human. The frequent characterization, especially by NGOs, of street children as lacking family and community makes them more vulnerable to material and physical violations at the hands of the police (Sondhi-Garg 2004: 91–101), by the ways that it (unintentionally) contributes to ideas about street children not fully being members of human society. Street children are anomalous not only to the category of 'children' but also to the category of public space. It is this double anomaly that renders them so vulnerable to violence at the hands of state authorities, particularly the police (Kilbride et al. 2000: 3; Sondhi-Garg 2004: 91–101).

In recent years there has been a proliferation of international concern about the problem of 'street children'. Statistics purporting to establish the extent of this 'problem' are very unreliable. In a World Health Organization report (2002) the estimate for the number of street children worldwide was given as between 10 million and 100 million (Sondhi-Garg 2004: 10). Such a huge range makes the figure virtually meaningless, useful only for its rhetorical purpose of establishing that this is a problem on an enormous scale. In Brazil, for example, a figure of 7 million street children is often cited. As Hecht points out in his excellent ethnography *At Home in the Street* (1998), this would mean that about 16 per cent of the child population are street children. He suggests that the figure is more realistically between 13,000 and 39,000. Although this claim itself seems rather arbitrary (the 39,000 figure is arrived at by assuming that only one third of children were counted during the period of the head count), the point is that accounts of the extent of the 'problem' are wildly overstated. Frequently the population of street children is combined with that of working children to produce phenomenal figures (25 million for Latin America) for a problem that, these reports imply, one would have to be either stupid or evil to ignore. This collapsing together of working children and street children is not only done to inflate the scale of the problem of street children. Rather, these two practices (working and living on the street) are both implicated in a third 'problem', children not having or taking their place within the family (Ennew 1995).

Street children are not usually discussed in the context of the family (Kilbride et al. 2000: 6), but it is precisely the relation of the child to the family that generates this category of the 'street child' (Nieuwenhuys 1999: 37); the street children are anomalous because they are children who are apparently without family. The UN defines street children as children for whom the street 'has become their home and/or source of livelihood and who are inadequately protected or supervised by responsible adults'. From this perspective it is the inadequacy of the family that accounts for a child being on the street in the first place. Factors that are regularly cited as leading children to live on the street include parental violence and neglect, single mothers, too many children (or too many fathers), step-families, and demands that children provide for their families (Kilbride et al. 2000: 5–6; Luiz de Moura 2002: 358; Sondhi-Garg 2004: 38–9).

Despite this widely held view of a break between the family and the child as the cause of children being on the street, most 'street children' are in regular, even daily, contact with their families, and many street children return home to sleep. Most children who are called street children by governments and charities live with their families, returning home frequently, often nightly (Myers 1989; Aptekar 1994; Sondhi-Garg 2004). The fact that these children are spending a lot, perhaps most, of their time away from home signifies their liminal or in-between social status somewhere between being a child and being an adult; it may not signify their abandonment by or of their family. Most street children are teenagers who have not quite left the dependency of childhood but nor have they transitioned to adulthood. One of the anxieties that street children produce is that they will never make a proper transition to adulthood either because they will be unable to survive on the streets or because they will grow older without being able to care adequately for themselves and their own children. In living on the street young people may not be entirely separated from their family home but their ties of dependence to their family, and perhaps the degree to which they are welcome at home, may have changed as they got older. Many street children talk of being told to leave home by their parents because they cannot continue to support them, and younger children are more in need of the scarce resources of the household, and perhaps of the safety of home. Nonetheless, for most street children leaving home does not usually entail a complete rupture with family life. Often street children do work in the street as vendors or casual labourers, or begging (Burr 2006). Many of these children will go home when they have made some money to contribute to their family's wage.

The very presence of children living and working, eating and playing, on the street, away from the protection of the family makes it very obvious that the boundaries between public space and private life are not as firm in reality as they might be in our imagination. If children can be at home on the street, if at times sleeping on the street is just as comfortable as sleeping at home, if food is more plentiful for a child on the street than for a child at home, what has happened to the private sphere, to the haven from a harsh world that the family is widely regarded as representing? The private space of the home and the public space of the street are in many ways not so different from one another if home is small and crowded and lacks basic amenities. What economic resources are needed to make a meaningful distinction between public and private space, and why do so many people clearly not have access to those resources? In Brazil, a country which regards itself as modern and developed, street children are shameful evidence of gross inequalities in wealth. They bring out into the public space of city centres the poverty that would otherwise be hidden in the private world of the family. The contrast between their poverty and the wealth of their compatriots in urban commercial and business centres potentially confronts government and the middle-class families whose support they depend on with the crisis of social reproduction that the poor are constantly facing (Marquez 1999; Kilbride et al. 2000: 78–89). It is this crisis of social reproduction that makes it impossible for them to either stay at home (Lugalla and Kibassa 2003: 16) or to provide them with the resources to make the transition to adult life.

Keeping children off the street: city curfews

Street child: the term conjures up an image of a child familiar from photographs of nineteenth-century waifs in the centres of the new industrial cities. It is an image of a child immersed in poverty, dirty and wearing ragged clothes, scared and unhappy. This image has probably not changed very much, but now the street child is always somewhere else – on the streets of Nairobi or Addis Ababa, Rio or Sao Paulo, Delhi or Bangkok. The street child is no longer a child of New York, London or Paris.

To the extent that the street child is a teenager who sometimes lives at home and sometimes does not, who is from a very poor family, whose home may not be more comfortable than the street, then, the phenomenon of 'street children' is more or less a problem of extreme poverty, but it also should be recognized that part of the reason that street children are a problem is because their presence on the street without any apparent purpose makes other people (younger and older) anxious. Young people may find that they have become a problem simply by being on the street. When thought of in this way it becomes apparent that street children in the developing world are not so different from children hanging around on the street in the cities of the developed world.

In the last two decades there has been a huge increase in the use of street curfews in cities in North America to keep children off the streets and out of public spaces. Juvenile curfews make it an offence for young people to be out in public after a specified time. Simply the act of being out in public becomes a criminal offence; no other offence has to be committed for the young person out after hours to be in breach of the law.

Juvenile curfew laws were first used in North America in the late nineteenth century against the children of immigrant families (Chen 1997: 134; Collins and Kearns 2001: 390; O'Neil 2002: 50). President Benjamin Harrison described them as 'the most important municipal regulation for the protection of the children of American homes, from the vices of the street' (cited in Lester 1996: 667). In the early twentieth century they fell out of use and were revived during the Second World War. Curfew laws remained on the statute books through the 1950s to the 1970s but were not generally enforced (Collins and Kearns 2001: 390). They were revived in the 1970s in response to a rise in political protests and violent crime and again in the late 1990s, partly in response to alleged increases in gang activity and juvenile crime (Chen 1997: 134; Collins and Kearns 2001: 390). Some cities operate both night and day-time curfews. The latter give police the right to 'question, search and, if necessary, detain any child or teenager found in a public place during school hours' (Collins and Kearns 2001: 393). In 2000 four fifths of cities in the USA with a population greater than 30,000 had a night-time curfew and a further 26 per cent had a day-time curfew (O'Neil 2002: 53). Curfews are not usually applied across the whole of the city. In Southern California, curfews justified by the need to combat gang violence are almost exclusively used in African American and Chicano neighbourhoods (O'Neil 2002: 53, citing Davis 1990). Most arrests for curfew violations in New Orleans in 1994 were of African Americans (O'Neil 2002: 61).

The proliferation of curfews has led to legal challenges on the grounds that curfews against young people contravene the Fourteenth Amendment, which guarantees equal protection of law. Many of the rulings on curfew challenges apply what is known, following a 1979 US Supreme Court case on whether a young woman needs her parents' consent to have an abortion, as the *Bellotti* criteria (Lester 1996: 671; Chen 1997: 154). The *Bellotti* criteria allow the law to treat children differently from adults because of 'the peculiar vulnerability of children', 'their inability to make crucial decisions in an informed, mature manner' and 'the importance of the parental role in child-rearing'. Curfews have been struck down for curtailing young people's First Amendment right to freedom of association. In *Qutb v. Strauss* 1993 the curfew did not restrict young people from all public space for all activities but had several exceptions including the exercise of First Amendment rights, travelling between states, running errands for parents and going to or returning from a place of work. The Dallas curfew was found by the Fifth Circuit Court to be an acceptable limitation on young people's liberty. Since that case many other cities have introduced curfews that include similar exceptions.

The use of the *Bellotti* criteria, especially the third item on 'the importance of the parental role in child-rearing', is significant for this chapter because it is about the ways that government intervenes in families. Since juvenile curfews make children's presence in public an offence, they deny parents the right to allow their children to be in public after certain hours. Often curfews make parents liable for their child's curfew violations (O'Neil 2002: 57). President Clinton claimed they were 'designed to help people be better parents' (cited in O'Neil 2002: 57). City authorities in the USA claim that the enactment of juvenile curfews is necessary to keep children safe and to lower juvenile crime (O'Neil 2002: 54; Chen 1997: 132).

The law's interest in keeping children safe 'originates from the state's custodial interest in ensuring the welfare and proper development of children. Minors are presumed to need the care of some protective guardian, a role usually filled by the parent unless state intervention is required. The state's custodial function establishes an authority over minors that the state cannot exercise over adults' (Chen 1997: 133). Chen contends that 'the state competes with the parent for control of her child, and as a result intrudes on the interests of both parent and child' (Chen 1997: 133). Although courts approach curfew ordinances as a conflict between the state and the minor, curfews also impinge on the rights of parents. In fact most curfew laws involve 'state intrusion into the family sphere' (Chen 1997: 133), and the state opposes the shared interests of child and parent.

In response to successful challenges to curfew ordinances on the grounds that they are unconstitutional city authorities enacted curfews with exceptions for minors that are with their parents, running errands for their parents, at work, attending school or civic activities and exercising First Amendment rights (Chen 1997: 136). Notwithstanding these limitations on the general scope of curfew ordinances, it is nonetheless the case that juvenile curfews challenge the right of children to be out in public at night (and in specific places in the day) and the right of parents to allow their children to do so. Curfew ordinances limit the liberty of children and young people, and this restriction has been allowed by US courts on the grounds that the child, 'unlike an adult, has a right not to liberty but to custody' (Chen 1997: 143, citing the ruling in *Gault* 1967).

The Supreme Court has not argued that children have fewer rights than adults but it has upheld restrictions imposed by states on minors that would not be legal in the case of adults. Chen argues that the development of minors' rights can be 'understood as a history of the conflicts among the state, parent, and child' (Chen 1997: 139). This was the approach that the Supreme Court took in the first part of the twentieth century. Early rulings on parents' rights to determine their children's education effectively claimed that 'any enhanced power the state exercised over minors derived from parental custody and authority' (Chen 1997: 141). Chen says that the premise that parents and children have similar if not identical interests 'continues to define the current understanding of minors' rights' (Chen 1997: 141). He notes that '[t]he family institution is so firmly embedded in American tradition that courts should, and generally do, presume that the parents are the best custodians and advocates of their children's needs. Until the state provides strong evidence showing that parents are failing to meet their basic responsibilities, courts should be very reluctant to allow the state to intervene' (Chen 1997: 160). The right of parents to raise their children without governmental interference has been recognized as a fundamental component of due process (Lester 1996: 682). This has extended to the courts refusing to give custody to the state in cases of alleged parental neglect. In *Re William 'EE'* the court refused to find child neglect although the children claimed that the 'respondents had hit them and their younger sister with sticks and tied them into their chairs with extension cords'. In *Re Bryan L* the Family Court in New York State did not find evidence of neglect that children were physically endangered during assaults. Similarly, when courts do find against the constitutionality of curfew laws, they are less likely to do so on the grounds that children have a right to equal treatment under the law (which in any case the *Bellotti* criteria refute) than to object on the grounds that curfews interfere with parents' rights over their children.

In the cities of the developed world the introduction of curfews may be compared with the anxiety over street children in the cities of the developing world. In both contexts the anxiety that the authorities and other citizens express is largely for the order of the street rather than for the safety of young people on the street. In a town in Cornwall, England in the summer of 2008 the police extended a curfew of 9 p.m. to all under-fifteens and 8 p.m. for all under-16s because 'many local people' asked for it (Morris 2008). These curtailments on the freedom of movement of children and young people are done in the name of encouraging good parenting and point to the ways that the state intervenes in family life through law and social policy.

Transnational adoption

Nowhere is the characterization of the family as a private concern more belied than by practices and discourses of adoption and fostering. The adoption and fostering of children immediately contests the naturalness of the family form by making it possible to do socially and legally what can, according to a particular discourse of childhood, only be accomplished biologically. The lack of biological ties in adoptive families is often a source of anxiety perhaps because of the credibility that is given to the biological over the social. Sara Dorow in her study of transnational adoption shows that adoptive parents often try to present their adoptive child as if they have some physical or mystical (pre-adoptive) connection with one another. She says that many of the Euro-American adoptive parents of Chinese babies she did her research with had fantasies about mysterious resemblances or mystical connections between themselves and their babies and often talked about the babies as destined to be in their adoptive family or as coming home (Dorow 2006: 233). Transnational adoption lays bare the multiple public forces (domestic laws on adoption and immigration, international laws on adoption, governance of population control, but also cultural mores) that act on and shape the putatively private space of family life.

The availability of children for adoption from one country to another, like street children, is a consequence of a crisis in social reproduction in child-sending countries. Most transnational adoptions are arranged from the sending countries' point of view, because families do not have the *material* means to provide for their children. This lack of resources is often a consequence of exceptional structural circumstances, for example war. However, for many families their inability to provide for their children is not exceptional but is a persistent consequence of structural poverty.

In the case of China, one of the major sending countries of transnational adoptees, the crisis in social reproduction is rather different than in most of the major sending countries. In China the state has attempted to resolve or forestall a crisis in social reproduction by forcing people to have fewer children and channelling the surplus capital saved into state-sponsored development projects with the intention that the state would meet the costs of social reproduction – a policy known as the 'iron rice bowl' (Leung 1994; Cook 2001).

In the first section of this chapter I discussed family planning as one of the ways that government shapes family life. International development agents from NGOs to UNICEF and the World Bank contend that one of the keys to promoting economic development is to limit the number of children born into poor families. Their hope is that education will persuade people of the benefits of having smaller families. As is well known, the Chinese government chose coercion over persuasion and imposed a one-child policy on families by making it illegal to have more than one child. In recent years this was changed to a one-son, two-child policy. If a family's first child is a girl then they can have a second child, but if the first child is a son then they cannot usually have a second child.

The Chinese government's adoption policy is essentially part of this strategy for population control and is inseparable from its one-child policy. The one-child policy is enforced through levying fines against 'over-quota' children and also by forced sterilization. This policy has produced a population of 'missing girls' (Croll 2000: 31–3) who are either unregistered and living with their birth families or unregistered and unofficially adopted. Many sources claim that missing girls are a consequence of gender-selective abortions and that 'for every 100 girls 120 boys are born' (Poncz 2007: 76). However, most of these sources ignore the fact that girl-children may not be registered so that the family can try for another child. These unregistered girls may mean that the sex ratio is not as unbalanced in reality as it is statistically. This is not to underestimate the impact on girls' lives of not being registered – registration is necessary to get all kinds of welfare including education. In one case that Johnson documents, a couple who already had a son adopted a girl but could not get a household registration or *hukou* for her. In withholding a *hukou* from her government officials were also withholding her access to school. The parents decided to place the girl in an orphanage intending to readopt her when the orphanage secured a *hukou* for her. However, they were not allowed to readopt her because they already had a son. The orphanage arranged for their seven-year-old daughter to be adopted by a family from the United States (Johnson 2005: 132).

The United States is the world's foremost receiving country of intercountry adoptions. In the period 1993–7 nearly half of all 100,000 intercountry adoptions were to the USA (UNICEF 1998: 3). In recent years the largest group of international adoptions has been of Chinese girls by white middle-class families in the USA (Volkman 2005: 82). These adoptions constitute about one third of all intercountry adoptees arriving in the USA. In 2004, of 23,000 intercountry adoptions to the United States, 7,000 were from China. Although international adoptions are a statistical minority, 'the practices of China/U.S. adoption – and the children themselves – have taken on forms of public and symbolic significance that exceeds what the numbers suggest' (Dorow 2006: 10).

The two-child, one-son policy is also enforced against adoptive parents. Many parents describe their ideal family as consisting of a son and a daughter. While sons are important in this as in all patrilineal societies because they carry on the family line and inherit property, daughters are thought of as more loving. However, a family whose only child is a boy cannot give birth to *or adopt* another child without attracting over-quota fines. These fines are substantial, and can be as much as two years' salary. In addition to which the family may in any case have their second child, regardless of whether it is a birth or an adopted child, removed from them by birth planning cadres. Nonetheless, such is the desire for a daughter that families often do take the risk and then absorb the cost of adopting abandoned girls.

The Hague Convention and the UNCRC

Intercountry adoption is regulated by the 1993 Hague Convention. It 'protects children and their families against the risks of illegal, irregular, premature or ill-prepared adoptions abroad. This Convention is intended to reinforce the UN Convention on the Rights of the Child (Art. 21) and seeks to ensure that intercountry adoptions are made in the best interests of the child and with respect for his or her fundamental rights, and to prevent the abduction, the sale of, or traffic in children' (http://www.hcch.net/index_en.php?act=text.display&tid=45).

The Hague Convention is a convention of the Hague Conference on Private International Law, which is a global inter-governmental organization that develops and services multilateral legal instruments. It has a similar role in private international law to that taken by the World Trade Organization in relation to global trade. It aims to facilitate legal security by resolving differences between the legal systems of countries in personal, family and commercial matters by working for the 'progressive unification' of these rules. The most widely ratified Conventions on family matters are those on international child abduction, intercountry adoption, maintenance obligations and recognition of divorces. Negotiations on a new global instrument for the international recovery of child support and other forms of family maintenance are currently in progress (http://www.hcch. net/index_en.php?act=faq.details&fid=47&zoek=child%20support).

The Hague Convention in Article 4 says: 'An adoption within the scope of the Convention shall take place only if the competent authorities of the State of origin – a) have established that the child is adoptable'. What makes a child adoptable is determined by adoption law in the state of origin and is therefore outside of the jurisdiction of the Hague Convention. The Hague Convention is primarily concerned with establishing that adoption should not be treated as a commercial transaction and that intercountry adoption should not be used as a cover for the commodification or trafficking of children. The Hague Convention only deals with clean-break adoptions whereas the UNCRC, reputedly because of objections to them from Islamic states (clean-break adoptions are not allowed in Islamic law), allows a variety of fostering and adoption arrangements.

The Hague Convention refers to its role in reinforcing Article 21 of the UNCRC. Although it does not mention them, other articles of the UNCRC are also pertinent to the regulation of intercountry adoption. Article 8 declares the child's right to 'preserve his or her identity, including nationality, name and family relations as recognized by law without unlawful interference'. Since transnational adoption involves the loss of one's nationality, the severing of ties with the child's birth family and a change in the child's family name and often also their given name, this article is clearly relevant to the regulation of intercountry adoption. Article 9 on the separation of a child from his or her parents is also relevant. Although these other articles of the UNCRC are relevant, Article 21 is specifically about adoption, and four of its five sub-clauses are about the regulation of intercountry adoption. Article 21 stipulates that 'the best interests of the child shall be the paramount consideration' in arranging adoptions, that domestic adoptions are preferable to intercountry adoptions and that where there are intercountry adoptions these should not be done for the financial gain of any party involved.

In Article 16 (b) of the Hague Convention the placement of the child with an adoptive family must 'give due consideration to the child's upbringing and to his or her ethnic, religious and cultural background'. This is similar to Article 20 (3) of the UNCRC on the care of children who have become separated from their family, which says: 'When considering solutions [to the care of separated children], due regard shall be paid to the desirability of continuity in a child's upbringing and to the child's ethnic, religious, cultural and linguistic background.'

Poverty and the circulation of children

To be adoptable a child should be orphaned, abandoned or have been taken into care. It may seem then a fairly straightforward matter to identify whether or not a child is adoptable. However, whilst it may be relatively easy to verify that a child is an 'orphan', it is much less clear how one would identify that a child has been 'abandoned'; how 'juridical terms such as "abandonment" and "negligence"' are translated into concrete practice (Fonseca 2002: 211). What constitutes neglect? In the United States, in 1994 the Speaker of the House Newt Gingrich suggested that the children of mothers on welfare should be put into orphanages (Ortiz and Briggs 2003: 50). A Harvard law professor and adoptive mother of two Peruvian children 'became a crusader against family reunification efforts in foster care policy, and a passionate advocate for adoption as a solution to poverty' (Briggs 2006: 616). A *Newsweek* article on an international adoption case in which a wealthy North American family's adoption of a Guatemalan boy was contested by the boy's birth family described the adoptive parents as one of 'the growing number of [North] Americans who go overseas to fulfil their dreams of parenthood', who 'believe that adoption – especially from an impoverished country – is an inherently good thing for the child' (cited in Briggs 2006: 629). Each of these instances suggests that poverty is often used by social workers and other figures of authority as a proxy for neglect.

Ethnographic studies of poor parents' child-raising practices, and, in particular, their use of informal fostering arrangements to manage periods of crisis in their ability to look after their children, suggest that what social workers and health visitors often characterize as neglect is not recognized as such by the children's community or the children themselves. Informal fostering arrangements between family members have long been recognized as a feature of working-class African American families (Brown, Cohon and Wheeler 2002). Informal adoption, child-shifting or, in Portuguese, *crian-cas em circulacao* 'is deeply rooted in the history of poor families in Brazil' (Hecht 1998: 90). In her study of informal fostering or 'child circulation' in a Brazilian favela, Claudia Fonseca found that short- and long-term fostering within favela households was common, with both children and adults using a social rather than a biological definition of mothering so that a child might easily have more than one mother. In her documentary film of interviews with the children and mothers in one poor Brazilian neighbourhood, one girl refers to her two mothers – the mother who gave birth to her and the mother who raised her. Some mothers put their children into temporary care in the state orphanage, FEBEM, until the crisis is over and the family once again has sufficient money to pay for their child's needs.

In environments where short- or long-term fostering is commonplace and children keep active ties with both their birth families and their foster families, signing a child over for adoption is understood very differently from the 'clean-break' interpretation that it is given in law (Briggs 2006: 628). In a different geographical context, Bledsoe (1990) explores how practices of fostering in West Africa are bound up with local concepts of the 'best interests' of the child that would probably be unrecognizable as such by contemporary Europeans, and certainly would be excluded as such in the terms of the UNCRC. In China before the passing of the 1991 Adoption Law informal or customary adoption of abandoned girls was an important alternative to abandoned girls being placed in orphanages (Johnson 2005: 124). The 1991 law restricted domestic adoptions to childless Chinese citizens over thirty-five (Poncz 2007) and increased the numbers of children being adopted internationally. Nevertheless, unofficial domestic adoptions outside of state-run orphanages are still common (Poncz 2007: 75 note 11).

The misrecognition of child circulation as neglect or abandonment has led to children being taken away from mothers by social workers and placed in national or international adoption. Although the Brazilian Children's Code (1990) states that poverty is not a sufficient reason to remove children from their families, '[m]any children who are withdrawn from their original families come from homes in which parental neglect is barely distinguishable from the effects of dire poverty' (Fonseca 2005: 158 note 4). Fonseca (2002) recounts just such a scenario, in which children in a town in Sao Paulo, placed in the state orphanage by their mothers who fully intended to take the children back home in due course, were given in international adoption to an Italian adoption agency. Over a period of six years more than 200 children had been regarded as abandoned and placed for adoption without their mothers' consent (Fonseca 2002: 211). This situation, in which poverty leads parents to place their children in orphanages or children are taken away from their parent(s) by the state through the agency of social workers because they 'neglect' to care for their children, is not of course unique to Brazil. In recent years the countries of the former Soviet Union and Soviet Bloc, especially Russia and Romania, have become major suppliers of children for transnational adoption. In both instances, one of the effects of the collapse of communism has been the loss of economic security that it provided and a dramatic increase in the numbers of families living in poverty. Similar problems in Romania were compounded by the government's population policies which aimed to increase population growth.

War and the transnational adoption of children

War often separates children from parents (Charnley 2000; Voutira and Brouskou 2000). While in the majority of these cases strategies for caring for separated or orphaned children will mostly be local (Charnley 2000: 114–20), dramatic increases in transnational adoption have mostly flowed from responses, ironically often in the enemy country, to the increase in orphaned and abandoned children during war. Children from Germany and Greece were adopted in relatively large numbers by families in the United States after the Second World War. A large cohort of Korean children was adopted during the Korean War, many of them the abandoned children of American servicemen and Korean women (Volkman 2005: 1). In 1975 in a few days 'Operation Babylift' took 2,000 babies out of Saigon for adoption in the United States (Volkman 2005: 83). The irony of children being made available for adoption in the belligerent country can hardly be overstated.

Summary: the family in public

The family, then, is shaped by multiple political and economic forces that regulate it materially and discursively. These regulations determine what kinds of relations between people are included and excluded from the concept of the family, what legal responsibilities parents have towards their children, what financial resources families get access to, what kinds of families are viewed as being legitimate or 'good' families and what kinds of families are non-legitimate or 'bad' families.

The intensely governed character of family life belies the commonsense notion that the family is a private space, a haven from a harsh world that people can retreat to and escape from to be themselves. The law, social policy, production and (social) reproduction all bear down on the family, attempting to shape how it in turn governs its members and especially its children. These attempts at ensuring the smooth socialization of children, the inculcation in them of particular habits, sensibilities and dispositions always produce an excess of failed socialization and failed incorporation, partly because all processes of normalization produce their constitutive outside and partly because of a global crisis of social reproduction that places unsupportable burdens on poor families. Street children and transnational adoptees are both, I suggest, the product of the crisis of social reproduction that makes the normative bourgeois family form an impossible achievement for many poor families. Both street children and transnational adoptees have been expelled from the family and are then reconstituted as abject subjects in need of rescue and reincorporation or removal. If the former (rescue and reincorporation) evoke discourses and practices of child-saving evident in adoption discourse, family reform and international campaigns to restore street children's 'lost childhoods', the abjection of the child expelled from the family can just as easily erase the humanity of street children and abandoned children in ways that legitimate their symbolic and real erasure – through violence or relocation – from public space.

Recommended further reading

Burr, R. 2006. *Vietnam's Children in a Changing World*. New Brunswick, NJ: Rutgers University Press.
One of the few ethnographic studies of street children.

Donzelot, J. 1980. *The Policing of Families*. Translated from the French by Robert Hurley. London: Hutchinson.
The key text on how the development of modern capitalism reshaped the family.

Hecht, T. 1998. *At Home in the Street: Street Children of Northeast Brazil*. Cambridge and New York: Cambridge University Press.
An early and compelling contribution to the ethnography of street and working children.

Mitchell, K., S. A. Marston and C. Katz. 2003. *Life's Work: Geographies of Social Reproduction*. Malden, MA and Oxford: Blackwell.
Originally published as a special issue of the journal *Antipode*, this collection is essential reading for anyone who wants to understand the concept of social reproduction and its salience to understanding children's lives.

Rose, N. 1999. *Governing the Soul: The Shaping of the Private Self*. London: Routledge.
An important theorization of the relationship between changing forms of governance and changing subjectivities, the chapters on the child, the family and the outside world are some of the best writing on the theorizing of contemporary childhood.

5

School and work

Introduction

What do children do with their time and what do governments want children to do with their time? This is one of the most critical questions in research on childhood and the answer to it is thought by many to be linked not only to children's wellbeing but to improvements in the health and well-being of future generations, and to no less an objective than the economic development of Africa and Asia. Getting children out of work and into school is seen as one of the most urgent tasks of development: for example, one of the eight Millennium Development Goals (MDGs) is to ensure that all children attend school and complete a full course of primary education.

In the contemporary world children can broadly speaking do one of three things with their time: they can work, they can go to school, or they can do neither (or both). Generally the literature on school and work assumes that if children work they do not go to school and if they go to school they do not work. This ignores the importance of leisure and play to children's worlds. Policy interventions that increase school attendance will not always lead to children doing less work – going to school may encroach on children's leisure time (and there is some evidence to suggest that this is what happens, as this chapter will show). Increasing school attendance may also fail to reduce children's workloads because they may have to combine work with school (Maitra and Ray 2002).

The emphasis on getting children in Africa, Asia and Latin America to attend school is not, however, entirely without its problems. Leaving work to attend school for most children in most of the world involves leaving family-based employment, typically in agriculture, or the family home to attend a poorly resourced school with barely qualified teachers where the teaching methods largely rely on rote-learning. Most children who do enrol in primary school will leave before completing the four years of education that is generally considered the minimum necessary to retain functional literacy. Smaller numbers of children will go on to high school and even smaller numbers on to university. The myth of universal schooling is that children are selected to continue their education on the basis of merit or ability. In practice whether or not children progress through the different levels of education is largely dependent on their class – and this is as true of developing as it is of developed countries (Galindo-Rueda and Vignoles 2005). All of these problems are well recognized by educationalists, yet the expansion of compulsory schooling is assumed to be the single most important indicator of a country's ability to achieve economic growth and development. International bodies like the World Bank and the UN, national governments and development NGOs all agree that school is a panacea for all kinds of problems including early pregnancy, poor sexual health, gender inequality and, of course, child labour. The Child Rights Information Network, for example, claims that 'the fulfilment of a child's right to education offers protection from a multitude of hazards, such as a life consigned to poverty, bonded labour in agriculture or industry, domestic labour, commercial sexual exploitation or recruitment into armed conflict' (www.crin.org). School has also become one of the central spaces of childhood – a place where children are thought to rightly belong.

The chapter begins by looking at the role of education in economic development and state development in the context of contemporary globalization. In the following section I show that education is important for the governing of a country. The state (which may then play an instrumental role in pursuing economic development) needs an educated class who can do the bureaucratic functions of government administration: governments need civil servants. If a government has a development strategy based on placing their country in the international economy at a high level, then it will need a labour force educated in engineering, design and science. If instead a country is trading in the global economy in primary agricultural goods then it will need a workforce educated in farming techniques. It can be seen from this crude contrast that some forms of knowledge can mostly be acquired through working whilst other kinds of knowledge have to be taught by specialists. In addition to ensuring that children and young people acquire the skills and knowledge that they will need when they enter the workforce, schools also have an important role in shaping children's view of the world and their place in it.

Education and globalization

The impact of education on economic development

School education is generally seen as essential for economic development. Despite the widespread conviction that expanding school attendance is a prerequisite to development, there is little empirical proof to support this claim. England, for example, had the first industrial revolution, but it did not make primary education compulsory for all children until the 1880s. The expansion of education to working-class children was a response to, rather than a stimulus for, economic development. France and Prussia introduced state-financed education much earlier than England. By 1800 most of the Prussian state had compulsory primary education. Despite their early state involvement in education, both France and Prussia were late developers in nineteenth-century Europe.

Some educational theorists (Green 1997) propose that the expansion of education occurs at points when the state is engaged in an exceptional period of consolidation and development. These periods of state development often follow the exposure of a weakness in the states' capacities that has been made apparent following a shock. Failure in war or the threat of revolution would be an example of the kinds of shocks that might stimulate a period of state development and educational expansion. The expansion of state-sponsored education in nineteenth-century Europe, Japan and North America for example can be traced to a need to consolidate state power following war or revolution. Nor is it difficult to say why this was so; education, after all, provides the state with administrators, bureaucrats, statisticians, planners. Education enables the expansion of the capacities of government by producing the kinds of people who can form the governing class.

The importance of school as a place for training civil servants and bureaucrats was also evident in the colonial period, when colonial rulers introduced public education in the colonized countries. School education was made available to relatively small numbers of children in colonial Africa and Asia, many of whom became civil servants in the colonial state. Indeed, the governing class of the postcolonial states came precisely from this group of students who had been educated in colonial schools, whether those provided directly by the colonial state or through Missionary schools that worked closely with colonial governments.

In postcolonial Asia formal education in school and university is thought to be one of the key drivers of economic growth in the region. The newly industrializing countries (NICs) of the late twentieth century, Hong Kong, South Korea, Singapore, Taiwan, Malaysia, Indonesia (and Brazil), had extraordinarily high levels of economic growth in the last quarter of the twentieth century. These rates of growth enabled the Asian Tigers (Hong Kong, South Korea, Taiwan and Singapore) to achieve living standards comparable with the G8 by the end of the twentieth century. There is considerable controversy about what combination of factors facilitated this level of growth, as well as about whether or not they represented a model of development that could be emulated by other developing countries or if, in fact, their experience was unique and could not be replicated. However, there is a general consensus in the literature that investments in high-quality and university-level education especially in information and communication technology were important drivers in the repositioning of these countries in the global knowledge-based economy. All four of the Asian Tigers have very high attendance rates at all levels of education from elementary to tertiary level. In South Korea, for example, well over 30 per cent of 18–30-year-olds are in university.

The Asian Tigers are all examples of developmental states. Liberal political theory predicts that states are inefficient and self-serving tools for development, claiming that development needs entrepreneurial individuals and a free market to flourish. The experience of economic growth in Asia has proved liberal theory wrong, although this theory continues to be at the heart of programmes for development in the rest of the world. In the case of Asia economic development was orchestrated and even managed by the state rather than the market. The state was able to take on this role for many complex reasons including the absence of a landlord class who might have opposed the development of a bourgeois economy, and the receipt of high levels of economic aid from the United States. This aid was provided in the expectation that Hong Kong, Taiwan and South Korea, all of which bordered communist states (China and North Korea), would be exemplars of capitalist development, as indeed they proved to be.

The impact of education on human capital

The impact of investments in education on economic development is not then particularly easy to untangle. Investments in education have been made by developmental states in an effort to catch up with early developers. In the nineteenth century that meant that France and Prussia invested in education so as to expand the state's capacities to direct development and to train people with the knowledge and skills that would enable these late developers to industrialize. In colonial Africa and Asia education was not so much a tool for economic development as a mechanism for developing a governing class in the colonies who would be loyal to the colonial power. In postcolonial Asia investments in education have continued to expand the capacity of the state, but they have also been strategically directed to inserting the Asian economies into the most valued levels of the global economy.

The belief that investment in schooling will lead to economic development is underpinned by human capital theory. Human capital theory claims that people should be considered as a form of capital analogous in its importance for economic growth to any other kind of capital formation. To accumulate human capital is to increase the quality of human attributes through investing in nutrition, health, and knowledge and skill acquisition. Although human capital theory includes investments in health and nutrition, it is education that has been analysed as the key investment (Sweetland 1996: 341). Human capital theory also accepts that not all education happens in school. It recognizes a role for informal education as well as work-based training. However, probably because of the increasing importance of specialized knowledge to the expansion of the global economy, school has been the most important educational input for human capital theory. The most important scholars in the field are Schultz (1971) and Becker (1964), both of whom received Nobel prizes for their theoretical work. These scholars, and especially Becker, have been enormously influential on research into the economics of education and the economics of child labour. The influence of human capital theory can also be discerned in campaigns against child labour. Although these campaigns tend to view abolition as a human rights issue that cannot be decided by cost–benefit analysis of the relative returns on school and work for children, many of the arguments put forward for abolition are implicitly claims about how work compromises the human capital development of individuals.

It is the presumed impact of education on human capital and the role of human capital formation in the context of a knowledge-based global economy that drives most research on access to education. How to improve school attendance is seen as closely linked to how to stop children working and, logically, children working are seen as an obstacle to the formation of human capital.

To understand the relationship between school and work it is necessary first of all to know something about working children: how many children are working? Where do children work? And who decides whether or not children work? It is to these questions that I now turn.

Working children

There is now a very large literature on working children. A joint ILO, UNICEF and World Bank project on Understanding Children's Work (www.ucw-project.org) has produced databases on children's labour from household surveys and rapid assessment that have been analysed in policy documents, country reports and, increasingly, in academic literature. Policy papers and academic papers and books have drawn on these data to develop and test theoretical econometric models of child labour, to describe gender differentiation in work and schooling, and to compare countries and sectors of employment. The following discussion is based on these sources, supplemented by Eric Edmonds' (2007) excellent review of the economics literature on children working, as well as the seminal study (1998) by Boyden, Ling and Myers, *What Works for Working Children*, and Manfred Liebel's more recent (2004) study of cross-cultural perspectives on working children.

How many children are working and where are they working?

It is not as simple as it might at first appear to say whether or not a child is working (Boyden et al. 1998: 20–3). Most children do not work for wages because they are working alongside their parents, often on their parents' land. Therefore a common definition of an adult worker – one who sells his or her labour power – cannot be applied to most working children or, if this definition is used, it will miss out the majority of children who are economically active, as well of course as those who make substantial contributions to household chores. Although the UNCRC and the ILO have attempted to provide a universal definition of child labour, the tasks that might be included as work, or hazardous or harmful work, are defined at country level.

According to the ILO about one in five of the world's 1.5 billion children are involved in production either for the market or for their – or their families' – own use (ILO 2006). Household chores, whether in the child's own or in someone else's home, do not count as economic activity. The decision to exclude domestic work from economic activity has been criticized, and given that in households with low technology it can involve many hours of work it is difficult to justify this exclusion.

The ILO has defined a sub-set of economic activity as 'child work'. These are activities that the ILO accepts as not necessarily harmful for children. They include a few hours of light work per week for children aged twelve to fifteen and all non-hazardous work for young people aged fifteen to seventeen. It is regulated by the ILO's Minimum Age Convention 1973 (No. 138) and in 2006 included 14 per cent of the global age group five to seventeen.

Hazardous work also known as the 'worst forms of child labour' includes any work that has adverse effects on safety, physical or mental health and moral development, or excessive hours of work in any occupation, including one that is otherwise safe. The definition of hazardous work is made by national governments but generally it would include all work (except domestic work) of forty-three hours or more in one week and all mining and quarrying. There are about 126 million children (8 per cent of the age group) working in hazardous conditions.

As might be expected, children work more hours as they get older. There is a large increase in participation rates in market and domestic work for boys at age ten and again at age twelve; for girls there are significant leaps at age eight (for domestic work), and at ages ten and twelve (for market work) (Edmonds 2007: 20). There are large variations between countries in what kinds of work children do as they get older, but there are also patterns that are interesting for understanding child labour (Edmonds 2007: 21).

Most economically active children work in agriculture, fisheries and forestry (69 per cent). The second most significant sector is the hotel, restaurant, wholesale and retail trades (22 per cent) and, when this can be disaggregated, children are found more often working in the wholesale and retail trades than in hotels and restaurants. Manufacturing is smaller than both, but still greater than mining or construction. Private households are significant employers of children in Kenya, Tanzania and Zambia. Edmonds notes that child domestic work in Africa has been little studied by economists. Only 9 per cent of children are working in industry, although it is industrial work – especially for export – that attracts the most international concern.

Most of the world's working children are in sub-Saharan Africa and Asia and the Pacific. One in four African children aged five to fourteen (nearly 50 million), and nearly one in five Asian/Pacific children of the same age (122 million), are working. The number of working children in Latin America and the Caribbean has declined considerably in recent years and is now about one in twenty (nearly 6 million).

UNICEF's MICS household survey asks if the child has worked in the *last week* and if they have attended school in the *last year*. This leads to perhaps unreasonably high levels of reporting of school attendance. Work outside the home is the *least* prevalent activity for all but three of the participating countries (Kenya, Venezuela, Azerbaijan); over two thirds (65 per cent) of children report doing domestic work. An important finding is that the countries with the lowest school attendance rates have the highest number of children who are neither in school nor in work. This shows that work is not the residual claim on children's time if they do not go to school (Edmonds 2007: 16). Countries with the highest rates of children working outside the home also have the highest rates of children working inside the home. This is consistent with the suggestion that child labour is not only determined by labour market demand. Participation in market work is highest in countries where domestic work is also high. The picture that Edmonds draws from his analysis of UNICEF's MICS data is of children engaging in several tasks for short periods, but not working long hours overall (Edmonds 2007: 16).

Gender and children's work

Children's work is largely hidden within what I call an 'economy of care'. What I mean by this is that children tend to do caring work – looking after siblings, housework, caring for animals, collecting water – that is low-skilled, unpaid, repetitive, and both essential to social reproduction and at the same time often invisible in calculations of work. Like 'women's work', children's work has a low status partly because children's status is low and their activities are correspondingly undervalued. If this is generally true of children's work it is particularly true of girls' work. In a UCW study of child labour in Latin America and the Caribbean from a gender perspective (Guarcello et al. 2006), the authors argue that the exclusion of household chores from the category of work, and the setting of the cut-off for including it as work as twenty-eight hours (compared to one hour of economic activity), are highly gendered and distort the picture of girls' labour activities. Hence, although other UCW country studies show that boys are more likely than girls to be economically active in Latin America and the Caribbean (the picture is more varied for South Asia and sub-Saharan Africa), these comparisons would look very different if household chores were included as economic activity, since these are more likely to be done by girls. Girls' work is more likely to be centred on the home and includes the care of siblings or other younger children, housework and the preparation (although less often the cooking) of food. Neither the girls themselves nor their siblings and parents are likely to think of these activities as 'work'. Generally, domestic work continues to be regarded as outside capitalist relations – important for (gendered) socialization but not an economic activity. The exception to this general configuring of domestic work as 'helping out' is in campaigns, for example by Anti-Slavery International, to rethink domestic labour outside the family home not only as work, but as unfree labour. Whilst Edmonds is correct that 'asserting that a child who works substantive hours in the provision of services in their home is not working is difficult to justify' (Edmonds 2007: 9), nor is it reasonable to claim that this is slave labour.

If most girls are working in the home, most boys that work are working in the rural economy either on family farms, in family work-teams or, less often, as independent wage-earners. Boys working in agriculture account for nearly three quarters of all boys' labour, and girls working as domestics outside their family home account for a similar proportion of girls' labour (although it is important to remember that girls' domestic work inside the home is not counted as work in most measurements). Girls' work frees up the labour of other family members; similarly boys' work on labour-intensive, unskilled tasks frees up the labour of adults for more skilled work, for production and for social reproduction. In addition, boys' work is regarded as an apprenticeship for adult labour (Nieuwenhuys 1994: 101).

Boys have higher participation rates in market work and lower participation rates in domestic work than girls. Within each category boys and girls are also likely to be involved in different kinds of work. In market work boys are more likely to be growing cereals whilst girls are more likely to be growing vegetables and rearing poultry. In Bangladesh only girls are involved in textiles, sewing handicrafts and private household services (Edmonds 2007: 18).

Who decides if children work?

The work of Gary Becker on the household has been enormously influential on research into why parents get their children to work. Becker's (1991) *A Treatise on the Family* considers the family as a unit of production similar to a firm, in which one member of the household (or adults acting as if they were one member) makes decisions about the allocation of resources and tasks to other members in order to maximize productivity and efficiency. Becker argues that families are the most efficient institution for increasing individual wellbeing because they optimize the possibilities for specialization. In contrast to feminist analyses that attribute gendered divisions of labour to patriarchy, Becker and other scholars following this neo-liberal model of household decision-making assume that there is no intent to discriminate against family members, but that even a small comparative advantage will be highlighted and developed in order to facilitate an organized division of labour in the interests of increased efficiency. What that means for a sexual division of labour is that an initial advantage – bearing and nursing babies – is codified into a comparative advantage over men and boys in caring for children. For divisions of labour across the life course in the household it means that children's different skills – whatever these are attributed to – are encouraged and developed in such a way that all members of the household benefit from each member's activities. So, for example, if a younger, cleverer sibling goes to school and an older child to work, both children benefit from each other's work; the older child's wage is shared and may even contribute to the costs of schooling, and the school-child's new knowledge and skills are made available to all family members. This rational-choice model of household decision-making has been very influential in the economic sociology of child labour.

These rational economic models of decision-making do not, however, take account of cultural, social and affective reasons for making decisions about whether children should work or go to school (or do neither). In order to understand decision-making about how children spend their time (in work, in school, doing household chores, caring for dependants, playing), it is necessary to think about the family or household as a unit because parents and children make decisions about their use of time in relation to the total needs of the household. Nonetheless, decisions made within the household cannot be reduced to the dimensions predicted by rational-choice theory. Decisions will be shaped by social and cultural norms – some of which may include, say, an expectation that girls do chores and care for siblings or that boys will contribute to farm labour on family-owned farms. Indeed, the (rather small) ethnographic literature there is on child labour shows that decision-making is so grounded in social and cultural norms as to appear entirely natural and unquestionable to both parents and children.

The assumption that decisions made in the household are unitary or dic-tatorial is increasingly being abandoned, but there is still a focus on parental decisions. More research is needed on the role that children play in making decisions about their use of their time. If, for example, children decide to make use of available employment opportunities, then anti-poverty measures that target parents may have little impact on child labour supply (Edmonds 2007: 45). Edmonds concludes: 'In general the role that attitudes and norms play in child labor is poorly understood. It is clear that child time allocation is in general elastic with respect to the household's economic environment, but it is not clear whether this elasticity is bounded by social attitudes towards work, whether there are some children who are espe-cially vulnerable in this regard, and whether this elasticity reflects changing norms or if norms are just one component of how child time allocation decisions are made' (2007: 47).

Why do parents put their children to work?

In their seminal paper (1998) Basu and Van also assume that parents decide whether or not their children should work and that they only send their children to work because their own wages are not sufficient to meet their subsistence needs. While some of the literature on child labour recognizes that some work may be non-hazardous and possibly even beneficial to children, the founding premise of much of the research is that work is undesirable for children and that, therefore, parents' decisions to send their children to work or keep them at home to care for siblings and do housework are made because of external constraints that make it more optimal for children to work than not to work.

Basu and Van's model assumes that parents are altruistic towards their children and that they would not send their children to work if they did not have to. This same principle does not inform many of the campaigns against child labour which assume that parents do not understand the value of investing in education or are neglectful (at best) of their children's welfare. Whilst Basu and Van's theoretical paper is an important corrective to this view, its underlying assumption – that child labour is essentially driven by poverty – is not completely sustained by other research. There is some research which suggests that increases in household assets may increase the likelihood of children working, particularly in family-owned businesses. Similarly, economic growth may multiply employment opportunities that children may decide to take advantage of.

Is child labour driven by a specific labour market demand?

The nimble fingers argument has been more or less discredited. The use of children's time for collecting activities, especially collecting water, is well documented. Several studies in different countries have shown higher rates of school participation where households have access to piped water (Edmonds 2007: 41). Children are more likely to work when families have productive capital and there are more opportunities for self-employment, although they may also be more likely to combine working with school attendance. Changes in technology also impact on child labour decisions when technology substitutes for child labour. Children work less in countries that trade more (Edmonds 2007: 42). Edmonds and Pavcnik find 'no support for the claim that trade perpetuates high levels of child labor in poor countries' (Edmonds 2007: 42). Other studies have found that booms in the world price of export crops leads to increased employment of children by land-poor labourers. Edmonds cites Kruger's (2007) study of the coffee boom in Brazil, in which she argues that in response to temporary booms families put children to work to take advantage of the new employment opportunities, and children return to school after the boom (Edmonds 2007: 43). The impact of international trade and child labour is therefore difficult to generalize and is country-specific.

If children don't go to work do they go to school?

Although child labour is apparently declining, the numbers of children who are neither in school nor in work may be increasing. The Human Development of India survey (1994) of rural households found that although school enrolment of 6–16-year-olds was 65 per cent (of which 4.1 per cent worked and studied), a further 25 per cent of children were neither working nor studying. Several of the UCW country studies report quite high rates of children neither working nor studying (e.g. 18 per cent for Guatemala). Biggeri et al. (2003) discuss this phenomenon and conclude that the time of some 'idle' children is in fact taken up by household chores, some are ill, and some are unemployed – that is, actively looking for work. However, after adjusting for these factors they still find that a non-negligible number of children are neither working nor at school. They propose a model that suggests that in certain conditions, essentially where the costs of education are high or the returns low, and the returns from work are low and the costs high, the optimal decision for a household may be for the child to neither work nor study. Biggeri and his colleagues initially took the UN cut-off of twenty-eight hours of household chores to calculate whether or not children are genuinely idle. As might be expected, once they applied a lower cut-off, twenty-one hours, they found that household chores do account for many more apparently idle girls. We may speculate then that the decline in child labour can partly be accounted for by a diversion of girls' labour into invisible household work.

The quality of school education also influences decisions about whether children should work or attend school. Research suggests that families are generally unlikely to send a child to school to learn what he or she would have learned 'at home', in any case. Nieuwenhuys (1994: 81) shows that in Kerala increases in school enrolment were connected with the policy of reservation and the expansion of both the number of government posts and the widening of access to them. In other words, parents were more likely to send their children to school to acquire skills and knowledge that they could not be trained in at home.

Poor rural children's schooling seems to be limited in general to those periods when they are considered too young to work or there is no particular need for their work. As and when such a need arises the child is likely to be withdrawn from school. In the absence of legal enforcement of compulsory schooling parents are apparently strategic about – rather than hostile to – school. However, the cultural presumption in rural economies seems to be that it is 'natural' for children in farming families to work, just as in urban economies the cultural presumption is in favour of school as children's 'natural' domain.

The impact of children's work on human capital

The previous section has shown that large numbers of children work and that they mostly work in agriculture (and therefore in rural areas). For the most part those who work in agriculture are not paid for their work, but this should not be equated with slave labour, as the campaigns for the abolition of child labour tend to do. Most children are not paid because they are working alongside their parents for an employer who pays the 'family wage' to the contracted adult, or they are working at home or on a family-owned farm or for a family business. There is still not enough knowledge about who decides if children should work, but two things are evident: firstly, that decisions about work are made for the benefit of the family rather than for individuals and, secondly, that in general, but not exclusively, parents get their children to work because their own wages or productivity are below subsistence level. The next section addresses the implications of children working for human capital looking at the impact on school attendance and achievement; the impact on health; and the future consequences of working for adult wages.

Impact of work on school attendance and achievement

The effect on human capital accumulation of children working is one of the main drivers of research into child labour. There are few studies of the impact of work on school achievement, but these do suggest that work impacts negatively on school performance. Work also impacts on attendance, unsurprisingly given that there are finite hours to allocate to work, school and other activities. Edmonds's analysis of UNICEF's MICS data suggests that about eight hours of work a week is compatible with school attendance and that the latter declines if the number of hours increases. Establishing whether these correlations imply causality is very challenging. One significant finding for social policy is that schemes that pay children to attend school do increase school attendance, but they do not lead to decreases in the number of children working by the same degree. A plausible explanation for this is that working children had time for leisure and that increases in schooling cut into their leisure time rather than their working time (Edmonds 2007: 28).

Impacts on health
Martin Woodhead's study of the possible implications of working on children's social–psychological development finds that working may have benefits for children comparable with those acquired in school. Generally studies focus on the impact on physical health and find that working may expose children to health hazards and may increase the child's nutritional needs leading to increased risk of malnutrition. Edmonds notes that work may have positive impacts on health, especially in the poor populations where child work is most prevalent. Additional resources may increase food availability, and the fact that the child is contributing to the household income may increase their participation in decision-making in the family. Generally there is no evidence that work on average has a harmful impact on working children. Edmonds notes that this might be because heterogeneity in the impact on health of working means that the worst effects do not show up in the data because of their statistical rarity. There is also so far little evidence on the impact of working as a child on future adult health. Edmonds concludes that 'evidence on specific mechanisms through which child labor might propagate through to adulthood seems to be largely speculative' (Edmonds 2007: 33).

Although knowledge about the harmful impacts of working on the health of young workers is fragmentary there is some quite concrete evidence from particular sectors. A Human Rights Watch report on child farm-workers published in 2000 documents the considerable risks and injuries to young farm-workers in the United States. There are about 800,000 farm-workers under eighteen years of age working in the USA, the majority as hired labourers. HRW's research was mostly done in Arizona. The majority of workers that they interviewed began working in the fields between the ages of thirteen and fifteen. All farm-workers, whether adults or youth, work long hours – twelve hours a day over six or seven days are routine. In peak harvest time the working day can be as long as eighteen hours. The main risks to the health of young workers are exposure to pesticides, heatstroke, musculoskeletal trauma and dangerous machinery. Children's bodies are more vulnerable to the toxic effects of pesticides than adults' and yet the regulations on exposure to chemicals are framed for adults. HRW says that the Environmental Protection Agency's (EPA) set periods for when workers can return to a field after pesticides have been applied are for a 154-pound man. HRW reports the case of a seventeen-year-old migrant farm-worker who collapsed and died from pesticide poisoning the day after he was soaked with pesticide sprayed from a tractor. Heat-induced illness up to and including death brought on by working in high temperatures with little or no access to water is another risk that young workers are especially vulnerable to. In June 2008 a young woman – seventeen-year-old María Isabel Vázquez Jiménez – collapsed and died on her fourth day of work in California. The contractor that hired her from Mexico, Merced Farm Labor, was issued three citations in 2006 for exposing workers to heatstroke, failing to train workers on heat stress prevention and not installing toilets at the work site, but the site still had no toilets, no shade and no drinking water (*The Guardian*, 5 June 2008). Children working in agriculture in the USA make up only 8 per cent of the population of working minors overall, yet account for 40 per cent of work-related fatalities among minors (Human Rights Watch 2000).

Future consequences of working
Analysis of the Brazilian government's large-scale household surveys that started in 1996 and ask when the respondent first entered the labour force provides most of the current evidence on the impact for an adult of having worked as a child. Emerson and Souza (2003) found that early entry into the labour force generally reduced adult wages by as much as 17 per cent. The exception to this is for adults who never attended school, who have higher wages than those who left school early. Emerson and Souza speculate that this is an effect of the additional experience that they accumulate in their work. In a study based on Vietnam's household survey Beegle et al. found that 'over a relatively short horizon (as might be appropriate in poor, credit constrained families), the value of increased earnings and the return to experience will outweigh the opportunity cost of foregone education' (Edmonds 2007: 31).

Impact on labour markets
Basu and Van's (1998) seminal study argued that, if children's labour and adults' labour can be substituted for one another, then children depress adult wages. If parents only get their children to work when their own wages are insufficient to cover their subsistence (what Basu and Van call the luxury axiom), then children's wages depress adult wages, which in turn means that children have to work because adult wages are insufficient to cover subsistence consumption needs. Whether child wages depress adult wages

is a critical question in the research on child labour, but 'direct evidence on whether child labor affects adult labor markets is scarce' (Edmonds 2007: 37). Given that child labour is mostly done outside formal labour markets, it seems less than plausible that it depresses adult wages. Edmonds argues that this is only likely to be the case where children are a substantial part of the active labour force. He then shows that children are a very small part of the active labour force even in countries where the economic activity rates for children are very high. There are only 'two countries in the world where children are more than a hundredth of a percent of the economically active population' (Edmonds 2007: 38). 'Is it possible', he asks rhetorically, 'that variation in the activities of less than a hundredth of a percent of the economically active population can influence equilibrium wages in the labor market?' (Edmonds 2007: 38). If child labour does suppress adult wages, then this has implications for parents' decisions about the costs and benefits of children working or attending school.

Summary on working children

Campaigns on child labour take it as axiomatic that children should not be working. Although the target of child labour campaigns is work that has 'adverse effects on the child's safety, health or moral development', in practice working below a minimum age, generally twelve years, is taken as a proxy for injurious work. Leaving aside what the ILO has identified as the worst forms of child labour (bonded labour, illicit activities, armed conflict, prostitution, pornography and trafficking), the reason for targeting other forms of labour for abolition (rather than, say, regulating them) is that they affect children's long-term development – specifically work is assumed to compromise children's future health and employment and the formation of human capital. There is little concrete evidence on either of these outcomes beyond causal inferences that are made about the employment and health of adults. Statistically, adult health and employment improves with each year of schooling, however, a simple inference that this can be attributed to the effects of schooling rather than that years of schooling are correlated with family income seems unwarranted. Nor is it entirely clear why school attendance is so clearly demarcated from work to the extent that, while school is increasingly the only public space that children are recognized as belonging in, work is entirely erased as a legitimate place for children. While such a statement might seem shocking and facile if we are comparing school to prostitution or soldiering, it may seem a more reasonable comparison if we compare school with, say, selling small goods on the street, parking cars, shoe-shining, shop work, waiting tables, child care, housework, shepherding, fishing and so on. Many of these are activities that most working children are involved in, and while it might be objected that they can involve long hours and are unpaid and boring, the same could be said of school for many, perhaps most, children. Nor is this a trivial point: so long as working children are only recognized as children who have lost their childhood and not as workers, it will be difficult and often impossible for them to be organized as workers for shorter hours, better pay, and better work conditions. Conversely, so long as school is presumed to be a good space for children, the damage and stress of studying for long hours, often under the tutelage of poorly trained teachers and in dilapidated buildings, will continue to go unrecognized. Contrary to the discourse of human rights approaches, it is only through the self-organization of workers that improvements in pay and working conditions have been secured. Self-organization has always been harder for marginal workers, as is evident from the tendency to lower pay, longer hours and worse working conditions for women workers and migrant workers. New questions about what kinds of knowledge, skills and subjectivities school *and* work give children, and how their work and study should be remunerated, need to be asked.

The impact of schools: schools as a moral technology

So far in this chapter I have discussed the correlations between school and economic development. School also has other functions – principal in which is the shaping of children's character or their socialization. It is to these other functions of school that I now turn. Although the connections between the school's role as a moral technology and economic development are not quite as clear as those between the school's role in disseminating bodies of knowledge/skills and economic development, such connections can still be made.

It may seem strange to think of the school as a technology. This is a concept that the critical theorist, Foucault, developed to think about how governments govern. Foucault's theory of government is that modern governments do not simply coerce or bludgeon people into accepting their rule but that they get people to govern or rule themselves. Governments concern themselves, he said, with regulating the 'conduct of conduct' – with getting people to feel that good conduct is at the heart of being a good person. Governments do this in many different ways – including through social work, school, health care, sexual and reproductive health care, policing and law. Foucault grouped all of these different ways together in his concept of 'technologies'. The reason why Foucault and others working with the same ideas (Foucauldians) call them technologies rather than, say, methods or policies is that they want to convey the sense that these activities shape human behaviour even though human beings – social workers, health visitors and teachers as well as clients, patients and students – might have entirely different intentions from those that are realized through these technologies. They are moral technologies because they are concerned with behaviour and with adopting and internalizing ideas about how a moral person should think and feel. School is not the only kind of moral technology, but it is a very important one in the lives of children.

From religious to moral education

The history of schooling begins with the school as a place for religious teaching and learning. For Muslims it involved learning classical Arabic and reciting the Qur'an and the Hadith; for Christians the Bible stories told at Sunday school were moral tales that instructed the child in how to live. These religious schools were the foundations of the secular schools that expanded everywhere throughout the nineteenth and twentieth centuries (Hunter 1994; 1996). In Egypt Islamic religious schools or *kuttabs* were the recruiting grounds for the preparatory and technical schools that were founded by the Ottomans when they restored their rule over Egypt in the 1820s. Later the British government accomplished the development of rural education in nineteenth-century Egypt and in England 'largely through the subvention of religious-based popular schools' (Starrett 1998: 32). It was these schools that were pressed into the service of both the dissemination of particular kinds of skills and knowledge and the production of a specific kind of subjectivity or moral character in the child. The conviction that the school was a site in which children could be trained to observe and reflect on their own conduct to the advantage of the political order continued throughout the British administration of Egypt (Starrett 1998: 72). Turning religious schools into secular schools was also the aim of colonial education policy in Indian schools during colonial rule. The British MP Macaulay was a key figure in the development of education policy in both India and Egypt. Demonstrating the importance to colonial policy of control over education Macaulay in his famous Minute on Indian Education said that the aim of colonial Indian education was to produce 'a class who may be interpreters between us and the millions whom we govern; a class of persons, Indian in blood and colour, but English in taste, in opinions, in morals, and in intellect' (Macaulay 1835).

Religious teaching and learning was reshaped from the inculcation in children of the habits of a 'way of life' to the teaching of religion as a separate and distinct school subject. In colonial India the British state subverted religious institutions, such as the Tols (Hindi religious schools for Brahmins) and the Madrashas (Islamic schools), through the provision of grants-in-aid that were conditional on religion being taught as a school subject and secular subjects being added to the curriculum (Langohr 2001). This use of grants-in-aid to get religious schools to teach religion as one subject in the curriculum was borrowed from England where from 1862 elementary schools could get grants-in-aid from the government if they taught reading, writing and arithmetic, rather than religious doctrine. Religion was constituted as 'a new historical object: anchored in personal experience, expressible as belief statements, dependent on private institutions and practiced in one's spare time' (Langohr 2005: 161, citing Asad 1993). In Egypt '[t]he traditional study of the Qur'an, whose purpose had been to learn how to use the sacred word in appropriate contexts now became the study of Islam as a moral system, a study removed from its living context and placed on the same level as other secular categories of knowledge' (Starrett 1998: 71; see also Mitchell 1988: 74–9).

Despite the success of Imperial governments, in both their domestic and colonial education policy, in subverting religious schools for secular purposes, the transformation of religion from a way of life to an object of knowledge was never quite complete. Religion might creep into the other school subjects, as when religious texts were used to teach literacy, but also, as Srivastava (1998) has shown, even in one of the most secular and prestigious schools in contemporary India, the Doon, a religious sensibility continues to influence the organization of the school and its timetable. The religious roots of secular education are also evident in England, where religion shapes many aspects of school including the rhythm of the school year (which continues to be punctuated by the celebration of Christian religious festivals). In the United States the religious right has made many attempts (some of them successful) to dictate the school curriculum, including insisting on the promotion of creationism/intelligent design in Science lessons (Apple 2008). Their success undermines the claims that schools are purely secular spaces. Their religious undercurrents are present in both their historical origins and their contemporary concerns about how schools can contribute to the moral instruction of the child.

The school might be thought of as a hybrid site of moral instruction in which the secular does not so much overturn the religious, or even hijack it for its own purposes, but displays the shared moral projects of both governments and religious authorities. Capitalism claims that some ways of being are natural to humans – that we are competitive, that we always put individual desires and needs before those of a larger group (neighbourhood or community), that we use rational (that is, not emotional) choice to minimize costs and maximize benefits to decide between courses of action. Despite the conviction of capitalists that all this is natural human behaviour, governments invest significant resources in education partly to produce the kind of person that values one side of the binary rational/emotional, individual/social, autonomous/interdependent more than the other. Underlying all of this is the persistent and religiously influenced injunction to be a 'good person'.

An adapted religious world-view informs many school subjects. Green claims that the extent of state planning in education and the emphasis placed on moral and social education are 'defining characteristics of the educational system of not only Singapore, Taiwan and South Korea but also Japan' (1997: 49). While these might seem ostensibly to be secular subjects, their claims to teaching 'ethics' or 'good citizenship' rely on the notion of a transcendental morality which is in fact a religiously derived ethics that has slipped its moorings from religious texts, places and times, to re-emerge as part of the liberal fashioning of the self.

English literature

One of the most significant effects of European imperialism on knowledge production has been the dissemination of European languages as the medium of instruction for secondary and tertiary education. The study of English as a school subject is always framed by the question: what is the connection between 'the curriculum and the "life" or "life-world" of students'? (Kress et al. 2005: 172). In the case of Anglophone postcolonial countries (e.g. India, Anglophone Africa), literacy in English has also involved the study of English literature/literature in English. The study of English literature across the English-speaking world 'consists of a *singularizable discursive formation* whose origin can be traced back to an ultimately imperial pedagogical imaginary' (Amoko 2001: 23; emphasis is his). This discursive formation, Amoko argues, constitutes and disseminates cultural capital through the medium of the school. It provides unequal access to linguistic or socially valued speech (Standard English) and to symbolic capital. In contrast to Said's emphasis on the content of the canon of Western literature, Amoko argues that the 'cultural capital[s] produced by English literature both in Western and non-Western contexts are ultimately more socially significant in their effects than the "ideological" content of literary works'

(Amoko 2001: 26–7). What he means by this is that, if a student graduates from school knowing what the canon of English literature is and able to display his or her familiarity with that canon, then this in itself is a form of cultural capital which can be converted into economic and social capital. The importance of education in the shaping of socio-economic class is therefore, Amoko is arguing, more important for understanding how power works than is the Orientalist discourse that Said focuses on in his seminal study.

English literature in colonial India was perceived by the British as a vehicle for inculcating in Indians, at least those Indians whose training in British grant-aided schools was intended to equip with the skills and disposition to staff the British administration, 'moral values for correct behaviour and action, it [English literary study] represented a convenient replacement for the direct religious instruction that was forbidden by law . . . A discipline that was originally introduced in India primarily to convey the mechanics of language was thus transformed into an instrument for ensuring industriousness, efficiency, trustworthiness, and compliance in native subjects' (Viswanathan 1990: 93).

Viswanathan argues that the 'history of education in British India shows that certain humanistic functions traditionally associated with literature – for example, *the shaping of character or the development of the aesthetic sense or the disciplines of ethical thinking* – were considered essential to the processes of socio-political control by the guardians of the same tradition' (1990: 3 – my emphasis). In British India English literature was to 'perform the functions of those social institutions (such as the Church) that, in England, served as the chief disseminators of value, tradition and authority' (1990: 7).

The introduction in the colonial period of English language instruction sought to secure, in a particular stratum of colonial subjects, a certain kind of attitude or disposition commensurate with rendering colonial populations and territories governable. English language teaching and learning in postcolonial contexts continues to be inscribed with a moral pedagogy. Students at English-medium schools in India are inducted into a practice of critical reading of a range of English language texts that will both smooth their path into tertiary education and orientate them towards 'reading and writing "critically" about social/textual issues, to working independently, to voicing opinions' (Ramanathan 2002: 144).

In many schools in the postcolonial world, elementary education (that is, from five to eleven) is taught in local, vernacular languages, but at tertiary level the medium of instruction is frequently the language of the formal colonial power. In India every state is obliged to provide both

English-medium and vernacular-medium education. At college level professional degrees (engineering, computer science, medicine and science)
are taught in English (Ramanathan 2002: 127). In order to prepare their
children for secondary and post-secondary education, parents who can
afford to do so will send them to private primary schools where the
medium of instruction is also English. Ramanathan has shown that in
Gujarat state in India students in Gujarati-medium schools have, perhaps
as one might expect, a less confident grasp of English than students in
English-medium schools. Her point is that these differences are not merely
technical, that they translate into differences, for example, in teaching practices (with Gujarati-medium schools teaching with traditional
methods) and in how students are encouraged to see themselves. She
says, for example, that texts for English in Gujarati-medium schools and
in English-medium schools 'foster more "individualistic" tendencies of EM
students, and the complete lack of them in the GM counterparts . . . The
inclusion and rehearsal of these [different textbook] activities encourage
EM, middle-class students to see themselves as individuals with opinions
that matter and that need to be articulated' (Ramanathan 2002: 137; see
also Srivastava 1998).

Literacy
Since English literature is the telling of stories that involve characters, often
experiencing and resolving moral dilemmas, it is perhaps quite easy to
grasp the idea that English is a 'moral technology'. This might not seem so
obvious for the act of learning to read and write itself. Literacy might seem
more like a technical skill than a 'technology' in the Foucauldian sense. One
approach that challenges this view of literacy as simply a technical skill is
the 'new literacy studies'. Brian Street, a key contributor to the new literacy
studies, says: 'Every literacy is learnt in a specific context in a particular way
and the modes of learning, the social relationships of student to teacher are
modes of socialization and acculturation. The student is learning cultural
models of identity and personhood, not just how to decode script or to
write a particular hand' (Street 1995: 141). What Brian Street is arguing
here is that the environment or setting in which literacy is taught conveys
cultural models about the self and others.

In arguing for seeing the setting in which literacy is learned, rather than
literacy itself, as a technology that shapes the students' ideas about 'identity and personhood', the new literacy studies are distancing themselves
from claims that learning to make marks on a page or decode a script can
be correlated with the acquisition of abstract and logical thinking. This is

what Street calls the 'great divide theory', the idea that people who can read and write think in qualitatively different (and better) ways to people who cannot read and write. The great divide theory says that literate people have better cognitive abilities, better facility in logic, understand abstraction better, are less concrete and have better higher-order mental operations than people who are illiterate. The new literacy studies, in contrast, want to argue that abstraction and logic are not cognitive skills that are restricted to literates or learned alongside the learning of literacy. They claim that differences in ways of thinking are linked to class and culture, and that literacy that is learned away from school (say, at home) will use different models of identity and personhood than those learned in school. The value of the new literacy studies is in thinking about ways that learning can be done outside the school context. This is important for education in developing countries, in many of which there are both logistical and cultural problems with improving access to school. It is also important for developed countries struggling with finding ways to educate a growing population of 'school refusers'.

Summary

In this chapter I have argued that school and work should not be considered as entirely oppositional sites or practices. They are both involved in similar processes in relation to the governing of childhood. The school's role in inculcating in the child the kinds of dispositions congruent with the formation of the subject as a rational, self-governing person can be contrasted to the role of work in integrating the child into existing and local economic structures and processes. As the local economy changes under the dual action of the national state and the expansion of global capitalism, it becomes increasingly difficult for working children to learn the knowledge and skills that the state needs them to have if they are to participate in this new configuration of the global and the local. The skills and knowledge and indeed the subjectivity that a child learns in a family-based economy, particularly a rural economy, become increasingly redundant and anachronistic (Katz 2004). The promise of education is that children will be able to be judged on their intellectual merit as individuals – their access to desirable work only being limited by their own ability to gain qualifications. For most (but of course not all) children this will turn out to be a hollow promise, since the insertion of national economies into the global economy does nothing to erode inequality but simply reconfigures it in new ways.

Recommended further reading

Edmonds, E. V. 2007. *Child Labor*. Cambridge, MA: National Bureau of Economic Research.
A comprehensive review of the literature on the economics of child labour.

Liebel, M. 2004. *A Will of Their Own: Cross Cultural Perspectives on Working Children*. London and New York: Zed Books.
A good complement to Edmonds' literature review, this book covers most of the qualitative studies of the lives of working children.

Srivastava, S. 1998. *Constructing Post-Colonial India: National Character and the Doon School*. London and New York: Routledge.
A brilliant study of the place of school in shaping children's identities.

Street, B. V. (ed.). 2001. *Literacy and Development: Ethnographic Perspectives*. London and New York: Routledge.
An important study for understanding the multiple contexts and sites of learning for both children and adults in the developing world.

6

Children and politics

Introduction

This chapter is about children and political activism. The idea that children might be involved in politics challenges many commonsense ideas about what it means to be a child (Stephens 1995; Brocklehurst 2006: 19; Wyness et al. 2004: 3). In earlier chapters in this book I discussed how childhood is thought of, especially in the developed world, as a time of innocence and dependence. In this view families and school should shelter children from the harsh world of politics. Political activism takes place in public, at work and on the street, and these are places where children are thought not to belong to.

I have also shown that the idea that children belong in particular places, say at home or in school, and therefore have little to do with economics or politics ignores the extent to which both family and school are shaped by law and public policy, and that children's lives are shaped by the politics of class, race and gender. So in fact it is not that children's lives and childhood can be separated from politics but a specific kind of politics – political activism – is anomalous to childhood.

This chapter challenges this view of children as unable or unwilling to be politically active. Drawing on evidence from China, the United States, Iran and South Africa, I show that children and young people have been active in politics. In addition to the cases that I focus on in this chapter many other examples of children and young people being actively involved in political movements come easily to mind, belying the dominant representation of children and political activism as incompatible with one another. In 1968, in a period of political turmoil in Europe and the Americas, there were protests by students about their government's policies on war, education and workers' rights (Carey 2005; Kurlansky 2005), and more recently even very young children have been caught up in political conflict in Palestine (Brocklehurst 2006).

The analysis of the case studies in this chapter identifies four key characteristics of young people's political activism:

- Firstly, that it is unusual for young children to be involved in politics and most young political activists are older teenagers.
- Secondly, that school is a central site of political mobilization.
- Thirdly, that the commonsense assumption that youthful political activism is rooted in generational conflict is not sustained by the empirical evidence.
- Fourthly, that political activism amongst youth is a minority pursuit, as it is for adults, except where the state is involved in orchestrating the total mobilization of society, usually in post-revolutionary contexts.

Young political activists: children or youth?

When children become politically active they are often spoken of as 'youth'. In this section I discuss why it is so much easier to think of 'youth' as politically engaged than it is to think of children in this way.

To be a 'youth' is to be somewhere between being a child and being an adult or, perhaps more to the point, to be neither fully a child nor fully an adult. Deborah Durham calls this an identity that straddles 'kin-based, domestic space and wider public spheres' (Durham 2000: 116). What she means is that youth has one foot in the spaces of childhood ('kin-based, domestic space') and one foot in the spaces of adulthood ('wider public spheres'). This position of being neither quite one thing nor another is sometimes referred to as a liminal zone or a liminal role. This term, liminality, means the space between, and has been widely used in anthropology and related fields to describe groups who are in a temporary space between two roles (Turner 1967). When young people who would usually be called children (say young people aged twelve and over) get involved in politics they enter this liminal zone – they are spoken of as youth: no longer children but not yet adults. On the other side of the boundary, young people who might be thought of as adults, say people aged eighteen or more, also attract this label 'youth' if they are involved in politics that are outside the normal, or acceptable, limits of political engagement. In studies of political activism, especially of communists and nationalists, people as young as twelve and as old as thirty-five are described as 'youth'.

Youth can also be thought of as a generational identity which will be different for each generation because of the wider social and political context in which they 'come of age'. Karl Mannheim (1972 [1928]) in his very influential essay 'The problem of generations' proposed that the experience of living in a particular historical moment forms a generation who acquire specific life experiences that differ from those of their parents' generation.

Awareness of this gap between their own experience and that which they have been socialized to accept produces what he calls a 'generational consciousness' in young people. This suggests that generational consciousness arises when there is a clear contrast between the experiences of the older generation and those of the younger generation, in other words in periods of wider disruption and change. Within generations, Mannheim contends, groups of young people coalesce around shared experiences, values and attitudes into 'generational units' who have the capacity (and will) for political action. In Africa the generations of youth that came of age during the relative prosperity of the 1960s and 1970s can be distinguished as a generational unit or cohort from those who came of age in the 1980s and 1990s and who had less access to formal sector employment (Burgess 2005: 20). Jean and John Comaroff have written of South Africa that 'the dominant line of cleavage here has become generation' (Comaroff and Comaroff 1999: 284), and John Illife has claimed that 'conflict between male generations [has been] one of the most dynamic and enduring forces in African history' (Iliffe 1995: 95; see also Carton 2000).

The term 'youth' is also used almost exclusively in respect of boys or young men. The category 'youth' is an almost entirely male identity. In large part, this is because girls have other opportunities than economic and political participation to establish their adult status (Nolte 2004: 62, 72). Gold reminds us that '[y]outh was a distinct stage of the Chinese life course only in elite families and then only for boys' (Gold 1991: 597), but the same might be said of youth in most other national cultures. Angela McRobbie (in McRobbie and Garber 1976), for example, has argued that most of the youth sub-cultures that attracted the interest of the influential cultural studies scholars of the Birmingham School were actually boys' sub-cultures.

Conversely, in many social contexts women never attain full adulthood since the access to independent resources that defines adulthood is not available to them. It is conventional to speak of youth as belonging simultaneously to two social roles and yet not completely to either; of having a public role and yet still being dependent (Durham 2000: 116). This definition is very gender-specific. It applies to boys and young men, and in fact has a good deal in common with definitions of 'women' who are also no longer children (girls) but still not fully adults.

If youth can be thought of as generational units whose common experiences in contrast to those who went before them coalesce into a shared identity, school has a distinctive role to play in the formation of this generational consciousness.

School as a site of political mobilization

Schools and universities have been very important sites for the political organization of young people. In chapter 5 I showed how schools try to educate children to be particular kinds of people, to hold certain moral positions and outlooks. This chapter shows that school is not always successful in producing in children the kinds of attitudes to authority that it might want to encourage. Once they are in school children are not only children, they are also students with interests in common with other students and a shared experience of the world. They become, in Mannheim's terms, a 'generational unit' with a shared consciousness. This is not enough to turn children into political activists, but if children do become politically conscious – often as a response to political conflict in the wider society – then schools are likely to be central sites for their mobilization. In South Africa, for example, the history of youth activism is virtually inseparable from the history of education.

If students are more likely than other young people to be political activists this is particularly true of university students. The political mobilization of children and young teenagers generally follows the level of political mobilization of society. That is to say, when there is a high level of political conflict in society children and young teenagers get involved in politics; older teenagers and young adults are more likely to get involved in politics even if society is not experiencing high levels of political conflict. Youth often take a vanguard or leading role in politics and push political issues to the front of the news agenda from where they may become mainstream political issues. This is what happened in the USA during the Civil Rights and anti-Vietnam war movements (Kurlansky 2005), in Latin America in the 1930s through to the 1950s, when student protests were 'the earliest and most significant bases of opposition to authoritarian governments' (Bundy 1987), and in the Mexican student rising in 1968 (Carey 2005). If youthful political activism takes this vanguard or leading role but then fails to engage the interest and involvement of a wider population, then it is likely to fizzle out.

The experience of higher education is one that, on a global scale, only a minority of young people experience, most young people being excluded from high school and university by social and economic conditions. The fact that most 'youth' activists are young adults, often university undergraduates and recent graduates, points to a particular reason for youths' political activism: their progression through the education system shapes their sense of self as individuals who are entitled to political and/or socio-economic rewards. Where there is an expansion of secondary and higher education and a rise in expectations of access to political, economic and social resources, the frustration of these expectations seems to lead to the increased political activism, and expands the scope for political mobilization, of students. In Remo, Nigeria the contraction of opportunities for secondary school and university graduates, combined with the availability of cheap arms and local support for youth activism, contributed to vigilante activism (Nolte 2004: 70). This would also explain why, once the expansion of education has stabilized and graduates obtain the anticipated benefits or rewards of having a university education, as is the case, for example, in Europe and North America, students have been less radical, and their activism has tended to be limited to single-issue campaigns on matters related to education (e.g. grants and fees).

In the rest of this section I show through four case studies how important school has been to the political mobilization of youth. The four case studies are the Chinese Cultural Revolution (1966–8), the US Civil Rights Movement (1954–64), the Iranian revolution (1979) and the struggle against Apartheid in South Africa (1968–94). These cases indicate that the importance of the school as a site of mobilization is not limited to any particular region or educational system – the examples are drawn from three continents over more than fifty years. They were all major political movements and events that involved literally thousands of children and young people and changed the history of their countries. In the Chinese case the government encouraged the political activism of its young citizens because it wanted to use schools and the young generation to smash the symbols of the old regime. In Iran and South Africa schools became centres of anti-government protest despite the best efforts of government to prevent this. In the US case school students were at the forefront of the struggle for political equality for African Americans.

The political mobilization of school students in the Chinese Cultural Revolution

The case of children and youth involvement in the Chinese Cultural Revolution has both similarities with and differences from those in South Africa and Iran. A key difference was that the teachers of Chinese students did not generally see themselves on the same side as protesting students, as many did in South Africa and Iran. Indeed during the Cultural Revolution teachers were the focus of student criticism and physical violence. However, as in Iran and to a lesser extent South Africa, the expansion of education had increased expectations about post-school careers, expectations that were unlikely to be fulfilled (Chan et al. 1980: 398–400). In this context, as in Iran, the frustration of rising expectations made students susceptible to political mobilization. A key difference with both South Africa and Iran is that the involvement of children and young people in the Cultural Revolution was not in opposition to the government but instead was initiated by the government.

The Cultural Revolution began in 1966 as a struggle for control within the Chinese Communist Party leadership in Beijing. It turned into a mass movement involving thousands of school children and university students, and ended in 1979 with the death of Mao and the arrest of his closest allies, the so-called Gang of Four. The end of the Cultural Revolution was the beginning of the reform period, known as Socialism with Chinese Characteristics, that led to the phenomenal growth of the Chinese economy and the insertion of China as a significant player in the global economy and in international politics.

The Cultural Revolution lasted more than a decade, but it was in the first few weeks that children and young people were most intensively involved in political action of a very brutal kind (MacFarquhar and Schoenhals 2006: 32–51).

The purge of the Beijing Communist Party leadership that started the Cultural Revolution was used by faculty staff at university campuses to settle old scores and improve their own position (MacFarquhar and Schoenhals 2006: 55–7). The protagonists of the Cultural Revolution were the Red Guards. To be a member of the Red Guards a student had to be from a 'red' family, a family in which the parents had fought in the 1949 Revolution and were Party Cadres. The first Red Guards attended elite, competitive-entry academic schools (Ye Weili 2005: 5); the first Red Guard organization was set up on 29 May 1966 by students at the elite middle school attached to Tsinghua University in Beijing (MacFarquhar and Schoenhals 2006: 87). The Red Guards put up 'big-character' posters on campus denouncing counter-revolutionary plots and incorrect interpretations of Party doctrine. The first 'big-character' poster was put up on the campus of Tsinghua University in June and it was reprinted in the *People's Daily*. It read: 'Beat to a pulp any and all persons who go against Mao Zedong Thought – no matter who they are, what banner they fly, or how exalted their positions may be' (MacFarquhar and Schoenhals 2006: 104).

This publication of the big-character posters was the signal for an intensification of the Cultural Revolution in colleges (MacFarquhar and Schoenhals 2006: 59). After the publication of the poster all schools in Beijing suspended classes. Even kindergarten staff, while continuing to care for the 'little successors of the revolution', became embroiled in the Cultural Revolution. The 'revisionist leadership' of the municipal Bureau of Education was charged (*sic*) specifically with attempting to train preschool children 'not to get into fights, not to swear at people, be polite, and be clean and tidy' (MacFarquhar and Schoenhals 2006: 60). On 13 June the Chinese Communist Party issued a decision to temporarily suspend classes in universities and schools nationwide so that 103 million primary-school, 13 million secondary-school and over half a million university students could 'devote themselves full-time to the Cultural Revolution' (MacFarquhar and Schoenhals 2006: 60). Party work teams encouraged criticism of teachers 'who were held responsible for "bourgeois" or "revisionist" curricula and pedagogy usually on the flimsiest of grounds' (MacFarquhar and Schoenhals 2006: 67).

On 28 July the Tsinghua University Red Guards sent Mao two big-character posters and requested a response. He replied: 'You say it is right to rebel against reactionaries; I enthusiastically support you' (MacFarquhar and Schoenhals 2006: 87). After Mao received the Red Guards from the balcony of Tiananmen in August 1966 the Red Guard movement 'swept the entire country' (Ye Weili 2005: 68). By the autumn the Red Terror that was the crucible of the Red Guard movement 'ranged from the destruction of private and public property, through expulsion of urban undesirables, all the way to murder' (MacFarquhar and Schoenhals 2006: 102). The initial target of the Red Guards, the 'ox ghosts and snake demons', were school teachers whose revolutionary credentials were far from assured; those who were from 'black' families and had been trained as teachers under the Imperial Regime. So-called 'black' families included former landlords, former rich peasants, 'reactionary bad elements' and rightists. 'Black' children were excluded from certain activities at school and from the youth sections of the Party (Ye Weili 2005: 52). The Cultural Revolution took the form of wall posters and struggle meetings. The latter often involved the public humiliation of the subject and frequently ended in an act of violence ranging from cutting hair, wearing dunces' hats, having boards hung from their necks with their 'crime' written on it or their name crossed out in red, to severe beatings and on many occasions murder. The violence of this campaign escalated very quickly. Teachers, intellectuals and former businessmen were targeted as 'bad class' elements. In Shanghai over 84,000 homes of bourgeois families were looted by Red Guards in two weeks, more than 1,200 of which were the homes of intellectuals or teachers (MacFarquhar and Schoenhals 2006: 117). Some were evicted and expelled to the countryside. In elementary schools in Beijing nearly 1,000 people were beaten and 'struggled' with between 1 June and 25 June (MacFarquhar and Schoenhals 2006: 124). In August and September, after the withdrawal of the work teams, over 1,700 people were murdered in Beijing. Police were instructed not to 'interfere with or suppress the student movement' and to 'stay out of schools' (MacFarquhar and Schoenhals 2006: 125). Teachers were tortured by students; at twelve schools a teacher was beaten to death, at one school two teachers were murdered.

In September Party teams were sent into schools to restore order. This was done without Mao's knowledge, and when he returned to the north he ordered the Party teams to leave. This began a period of factionalism within the Red Guards. Mao declared the 'bloodline' of inherited revolutionary deficiency to be incorrect, saying that anyone who fought for socialism could be a Red. This swelled the ranks of the Red Guard but also increased the fervour of the Terror as students from 'black' families sought to prove their revolutionary credentials by joining in the Terror, often denouncing their own families.

The desire on the part of so many urban youth and children to participate in revolutionary activity may be attributed in no small part to their education under communist rule. In the period from 1950 to 1959 elementary education expanded phenomenally and the curriculum was organized around the dual elements of self-sacrifice for the national/collective good and the personal striving for achievement of each student. Elementary-school children were enrolled not only into school but also into the Young Pioneers, and in both places they learned the language of revolutionary struggle but without a context in which to practise it. The Cultural Revolution was exceptional in many ways, but the language of class struggle and building socialism would have been very familiar to students from earlier campaigns, for example Mao's 1962 call to 'never forget class struggle' and the introduction of the 'revolutionizing movement' in schools in 1964 and other similar political campaigns (Weili 2005; Wen 1995: 2).

The student campaign or the Red Terror was ended by the start of two more government-initiated programmes: the 'linking-up' campaign and then the 'down to the countryside, up to the mountains' campaign. This campaign involved the voluntary and forced migration of millions of 'young intellectuals' or high school graduates to the countryside over the ten years from 1968.

School students and the struggle for racial equality in the USA

In 1954 in *Brown* v. *the Board of Education* the Supreme Court ruled that 'in the field of public education the doctrine of separate but equal has no place' (cited in de Schweinitz 2004: 191). This decision, which effectively began the dismantling of segregation or what is known in the States as Jim Crow, was violently resisted by most whites in the Southern states. This ruling effectively put the responsibility for dismantling Jim Crow and resisting the racism of Southern governments in the hands of school children and, as is well known, many children took up that challenge with great courage and determination (de Schweinitz 2004: 353).

The most famous struggle to integrate schools was in Little Rock. The local paper, the *Arkansas Gazette*, asserted before the campaign started: 'We do not believe any organized group of citizens would under any circumstances undertake to do violence to school children of any race' (cited in de Schweinitz 2004: 219). Given that violence against black children was an endemic part of Jim Crow (Ritterhouse 2006), a belief that white parents would be reluctant to 'do violence to school children' was, as it turned out, entirely unwarranted. In Little Rock and elsewhere in the Southern states African American children, in their efforts to end segregation and institutional racism, endured verbal abuse and physical assaults from white adults. One of these students, Dorothy Counts, withdrew after four days of 'name calling, pushing, spitting, being ignored by teachers and other, more serious acts of intimidation' (de Schweinitz 2004: 222). In 1956 the Rev. Fred Shuttlesworth, his twelve-year-old daughter Ruby and other black students were beaten by a group of white men as they tried to enter Birmingham's all-white Phillips High School (de Schweinitz 2004: 253). Several schools chose to close down rather than implement the Supreme Court's decision. In September 1963 a Sunday school in Birmingham was bombed by white supremacists and four black children were killed.

Young people in the 1950s through to the mid 1960s were important in mobilizing against Jim Crow and organizing the Civil Rights Movement. The *Brown* ruling was one of a series of events in the history of the struggle against racism that galvanized African American children and youth. Their political consciousness had been developed through their daily experience of racial injustice (de Schweinitz 2004: 347). Rebecca de Schweinitz (2004) contends that watching television news and images of school students confronting the racism of whites to force the implementation of the *Brown* ruling politicized a generation. Robert Coles cites one young black activist who told him: 'I used to have dreams about that . . . We'd sit and watch that on that television set, and we'd get angry and my grandmother would say that those kids shouldn't try to go to that school and my mother wouldn't say anything and my father would curse those whites and say we should stay away from all of them . . . they can't be trusted, they're no good . . . I'd go to bed and dream that I was one of those nine kids in Central High and that Faubus came over to the school and I killed him with a machine gun' (de Schweinitz 2004: 354).

Rebecca de Schweinitz, recounting the history of a school strike that aimed to end separate and unequal education for black students in Farmville, Virginia, which was led by then sixteen-year-old Barbara Johns, comments on the importance of school as a place of shared experience that allowed the possibility of collective political action. Children and young people, she points out, 'more commonly experienced the strictures of Jim Crow collectively – such as when they went to school or recreational facilities together . . . their everyday shared experiences with segregation helped them see the collective nature of those constraints and encouraged them to confront Jim Crow collectively as well' (de Schweinitz 2004: 375). James Bevel, an SNCC organizer, has noted that students 'had a community they'd been in since elementary school . . . if one of them would go to jail, that had a direct effect upon another because they were classmates' (cited in de Schweinitz 2004: 378).

Students and the Iranian Revolution

The mobilization of school students in revolutionary Iran bears comparison with that of students in Apartheid South Africa. In both cases the school as a site of shared experience and a place which produces a sense of shared identity in a mass of people worked to the advantage of the political opposition. Arguably a crucial difference between the two cases is that most school students in South Africa were mobilizing in support of the ANC and an even greater number for majority rule, whereas in Iran the opposition forces were much more fragmented and fractured. Once the government was overthrown in South Africa the dismantling of Apartheid and the establishment of majority democratic rule was a goal agreed on by the ANC, Inkatha and the Black Consciousness Movement. This outcome, where young activists' interests were aligned to those of the movement that finally took power, was not so clearly the case in Iran. The Islamic left was completely excluded from the post-revolutionary government. The Islamic right took control of the government and continued to include and mobilize young activists after the revolution, and has continued to do so right up to the present day (Varzi 2006).

The Shah of Iran was overthrown by a coalition of Islamic and communist forces in 1979. This was not the first time that the Shah had faced organized opposition to his rule; it was the first time that he had failed to crush it. In 1963 a wave of anti-regime activity had forced the Shah into a programme of modernization and reform, known as the 'White Revolution', intended to placate the opposition. Despite these reforms in the years after 1963 workers' strikes were frequent and students were 'at least as great a political threat' as workers, since 'most students were too young and idealistic to have been co-opted by the regime, and they had many grievances' (Keddie 2003: 218). Student protests and strikes were frequent, particularly in the main cities. Many of their grievances were about academic and educational issues, but once the 'national protest movement broadened in 1977–78, students had the habits, inclination, and experience that helped make them important participants in the revolutionary movement' (Keddie 2003: 218).

A key turning point in the revolution was an attack in early 1978 by government security forces on a protest in Qom of theological students against the publication of an article in a semi-official newspaper criticizing Khomeini (who would later become the leader of the Islamic Republic of Iran) as 'an adventurer, without faith, and tied to the centres of colonialism . . . a man with a dubious past.' (Keddie 2003: 225). Seventy students were killed in two days. In February 1978 a riot at Tabriz began as a commemoration of those killed at Qom. It was '[l]ed by youths, who attacked the banks, the headquarters of the Shah's Rastakhiz party, cinemas, and liquor stores' (Keddie 2003: 228). Radical students from Tabriz University joined. About 100 people were killed and over 600 were arrested.

The fall of the Shah was accomplished by the activity of different groups, mostly Islamic but politically diverse. In the early days of Khomeini's rule this broad base of the opposition was acknowledged by Khomeini's decision to invite several parties and groups into government. However, this did not include any leftists, and both the Islamic leftist Mojahedin-e Khalq (MK) and the Marxist Feda'iyan-e Khalq, despite both parties being 'partly responsible for the revolution's victory' (Keddie 2003: 243), were excluded from government. These parties were mostly made up of high-school and university students (Keddie 2003: 243).

Immediately after the overthrow of the Shah one of the Islamic opposition forces, the Mojahedin, formed a new group, the Organization of Young Mojaheds, to recruit young members, especially high-school and college students. The Mojahedin 'drew most of its recruits not just from the intelligentsia, but from the young male members of the intelligentsia' (Keddie 2003: 227). Students in secondary, vocational and technical schools were a small minority of the general population (3 per cent) but provided nearly half (45 per cent) of the ordinary members (the rank and file) of the Mojahedin (Keddie 2003: 227).

Importantly, and not unrelated perhaps to the young age of their members, neither the Mojahedin (MK) nor the Feda'iyan-e-Khalq had any significant economic support. The new regime moved quickly against them. Khomeini's army, Hezbollah, attacked the Mojahedin's headquarters, which they eventually had to leave. In 1981, following the murder of some of their members by Hezbollah, they began an unsuccessful armed struggle against the regime; thousands of their members were executed by the new Islamic government (Keddie 2003: 253), and the Mojahedin leadership fled into exile.

The political mobilization of leftist Iranian students in the revolution did not ensure the inclusion of these young people in the revolutionary settlement. This indicates a weakness of young activism, which is that it can only succeed if it incorporates or is incorporated by a larger movement. The left (Islamic and secular) lost the Iranian revolution to the Islamic right; it was inevitable that students on the left would also be excluded from the revolutionary settlement. After Khomeini took power the government began to mobilize youth in defence of the Islamic revolution and the state (Varzi 2006).

Political mobilization of school students in Apartheid South Africa

In Apartheid South Africa the school operated as a key site for the practice of Apartheid. The division of South Africans into new racial categories was made possible in part by enforcing the racial segregation of schools and through the teaching of a deeply racist curriculum (Dolby 2001: 21). Although segregated schooling can be traced to the beginnings of Dutch colonization in the mid seventeenth century, it is at the beginning of the twentieth century, following the Anglo-Boer War, that the state instigated a series of Acts that 'provided for compulsory, and racially segregated, education for white children' (Dolby 2001: 20), and from 1922 African education was wholly financed through African taxation. Following the National Party's victory in 1948 a series of Acts designed to inscribe Apartheid into the legal framework of South Africa was implemented. The Bantu Education Act (1953) was followed by other educational Acts which 'established the segregated and unequal system of mass schooling that, as Cross and Chisholm (1990) argue, became the basis for the construction of racial and ethnic subjects' (Dolby 2001: 22).

In 1968 the South African Student's Movement (SASM) was formed. This organization's demands focused on the need for student representation and for improving matriculation results. Even these demands, which were limited to specifically educational issues, faced opposition from teachers and principals. When the Movement formed an alliance with the Society for African Development and was renamed the African Student's Movement, it developed a broader political agenda (Diseko 1991: 55).

In 1976, in a continuation of the government's policy of using schools as key sites in the production of racialized subjects, Afrikaans was introduced as a medium of instruction. This initiative was met with school boycotts that led to the Soweto uprising (Brocklehurst 2006: 129). One of the most iconic images of youth opposition to Apartheid is the photograph of Mbuyisa Makhubo carrying Hector Peterson's dead body, with his sister, Antoinette Sithole, running along beside him. Following the Soweto uprising schools became a 'key site for political organizing and resistance' (Dolby 2001: 23). In the 1976 Soweto riots 10,000 students and young children were involved and twenty-five students killed by security forces (Brocklehurst 2006: 132).

The Soweto uprising was the beginning of concerted action by children and youth to overturn Apartheid. In 1979 the Congress of South African Students (COSAS) was founded and organized school boycotts throughout the 1980s. Between 1970 and 1986 up to 1,000 children were shot dead. An eyewitness account captures the feeling of these times: 'by the mid-'80s, townships like Diepkloof were buzzing. Meetings . . . were happening on every corner. Crowds of people marched in protest against poor service delivery, the collapse of schooling and the detention of activists. Barricades set up mainly by youth were burning on the streets. And, visible everywhere, were the security forces' (Marks 2001: 35). These school boycotts were organized by students, usually without consulting parents, many of whom were opposed to them, fearing the effect that they would have on their children's education.

During the State of Emergency the role of the school as a place where the government could control children and through them the wider community increased. In Diepkloof, Soweto, school-age children who were not in school were liable to be arrested. In Durban townships, students who were known to have organized boycotts in the mid 1980s were not readmitted to school. Some schools would not admit students whose previous schools had been involved in boycotts. 'In short, for one to be admitted to a school, it was important to display good conduct by appearing not to be involved in any form of politics' (Dlamini 2005: 96).

Despite the attempts by the government to stop schools being spaces of political activity, the common experience provided by school continued to facilitate the political organization and mobilization of young South

Africans. Most of the township youth who joined political organizations in this period were at school, as were their leaders (Marks 2001: 49). Resistance to Apartheid in black schools and the activities of the Black Consciousness Movement (BCM), Azanian People's Organization (AZAPO) and the African National Congress (ANC) came at a point when the state itself was confronting economic and political crisis. The National Education Crisis Committee (NECC) was formed and called for a democratic and non-racial 'people's education'. In 1990 a new model for limited school desegregation was announced. Although it fell far short of meeting the demands of African nationalists or communists, it was a sign that Apartheid was unravelling; three years later in South Africa's first general election the ANC took power.

In her study of the Charterist youth movement, *Young Warriors: Youth Politics, Identity and Violence in South Africa*, Monique Marks affirms the connection between political engagement and school attendance. Dropout rates in high school were high, particularly in grades 9–12. Schools were poorly resourced. Corporal punishment was routine. Violence against staff was also common, and often politically motivated. The security forces were present in the schools. In his foreword to Marks' book Makgane Thobejane describes how

> [t]he involvement of youth in politics in Diepkloof [a district of Soweto] began with a concern about how our parents were being exploited in terms of rent. In 1980, during an assembly at Bopa Senatla High School, a certain Mokgomotshi Mogodire took over the reins. He disconnected the telephone and addressed 500 of us regarding the high rentals. We immediately agreed action was required. We marched to other high schools and converged at the local municipal offices, which were effectively stopped from operating. When I excitedly reported the incident to my parents that night, they pointed out that they paid the rent, not me. This only motivated me to continue our struggle.
>
> (Thobejane 2001: vii)

As this quote suggests, youth involvement in politics came by way of 'adult civic struggles' (Marks 2001: 38), but it was the spatial organization of schools, their potential for the assembling of young people into a collective through their shared experience of school and neighbourhood, and the space it provided for people to meet together, that made it possible for young people to engage with civic struggles as an independent collective body – school students – rather than as the sons and daughters of their parents.

Schools and politics

Iran and South Africa are both excellent examples of how the school becomes a site for political mobilization. In both these cases the intention of government to use schools to make students compliant 'citizens' produced the opposite effect. Schools 'became an epicentre and vehicle of political mobilization' (Brocklehurst 2006: 136). The overt political interference in schools by government had the effect of politicizing and mobilizing students *against* the government. The conflict between state and society was deep and sustained over many decades. This meant that many teachers who had been involved in politics and had experienced government oppression when young felt that they had a duty to encourage and support students in taking a critical view of school life and of politics. Of course, not all teachers are potential revolutionaries! Nonetheless, when teachers are politically committed, school is more likely to become a site of political consciousness-raising and activity against the regime than a place for the smooth transmission of dominant ideologies to students. This may also explain why in post-revolutionary regimes, where teachers have been appointed by the new regime and are generally pro-government, schools are less likely to be sites of anti-government opposition.

Whilst revolutionary regimes may welcome the support and energy that students bring to revolutionary politics, once the regime is securely in power these same students can become politically dangerous – demanding their place at the table. In response, revolutionary regimes have sought ways to deploy activist students safely away from the centres of political power. All revolutionary states have mobilized youth by sending them to rural areas as labourers, literacy educators and agricultural extension workers. In Iran the Jehad-e Sazandegi (Reconstruction Jihad) 'mobilized youth by sending them to rural areas to aid the poor with cheap or free housing and sanctioned some seizures of urban homes and rural lands by the poor' (Keddie 2003: 246). In Ethiopia the National Development through Co-operation Campaign (the Zemecha) 'mobilised the entire body of some 50,000 secondary and university students and teachers to go out into the countryside, propagate the aims of the revolution, encourage literacy and, once the land reform had been decreed, explain it to the peasants' (Clapham 1988: 49). In China the send-down campaign sent a generation of urban middle-class children to the countryside to learn 'revolutionary practice' from the peasantry.

As a generation, youth have responded to these calls ambivalently. Some have welcomed the opportunity to engage in what they think of as revolutionary action, extending the revolution to the rural 'masses'. As Clapham comments of the Ethiopian literacy campaign, the Zemecha that came after the revolution, 'Since it offered students the chance to participate in spreading the revolution to the countryside which they had demanded, they could scarcely refuse to take part, and many did so enthusiastically' (Clapham 1988: 49). Others have gone reluctantly or have been coerced into going to the countryside. Whatever the reality of youth propensity to radical political action, it is clear that regimes generally believe that youth are more radical, and therefore potentially more disruptive, to post-revolutionary states than adults are. If the aim of sending youth to the countryside is to extend the revolutionary state's capacity outside of the urban centres, it also removes students from the cities, where they could threaten the regime (Clapham 1988: 49).

Political mobilization and generational conflict

When a new regime seeks to overturn the old order, it recruits young people to the task of smashing the symbols of that order. In this moment young people are offered the reins of power, and many of them, as we saw in the example of the Chinese Cultural Revolution, take up this offer with great enthusiasm. The revolutionary state seeks to mobilize youth on the side of the regime so as to consolidate the power of the new regime by breaking people's attachment to pre-revolutionary symbols and social relations. Central to this is the breaking of relations between children and adults as they are organized within the family. Like other revolutionary states, before and since, the Chinese Communist Party sought to usurp 'the prerogatives of the family' (Gold 1991: 597). In such moments children and youth are encouraged to break their ties with their parents and other symbols of parental authority (teachers, for example) and to reorientate their sentimental or affective ties from their families to the symbols and actors of the new regime. Love, one might say, is transferred from mother / father to *the* father/mother or the fatherland/motherland. During the Cultural Revolution and the Nazi rule in Germany (Brocklehurst 2006: 49–82) this turning away from the mother/father to the *patrie* was accompanied by extreme acts of violence and rage, many committed against precisely those persons, teachers and parents (perhaps especially fathers) who could have demanded respect from their young attackers before the revolt. One might say that at these points the state encourages the expression of generational resentment. In breaking their ties with their parents, they break with their parents' attitudes, with their parents' habituation with the old order; they refuse to countenance their parents' doubts about the morality of the new order.

The investment of a new regime in securing its rule through the inculcation in the ruled of a reinvented public morality is met by the investment of the young in asserting their 'will to power'; a will that is normally frustrated precisely by their youthful status. Youth should not be thought of as inevitably on the side of 'right'. Although they are often on the side of those whose claims to power are tenuous and fragile, a condition that echoes their own lives, and therefore more often on the side of the usurper or the contender than the incumbent or the established, it is as well to remember that the usurper is not always progressive.

Deborah Durham claims that 'youth enter political space as saboteurs; their potential for political sabotage comes from their incomplete subjugation to contexts and co-opters, and to their own power for action, response, and subversion in contexts of political definition' (2000: 113). Keddie makes a similar point about young Iranian activists who 'were too young and idealistic to have been co-opted by the regime, and they had many grievances' (Keddie 2003: 218). As Kazem Mohammadi-Gilani, a key member of the Young Mojaheds, was executed in 1981 with his younger brother, fighting the Islamic republic they denounced their father as 'reactionary, anti-Islamic' and a 'bloodthirsty executioner'. Abrahamian comments that '[t]he Gilani household in many ways epitomized the generational conflict within religious orientated traditional families that had enthusiastically supported the Islamic Revolution' (1989: 179). In South Africa, Chikane claims that in 1976 there was very little support from parents for their children's demands. Apart from the Soweto Parents Association, 'the children were organising their own struggle with their own leadership, irrespective of the wishes of their elders' (Chikane 1986: 340). He claims that the 'failure of parents to struggle with their children and to provide leadership widened the generation gap. The more radical children almost lost confidence in their parents' (ibid.). Durham's account concurs: 'The youthful militants of the ICU, the radicals who formed the Independent ANC, and the young intellectuals of the ANC Youth League all chafed against the restraint and moderation of their elders; they were the precursors of the Black Consciousness ideologues, the enrages of 1976, and the township comrades of the 1980s . . . a self-aware age-group sought generational unity, [and] distanced themselves from their parents, and spoke for "we, the youth of South Africa"' (2000: 310).

However, it is equally clear that not all youth political activism involves the severing of ties between parents and children. In the cases of both South Africa and Iran there was, on the part of many activists, a frustration with the political tactics adopted by the older generation. However, this frustration did not always translate into a rejection of the older generation's rights over the younger generation or of the political or religious sensibilities of their parents' generation. Their disagreement was over tactics, not principles. In the context of Northern Ireland, Helen Brocklehurst argues that conflicts between generations were less important than conflicts between Catholic and Protestant neighbourhoods and their political and military organizations (Brocklehurst 2006: 96). In Iran the Mojahedin attracted young followers because of its adaptation of Shi'ism to a revolutionary programme. The young intelligentsia, many of whom were the children of the traditional middle class – tradesmen and shopkeepers – were deeply attached to Shi'ism but rejected its clerical interpretations. Joining the Mojahedin, unlike joining a secular Marxist party, 'did not necessitate severing ties to family values, household customs, or childhood beliefs' (Keddie 2003: 230). In her study of youth identity in post-revolutionary Iran, Varzi says that at the beginning of the Iran–Iraq war during Friday prayers 'teenagers were encouraged to ask their parents' permission to go to the front. Mothers were congratulated for giving up their sons . . .' (2006: 66). In Nigeria, Insa Nolte has shown that youth organizations are embedded in religious or ethno-nationalist movements (2004: 62) and shared a common agenda with older generations. Similarly, in Cape Town children and young people who supported the ANC were reluctant to be seen to be critical of their elders, many of whom supported Inkatha (Dlamini 2005). In the townships there were cross-generational sub-cultures (Diseko 1991: 44). There is also substantial evidence that youth activists, particularly leaders, were politicized by their elders.

A study of the psychological impacts of the struggle on activist youth in a South African township shows how the support of parents for the struggle increased the psychological resilience of young activists in the face of the trauma and violence of this period. The author, Gillian Straker, discusses, for example, the case of a particularly resilient young man, Ricky, who became involved in the movement when he was thirteen. His father had been killed in a conflict with his employers. His father's death

> reinforced for Ricky a sense of the injustice of the circumstances governing the lives of blacks in South Africa. This sense had been fostered in him . . . by his grandmother, whom he remembers as an assertive woman, a leader in the community, and a great storyteller. Every night she would

tell them traditional tales; but she would also tell them stories of her own life, such as her presence at the signing of the Freedom Charter, or of the march on Pretoria of 50,000 women to protest against the [Pass] laws . . . She described the massacre at Sharpeville of 1960 and spoke of people she knew who were connected with Mandela. Thus inspired, Ricky's political education was initiated at a very young age within the family circle.

(Straker 1992: 24)

Similarly another youth leader, Sisi, believed 'that what helped her become involved [in the struggle] was the degree to which her home was politicised' (Straker 1992: 30). Her aunt was a trade unionist and her contact with cousins from Soweto and Bethal kept her informed about the events in other townships. Adult support, and political activism, for example when councillors' houses were attacked, reassured youth about the morality of their actions and reaffirmed the legitimacy of violence as a means to equality and justice (Straker 1992: 103). Indeed, the turning point for youth activism in South Africa came with the formation of the United Democratic Front in 1983 because it both recognized and consolidated cross-generational alliances. It brought students, workers and township residents together in their struggle against Apartheid. In September 1985 the Soweto Parents Crisis Committee (SPCC) and other parent–student– teacher committees in other parts of the country were formed. Chikane's assessment of the impact of these new alliances on parent–child relations underscores the point that youth activism is not always also generational conflict: 'At the end of 1985 the SPCC convened a national consultative conference in Johannesburg . . . to address the education crisis. All over the country thousands of children were boycotting classes. They and their parents were calling for the withdrawal of the troops from the townships, the lifting of the State of Emergency, the release of student and other leaders from detention, and the postponement of the final annual examinations' (1986: 343). The formation of Parent–Teacher–Student Associations in 1985 was a further sign of the recognition of the need to both form alliances and acknowledge the hardships their parents had faced in living through Apartheid.

The evidence offered in this chapter then does not support the commonsense assumption that generational conflict is the motor of youthful activism or that youth are more revolutionary than their parents. In fact, often the involvement of youth in political activism takes a distinctly conservative turn where youth seek to police a return to moral order that they feel has broken down.

Young moral guardians

There is a substantial literature in developmental psychology that theorizes the development of morality in children. Typically, these studies pose a causal and more or less linear relationship between increasing age and increasing moral understanding. Underlying these models is a supposition that children acquire moral understanding from adult members of society in socializing institutions, in particular the family and the school, and over time internalize ethical codes into their own sense of self. In periods of intense political activism, particularly arising in the context of political conflict, especially war and revolution, the role of moral guardians is often taken up by children and youth. Diamant in his (2000) study of politics, love and divorce in China from the revolution to 1968 proposes a thesis that sexuality – or more accurately sexual Puritanism – was an important element in explaining the role of young people in the Cultural Revolution. Furthermore, he suggests that the role of youth as moral guardians is a pervasive feature of strong religious or ultra-nationalistic political move- ments. Youth, he says, 'can easily cast themselves as "cleansers" of the national community largely because of their own naiveté, black-and-white worldview and innocence with respect to the complications of love and passion' (Diamant 2000: 215). The Red Guards called for a ban on under-24s' smoking and drinking and denounced the vulgar language as 'intolerable to the ear and extremely shameless' (MacFarquhar and Schoenhals 2006: 114). In the contexts discussed in this chapter it is evident that children and young people often perceive themselves as involved in a project of moral renewal. It is not that they reject the normative values of their communities but that they feel that the older generation have forgotten or abandoned an ethical life. In these contexts, youth explicitly frame their role as that of moral guardians of the community, inverting the classic moral context governing parent–child or adult–youth interactions. In Nigeria the role of moral guardians of the community was already invested in young people in the pre-colonial period and this was reworked in the postcolonial period, invoking rather than breaking with traditional concepts of relational cat- egories (Nolte 2004: 65). In Apartheid South Africa, although relationships between youth and adult activists were sometimes strained, the youth activists saw themselves as part of a community. In this role they often positioned themselves as the moral guardians of the townships, insisting that comrades should be self-disciplined and subjecting both comrades and other youth to the codes of discipline of the activists (Marks 2001: 62). In revolutionary and post-revolutionary Iran the role of moral guardians has been taken up by the young soldiers of the Revolutionary Guard, the Basij (Varzi 2006).

Summary

Young protagonists engaged in political activity are more likely to be teenagers than children in early or middle childhood. Whilst pre-teenage children have been involved in political activity this generally only happens when there is a specific configuration of events. In particular, children are more likely to be mobilized for political activity by government interventions, as is the case with the Young Pioneers and the Young Red Guards in China, than they are to take up politics in opposition to the government. The exception to this – in a pattern that bears comparison with the mobilization of children in war – is where the longevity of the conflict leading to the death or imprisonment of older generations means that the leadership of the movement falls to young people and the mass mobilization of the young brings with it children who would normally be considered too naïve and inexperienced to be directly involved in political activity. This was the case in the ANC's struggle against the Apartheid regime and is also evident in the changing age profile of the protagonists in the first and the second Intifadas in Palestine.

Young people are also more likely to be politically mobilized when they are in secondary school or university. This means that in most contexts politically active youth are likely to be better off than their generation as a whole. This also points to one of the clearest explanations for why youth are often more politically active than older generations: they have rising expectations that are frustrated by their material situation so that, for example, increased school enrolments (rising expectations) accompanied by diminishing opportunities or opportunities that do not keep pace with the increased numbers of high school and university graduates (frustration of expectations) are fertile ground for young people to become politically active.

Generational conflict and resentment, which are widely regarded as a key reason for young people to become politically active, actually seem far from conclusive on the evidence offered here. While young people in many politically charged contexts accuse their parents' generation of quietism, this accusation only makes sense because of the presumption that their parents *should* be more politically involved with the (shared) cause. In the Red Guards and in the ANC (and other anti-Apartheid organizations) young people were more likely to be politically active if their parents were, or had been, also politically involved. When parents and children are on opposite sides of a political conflict it seems that they often (although by no means always) try to depoliticize or contain their relationship – as Dlamini found with young Zulu ANC members whose parents were affiliated to Inkatha, or the young Mojahedin in Iran who tried to integrate their politics with their parents' world-view.

The activism of the young, in contrast to the quietism of their elders, is often explained by the purity of youth in the political context – they have not been compromised or co-opted. However, before reproducing a well-trodden path of youthful political innocence and enthusiasm versus elders' political corruption and cynicism, it is as well to remind ourselves that in all the contexts discussed here youth were, like their elders, a minority in political struggle, and that not only were older generations also still involved in the struggle but in many instances they provided the leadership for it. Indeed, when the leadership of political movements is only in the hands of young people – as with the Red Guards, the ANC during the notorious 'necklacing' period, the young Bahiris policing Islamic morality in the Iranian revolution – it often displays a spectacular excess and a politics of terror which the protagonists may later look back on with incredulity and remorse. The innocence of youth does not mean that they are more politically engaged than their elders, but it does often translate into a moral Manichaeism that allows them to take up the role of moral guardians with great enthusiasm.

The involvement of youth in spectacular acts of terror – often in the name of moral rectitude – should also alert us to the dangers of thinking of youth as the new political saviour. Whilst there is, as this chapter has shown, ample evidence that youth are open to political mobilization, there is nothing automatically progressive about their political engagements. They are as likely to be on the side of reactionary, conservative, politics as they are to be on the side of progressive, radical, politics.

Recommended further reading

Abbink, J. and I. Van Kessel (eds.). 2005. *Vanguard or Vandals: Youth, Politics and Conflict in Africa*. Leiden: Brill.
An important contribution to the literature on the role of youth in conflict in Africa, with an excellent introduction by Jon Abbink on concepts of youth in the African context.

Brocklehurst, H. 2006. *Who's Afraid of Children: Children, Conflict and International Relations*. Aldershot: Ashgate.
The first study of the place of children in international relations theory.

Cole, J. and D. Durham (eds.). 2007. *Generations and Globalization: Youth, Age and Family in the New World Economy*. Bloomington and Indianapolis: Indiana University Press.
A new turn in childhood studies towards understanding childhood as a moment of identity in the life course that has interesting parallels with old age.

Howman, A. and F. de Boeck (eds.). 2005. *Makers and Breakers: Children and Youth in Postcolonial Africa*. London: James Currey.
A significant collection on youth and conflict in Africa, with an excellent review of the role of youth in contemporary African politics and conflict by Jean and John Comaroff.

7

Children and youth at war

Introduction

This chapter is about children, youth and civil war. It is in two parts. The first part describes contemporary civil war and the second focuses on child soldiers. The section on contemporary civil war looks at how contemporary war differs from historical conflicts. It explains civil war in terms of the failure of the state to maintain its legitimacy and control over territory after the shift in international relations that followed the end of the Cold War in 1989. It takes civil war in Africa and especially in Sierra Leone as exemplary of these kinds of conflicts and of the involvement of children in them. My account of contemporary war is intended to broaden the picture to give a more comprehensive understanding of why so many children are fighting in rebel and government forces around the world. The second part of the chapter on child soldiers explores why children fight and how and why boy soldiers have been responsible for the most brutal atrocities of modern war. This section concludes with a discussion of how to heal the trauma of children's involvement in war.

Contemporary war

When the Cold War ended in 1989 with the collapse of the Soviet Union, many people viewed the ending of conflict between the Soviet Bloc and the capitalist countries as a new opportunity to establish a global consensus for peace. Liberal theorists declared that this was the 'end of history' (Fukuyama 1992) and the beginning of a 'new world order' (Kagan 2008). There was to be no more conflict except perhaps for mopping up isolated pockets of resistance to the triumph of liberalism. In 1993 Samuel Huntington published his highly influential and somewhat apocalyptic article 'The clash of civilizations?', which argued that the next conflict would be between Christian and Islamic civilizations, but his article was hardly in touch with the mood of the times, which was overwhelmingly optimistic about the possibilities for ending conflict. In the spirit of this new hope for a post-conflict global order Martin Shaw speculated, in a collection edited by the international relations scholar and cosmopolitan theorist Professor Anthony McGrew, that armed forces might be 'transformed into peace-making rather than war-fighting institutions, tools of a more democratic global order' (1997: 43).

The print was barely dry on these optimistic assessments when it became clear that the legacy of the collapse of the Soviet Union and the end of the Cold War would not be a lasting global peace but a proliferation of seemingly intractable contests between governments and rebels for control of fragile states and lucrative trade routes – both legitimate and criminal. In the first ten years after the Cold War there were twenty-five conflicts in Africa alone in every part of the continent (Goulding 1999: 158); only four of these were classic interstate wars, the rest were internal or civil wars. Of ninety conflicts that occurred in the period 1989–93, over half were still active in 1993, and all were internal conflicts. Fifteen of eighteen conflicts fought in Europe from 1989 to 1993 were in the countries of the former Soviet Union and Yugoslavia.

Mary Kaldor has argued that these post-Cold War conflicts are a new kind of war. Their distinguishing feature, she says, is that they deliberately target civilians (Kaldor 2001). Jo Boyden and Joanna de Berry have also claimed that conflicts increasingly involve civilians (Boyden and de Berry 2004: xi). Modern warfare is marked by the murder, torture, rape, mutilation and detention of civilians. Peter Singer also claims that in contemporary wars 'the ancient distinction between combatants and civilians as targets of violence has arguably disappeared, or, even worse, swung the other way, creating a new pattern of warfare' (2006: 4).

Others disagree that a clear boundary can be drawn between new wars and old wars, where the latter are rule-bound and fought in demarcated territories over clear political goals (Rosen 2005: 10; Kalyvas 2001). Nonetheless, regardless of whether or not 'old' wars also targeted civilians and were less rule-bound and orderly than the 'new war' proponents suggest, contemporary civil war is undeniably characterized by the terrorizing of civilian populations and their forced recruitment into militias and armies.

Many of these civilians are children; war has a disproportionate effect on them because of their size and vulnerability. Targeting children has now become a tactic of war; Singer cites examples from Serb snipers during the siege of Sarajevo who deliberately shot at children and Rwandan radio broadcasts before the 1994 genocide urging Hutu killers not to 'forget the

little ones' (Singer 2006: 5). Alicia Honwana in her ethnography of child soldiers in Angola and Mozambique claims that the 'scale of the contemporary
problem is unprecedented, both in the numbers of young people involved
and in the degree of their participation' (Honwana 2006: 27). The figures
confirm their statements: in the last ten years of the twentieth century
more than 2 million children were killed in war; 6 million were disabled or
seriously injured and 1 million were orphaned; almost 25 million lost their
homes (Singer 2006: 6). These figures far exceed the 300,000 child soldiers
who are fighting in contemporary conflicts around the world.

The 'new wars' thesis is not in any case only about the targeting of civilians; it is also about the motivation for war. 'Old wars', so the argument
goes, were fought for specific political objectives by clearly opposing sides.
War, in Clausewitz's famous dictum, was the continuation of politics by
other means. In contrast, contemporary civil wars are about 'the continuation of economics by other means' (Galperin 2002: 113, citing Keen 2000:
27). This thesis, often glossed as the thesis of 'greed not grievance', has most
forcefully, and influentially, been argued by Paul Collier of the World Bank's
Development Research Group (see Collier and Hoeffler 1998; 1999; 2000;
and Collier 2000). Of course, no such neat division between the economic
and the political really exists: is the war in Iraq about oil or democracy –
many people think it's the former; the First World War is widely acknowledged to have been an inter-imperialist conflict in which European powers
fought over their 'right' to keep or extend their overseas Empires. What
does divide the new from the old wars is that the latter were mostly fought
between nations whereas the former are being fought within nations.

In 1994 Robert Kaplan published his very influential article on 'The
coming anarchy', in which he argued that many long-standing internal conflicts are strategies to control particular resources, especially trade routes.
He claimed that war is functional to the pursuit of these goals. One of the
reasons his article has been so influential is because it offers a convincing
explanation of the seeming intractability of internal conflicts. In Angola,
Congo and Sierra Leone control of trade in diamonds, oil and other miner-
als (including cobalt, used in the making of mobile phones) has allowed
all sides in these conflicts to profit from war (Arnson 2006; Keen 1998). In
Colombia the long-standing conflict between the state, paramilitaries and
the FARC has been financed, in part, by the trade in illegal drugs. War is
especially good for smuggling because of the breakdown of state control
over trade routes and the close and well-documented connections between
war and organized crime (Kaldor 2001). In a similar argument David Keen
has claimed that 'war is not simply a breakdown in a particular system, but a

way of creating an alternative system of profit, power and even protection' (Keen 1998: 11). Globalization and the extensive opportunities it provides for warring parties to control profits from legal and illegal trade networks also has to figure centrally in any analysis of the sources or persistence of conflict (Arnson 2006: 9–10). It is these new global networks that make war and the cover it provides to organized crime so profitable. Carey makes a similar point when she says that 'the objective of fighting may not, in fact, be to win . . . Open conflict and its subsequent chaos may be considered ends in themselves' (2006: 99). Christopher Clapham, who has written extensively over many years on conflict in Africa, says that warlord insurgency is 'directed towards a change of leadership which does not entail the creation of a state any different from that which it seeks to overthrow, and which may involve the creation of a personal territorial fiefdom separate from existing state structures and boundaries' (Clapham 1998: 7).

Failed states at war

The neo-liberal state

Certain characteristics distinguish state power from other kinds of power. State power operates through 'a set of organizations invested with the authority to make binding decisions for people and organizations juridically located in a particular territory and to implement these decisions using, if necessary, force' (Rueschemeyer and Evans 1996: 47). While liberal theory has long recognized the importance of the state or political authority to the orderly conduct of economic relations, it also views the state with deep suspicion. It fears that the state, with its monopoly on the legitimate use of violence, will become a monster devouring society and the economy. To prevent this from happening liberal theory proposes that states must agree to limit the scope of their power. This mechanism, the 'rule of law', is a set of constraints that the law places on the rights of the state to exercise power. In order for this to happen, the law-making functions of the state (the judiciary) have to be separated from its other functions. Liberal theory also advocates that the state should be separated from the economy and its role limited to ensuring the smooth operation of market forces – for example, through enforcing contracts or limiting the growth of monopolies and cartels that distort the market. Liberal theorists view the state as an obstacle to economic growth. They say that it stifles entrepreneurship and is grossly inefficient, especially as compared to the market, in making economic decisions and distributing resources. Liberal theory is at the centre of the models of economic development used by both the International Monetary Fund (the IMF) and the World Bank. It is because of the commitment of these two institutions to liberal theory that they attach conditions to their grants and loans that force states to restrict the role of government in the economy through privatization and trade reform.

The neo-patrimonial state

The liberal concept of the state is very unlike the postcolonial state in most of sub-Saharan Africa. The postcolonial African state has not everywhere had 'the authority to make binding decisions for people and organizations in its territory' (Rueschemeyer and Evans 1996: 47). It has not had a monopoly on the means of violence. It has not had a clear separation of powers or subjected itself to the rule of law and it has been deeply involved in the economy. The African state has been characterized as 'broken-backed' and as an edifice floating above society and yet parasitic on it. It is said to be simultaneously weak and coercive; deriving its right to rule not from the delegation of sovereignty by the people it rules over, as it is supposed to according to liberal theory, but from a combination of violence and rewards and the support of the international system (Jackson 1991).

The rewards that these weak states give to their subjects include government jobs, trading networks, land, political prestige and protection. In return those in political power get left alone to accumulate private wealth through their privileged access to state resources. This kind of relationship between state and society is known in political science as a 'neo-patrimonial state'.

The neo-patrimonial state then is something of a corrupt and parasitic entity. Certainly this is the view of the World Bank and the IMF who, since the end of the Cold War, have put conditions on grants and loans to force African states to privatize their assets and liberalize their economies in an effort to stimulate economic growth through the market and limit the scope for government corruption.

Not everyone agrees that the neo-patrimonial state is entirely dysfunctional. The political scientist William Reno, who has written about the African state and especially about the state in Sierra Leone (1995; 1998; 2000), says that neo-patrimonial states are viable so long as the governing class has personal control over sufficient public resources to satisfy organized opposition and reward collaborators.

William Reno based his claims about the viability of the neo-patrimonial state on what happened to states like this after the World Bank and the IMF dismantled their access to public resources. In the cases that he analysed, Sierra Leone, Liberia, Zaire and Nigeria, 'less government has contributed not to better government but rather to warlord politics' (Reno 1998: 8; see also Hibou 1999). This is because, as the state was forced to withdraw from control of trade or lost the ability to pay civil servants' wages or to raise the salaries of the army, the sites for conflict and competition for power and economic resources expanded. Governments looked to intensify their control of trade to compensate for the loss of other resources, like international aid. Whereas in a state-controlled economy governments could raise funds through taxing trade, now, with the insistence of neo-liberal institutions that tariffs and taxes should be lowered or abolished, governments started to get directly involved in organizing trade. Reno argues that weak states are very attractive to global markets because capital can do things in such states that stronger and more regulated states would resist. The contest for control of commerce in such a climate may be very violent, and violence can also provide opportunities for commerce, especially illicit trade, because it covers up the traces of transactions. For Reno, in neo-patrimonial states politics is an 'often violent contest to control commerce' (Reno 1998: 26; Bayart 1999: 44) and the global market – especially the trade in illegal goods – provides opportunities for insurgents to accumulate wealth and political power (Reno 1998: 30; Berdal and Malone 2000; Singer 2006: 49–51; Honwana 2006: 46).

Civil war in Africa

Nowhere have the naïve claims of the 'new world order' that followed the end of the Cold War been more thoroughly discredited than in sub-Saharan Africa. Several countries in Central, West, North East and Southern Africa have been the sites of brutal conflict since the end of the Cold War. Although Rwanda, the Democratic Republic of Congo (formerly Zaire), Sierra Leone, Liberia, Sudan and parts of Uganda and Ethiopia are hardly alone in the international system as regions of internal conflict, they have been amongst the most terrible and the most spectacular.

These African states are exemplars of the impact of war on children because of the demography of the continent. In common with Asia and Latin America, Africa has a much greater number of young people, and young people are a much larger proportion of the total population than in Europe and North America. People under the age of fifteen are only 18 per cent of the total population in the 'developed world', whereas they account for a third of the population in both Asia and Latin America. Africa, with

43 per cent of the population or 338 million young people under the age of fifteen, continues to be the youngest region (http://www.prcdc.org/summaries/intlyouth/intlyouth.html).

Africa is not of course the only region where children have fought or are fighting in wars: in the Middle East and Central Asia children have fought in Iran, Iraq, Afghanistan and Palestine (Rosen 2005: 91–132); they have fought in conflicts in Central and South America, especially for the FARC and in the rightist paramilitary forces in Colombia; in Europe in Serbia, Kosovo and Turkey; and in Asia in many anti-government insurgencies, but especially in Northern Sri Lanka with the Tamil Tigers and in Myanmar (Singer 2006: 15–34; Honwana 2006: 27, 30–1).

Although Africa has not been the only region where children have joined militias and government armies, it is nonetheless true that African states have been at 'the epicentre of the child soldier phenomenon' (Singer 2006: 19). Children have fought in wars in Angola, where as many as one in three children joined the army; in Liberia, where some 20,000 children fought in the Liberian war. In Northern Uganda as many as 14,000 children are in the Lord's Resistance Army – most having been abducted; in Rwanda thousands of children participated in the genocide in 1994; child soldiers make up perhaps a third of combatants in the conflict in the Democratic Republic of Congo (Singer 2006: 19–21; Honwana 2006: 29–30). In Sierra Leone thousands of children fought in the government army and with rebel militias (Zack-Williams 2001: 79). The brutality of the conflict and the extensive involvement of children have made the Sierra Leone war synonymous with child soldiers.

The civil war in Sierra Leone began in 1991 when a small rebel group calling themselves the Revolutionary United Front (RUF) crossed over the Liberian border and entered eastern Sierra Leone. This small force of perhaps no more than thirty people was a mixed group of ideologically motivated former university students, and mercenaries from Liberia and Burkina Faso. They proclaimed their goal to be the overthrow of the corrupt government. In 1992 junior officers led a successful coup against the government. They acted entirely independently of the RUF, and their success meant that the RUF no longer had a *raison d'être*. The RUF retreated to the forest, from where they re-emerged in 1995.

Lacking the support of the civilian population, the RUF increasingly relied on the abducting of young people, including children, into the rebel forces as fighters, but also as cooks, cleaners, farmers, mothers and 'wives'. Their camps in the forest were well organized and included schools, fields, mosques, churches and compounds. There was a harsh disciplinary code that was weakly enforced, at least in respect of the prohibition on rape. Rape was forbidden in the disciplinary code and yet almost all girls in the rebel forces, regardless of whether they volunteered or were abducted, were raped. Rape was used to force girls into relationships with men and many girls, having been raped, then became the 'wife' of the man who raped them.

In 1997 the RUF published a document, 'Footpaths to democracy', that set out their ideological position, a combination of socialist and populist platitudes that bore little or no resemblance to their relations with the civilians they were supposedly fighting to liberate. The RUF's tactics became increasingly brutal as the war went on, including the amputation of limbs, and rape. The hallmark of the war in Sierra Leone was the brutal simplicity of the terror that it visited on the civilian population. The soldiers of the RUF used machetes to hack off the arms of thousands of civilians. The horrific image of these vicious amputations was rendered all the more harsh by the fact that many of the perpetrators were very young: perhaps as many as 80 per cent of all soldiers were aged seven to fourteen (Singer 2006: 15).

The last ceasefire between rebel and government forces was signed in 2001 and brought to a close ten years of a most brutal conflict.

International crime, diamonds and 'casino', or 'occult', capitalism

There are many, often conflicting, interpretations of the RUF's violence, and of whom the RUF were and why they were fighting at all. Were they fighting to make for a more just and equitable division of resources between different generations and different regions, as they claimed (Richards 1996)? Or were they fighting to get control of the state so that they could use it to convert public wealth into private wealth, as the current government had done (Collier and Hoeffler 1998; 1999; Collier 2000; Smillie et al. 2000)? Did they not care what happened in the rest of Sierra Leone so long as they kept control of the diamond producing south-west?

If the RUF were fighting to keep control of the diamond producing south-west then ongoing conflict would help rather than hinder them in their aims. When it did not the RUF could negotiate a ceasefire. This is what happened in 2001 when the RUF finally did negotiate a permanent ceasefire; it seems likely that this was because they and their ally, the Liberian warlord Charles Taylor, decided that control of newly available flows of international aid would be more lucrative than control over trade in diamonds and guns.

Whether or not it was the aim of the RUF to propagate war so as to control the trade in diamonds, the money raised from smuggling diamonds has been absolutely key to the ability of the rebels to carry on fighting and was the single most important factor in making it possible for the conflict to continue. When a Canadian NGO published its report showing the connections between the diamond trade, international crime, the war in Sierra Leone and the involvement of children in that war, it seemed to unlock the key to the resolution of the conflict: end the rebels' access to the diamond trade. The publication of *The Heart of the Matter* (Smillie et al. 2000), which identified 'conflict diamonds' as central to the motivation and ability of the rebels to continue the war, was probably one of the two most important events that led to a wave of international action to end the war. (The other event that galvanized international public opinion was the vicious and brutal assault on Freetown by the rebel forces in 1999, in which they mutilated thousands of people.)

   The Heart of the Matter broadened the analysis of the war as a national or regional conflict to explore its global dimensions. In particular it attended to the connections between diamond smuggling, gunrunning, and international crime. It also exposed the lines of connection between organized crime and global capitalism. If the former is ungoverned, rapacious and criminal, the latter is supposed to be rule-governed, rational and normative. What *The Heart of the Matter* exposed was that no such neat division between criminal capitalism and regular capitalism could be maintained (Nordstrom 2007).

   Susan Strange used the term 'casino' capitalism to capture the ways that circuits of finance capital generated unproductive wealth out of the willingness of finance capitalists to chase financial risk with the expectation of high returns. Comaroff and Comaroff make use of the same concept together with 'occult' capitalism and 'millennial' capitalism to analyse the unproductive character of contemporary global wealth and the interweaving of criminal capitalism (organized crime) and regulated capitalism (1999; 2000). In their analysis the production of wealth takes on an occult or magical quality that mystifies the observer. Into this landscape saturated with the promise of magical and almost unimaginable rewards step the figures of the diamond miner, the gold miner, the drugs smuggler, the gunrunner, the child soldier.

Why do children fight in wars?

In the first section of this chapter I have shown that since the end of the Cold War there has been a proliferation of internal wars, especially in Africa. I have explained these wars in a general way, as largely a result of pressures on neo-patrimonial states resulting from global processes that have produced new conflicts between different groups for control of economic resources. I have suggested that war is often functional to the ability of different armed forces to control trade routes and especially for rebel forces to profit from their entanglement in networks of organized crime and illicit trade. The next section explains why and how children and young people come to fight in these wars.

Cultural explanations

The extraordinary expansion of the numbers of children fighting in rebel wars in Africa has led some theorists to attempt a cultural explanation for this phenomenon: to claim in effect that Africa has a culture of youthful militarism. Okwir Rabwoni, himself a former child soldier and a senior member of Uganda's now ruling party, the National Resistance Army (NRA), makes this point in his contribution to *Young Africa* (2002: 162). This explanation has also been put forward to account for the large numbers of children fighting in the war in Sierra Leone. In Sierra Leone, when children reach young adulthood, they are more likely than not to be initiated into a secret society. Some of these are hunter societies that train initiates in the arts of hunting. In West Africa the roles of hunter and warrior often overlap (Ferme 2001: 27; Leach 2000; Shepler 2005a: 100–3). One of these secret societies in Sierra Leone, the Kamajo, was refashioned during the civil war into Civil Defence Forces (CDFs). In their adaptation or mutation into civil defence forces they shifted from being hunter societies and became 'by and large a modern guerrilla force trained and armed for modern warfare' (Ferme 2001: 27). Notwithstanding this metamorphosis, the members of the Kamajo-CDF still had to be initiated into it through a very truncated form of traditional initiation rites retaining the connection between African secret societies, youth and militarism. One of the elements of initiation is the child's withdrawal from the village and their immersion into the bush – a place perceived as outside culture and steeped in magic. Richards (1996: 81) claims that when the RUF abducted children and took them into the bush (where the RUF camps were) they were making a kind of reference to these initiation rituals and thus attempting to legitimate these abductions by making them akin to a rite of passage.

Initiation into warrior or hunter societies is now and was historically a route by which young men came to be fighters, but despite the arguments cited above it should also be remembered that initiation is precisely about making the transition from being a child to being an adult. In precolonial

Africa boys did not fight until three or four years after puberty (Bennet n.d.). Of course, this could still mean people as young as fifteen might be eligible to fight in wars, but it does not mean that they were perceived to be children.

If initiation into adulthood or at least out of childhood can occur three or four years after puberty this means that the legal definition of a child as a person under eighteen years is not at all congruent with local definitions, unsurprisingly. Although the argument that children have always fought in war seems illogical – if children can fight in wars then what exactly makes the difference between being a child and being an adult – it does seem likely that people much younger than eighteen might be considered adult enough to fight.

More generally some people have suggested that children everywhere have always fought in wars (Rosen 2005), and that the enlisting of children in war is not peculiar to Africa or to African initiation rituals that mark the end of childhood. There is a good deal of disagreement about this, with scholars arguing directly opposing points about the same conflicts. Historically, for instance, in the Napoleonic wars in Europe (Cardoza 2002) and the American Civil War there is evidence of children being involved as soldiers (Werner 1998), but most of the tasks boys had in the European military in the seventeenth and eighteenth centuries were ancillary roles – drummer boys and 'powder monkeys' (small boys who ran ammunition to cannon crews) (Singer 2006: 11). Peter Singer in his recent book *Children at War* claims that only 247 boys fought in the American Civil War (Singer 2006: 15). But Rosen says that the number of children fighting in the Civil War on both the Union and the Confederate sides was in the order of 250,000 to 420,000 or about 10 to 20 per cent of soldiers' sides (Rosen 2005: 5, citing Werner 1998: 2, 9). These startlingly divergent statistics can only mean one thing: the debate about whether children have always fought in wars is highly ideological, and any statistics that authors use to establish their case should be treated with scepticism.

Many nations see it as normal that young people should become soldiers. Many governments, including the UK and the USA, allow recruitment of sixteen-year-olds into the armed forces. Many governments also have some kind of cadet force that under-sixteens can join. Whilst these are not training children to be combatants, they do militarize children, including training them in shooting, and involving them in military parades.

Alicia Honwana maintains that 'the recruitment of children into the military in war represents a real rupture of historical continuity, a profound disruption of social order, and a violation of moral norms' (2006:

45). If cultural norms about children not fighting are shattered by the use of child soldiers as it seems they are, then why do children fight? Two related reasons can be discerned as most prominent in the policy and academic literature on war-affected children: a crisis of social reproduction and generational resentment. The former describes the general breakdown in society's ability to reproduce itself; a breakdown caused by myriad factors including the deepening of poverty, the AIDS pandemic, and the displacement of people by conflict and by the search for work. Generational resentment is related to this crisis in social reproduction, but it specifically describes the feeling of youngsters that they are losing out to their elders in the struggle for resources in contexts of increasing scarcity.

A crisis of social reproduction

The main reasons why children fight are to escape poverty, to secure protection, to enact revenge, and for political or ideological reasons. A crisis in social reproduction or in the ability of societies to maintain functioning social relations and networks and to provide for dependants explains why children feel the need to fight to escape poverty and to secure protection. As Alicia Honwana rightly comments, when 'conflict, migration, and poverty cause families to dissolve and communities to disintegrate, the young are forced to improvise their own survival strategies, becoming street children in cities or joining gangs, armed groups, and the military' (2006: 28). Surveys of demobilized soldiers in the Democratic Republic of Congo found that almost 60 per cent joined because of poverty (Singer 2006: 62).

Poverty and disease also cause a breakdown in family relationships and in the ability of the family to care for its dependants. War increases the likelihood of children being separated from their parents and this makes them vulnerable to abduction, but also can make the army seem like a safe space; in a situation of conflict children argue (not unreasonably) that it is better to be a soldier with a gun than a civilian being threatened by a soldier with a gun. Children in refugee camps are easy targets for recruiting armies.

In some cases children might not have to fight with the rebels, they might just tag along with armed forces for protection and food – such was the case with the large numbers of children who attached themselves to the then rebel leader Museveni (now President of Uganda) and the NRA (Furley 1995: 28).

Poverty and a general crisis in social reproduction, for example in the dissolution of networks of family support, thus make children vulnerable to abduction and to 'voluntary' enlisting. Brett and Specht's (2004) *Young Soldiers: Why they Choose to Fight* shows that children are not always abducted into militias and armies; some choose to fight, albeit within a very limited range of choices. There is a lot of evidence that perhaps two out of every three child soldiers joined armed forces without any direct coercion or threat of violence (Singer 2006: 61). Children and youth do not only volunteer in rebel and government forces to escape poverty and to secure protection; increasingly, at least in Africa, many youth enlist in an attempt to secure positive advantages for themselves and their generation and to challenge what is widely perceived as a corrupt gerontocracy. It is to this issue of generational resentment that I now turn.

Generational resentment and conflict in Africa

Whether or not the war in Sierra Leone was fought over diamonds, it is quite clear that since they were discovered in 1926 diamonds there have symbolized the possibility of acquiring sudden and unimaginable wealth and escaping the routines of agricultural labour. Martha Carey argues that '[y]ouths, already marginalized geographically, psychologically, and economically, saw their future as bleak when juxtaposed to the possibilities advertised by the global market economy' (2006: 111). The discovery of diamonds could enable a young man to escape the control that seniors had over his labour and enter into the increasingly desired circuits of global capitalism.

The distribution of political power and control of economic resources along generational lines in Africa has led to an analysis of youth 'almost as a political class for themselves' (Shepler 2005b: 125). Increasingly, particularly in relation to conflict in Africa, scholars are suggesting that 'child' soldiers are expressing their dissatisfaction with the distribution of economic and political power between the generations and, in particular, the exclusion of youth from politics. If this claim is correct it is difficult to see how such antagonism can be resolved when resources are constantly shrinking. With ever smaller possibilities for acquiring adult or senior status and ever more pressing demands from the global economy, young people in Africa are now forming, according to Jean-François Bayart, a 'juvenile underworld' (1993: 240). As Jon Abbink remarks, 'Being young in Africa is widely and consistently perceived as problematic in essence. Social analysts, policy makers, NGOs, Governments and international organizations all reiterate that African youth is in deep trouble and enmeshed in violence' (2005: 2). Danny Hoffman claims that the Sierra Leone civil war has been widely attributed to a 'crisis of youth' (Hoffman 2006: 3). Christian Geffray (1990) makes the same claim in relation to the Mozambique civil war (cited in Furley 1995: 34), as does Alex Vines: 'Other disenchanted social strata – the young in particular, who have been unable to obtain secondary school education or upward mobility in the village structure because it has fallen into the hands of the dominant lineage's elders – probably find life with [the rebel opposition in Mozambique] Renamo offering the only alternative, providing some excitement and the potential authority denied to them in their villages – albeit by the barrel of a gun' (Vines 1991: 119). More generally Abbink notes that 'young people and rebellious groups in Africa consistently phrase many of their problems in terms of generational opposition' (Abbink 2005: 3).

The problem of generational conflict is hardly unique to Africa, but particular mechanisms for dealing with this conflict are widespread across sub-Saharan Africa, in particular the use of age systems and rituals to mark the transition from childhood to young adulthood (Abbink 2005: 4); when these rituals are disrupted or delayed youths can feel that they are being excluded from access to wealth (money, land, cattle or diamonds) that their elders enjoy. Youths (or juniors) are expected to defer to seniors (Abbink 2005: 5; Hoffman 2003: 296). Hoffman claims that '[t]he exploitation, real and imagined, that comes with the systems of patronage in Sierra Leone and elsewhere in postcolonial Africa is experienced by youth as the machinations of their elders' (2003: 304). If the 'spoils of modernity' (Hoffman 2003: 304) are perceived by youth to always be going to someone else, 'militarization increasingly presents itself to some as a way to opt out, to subvert the injustices of patronage by violently levelling the field' (2003: 304). The Sierra Leone war provided young people with an alternative source of patronage (Richards 1996). In that conflict the allegiances of the young to particular armed factions were unpredictable, with many youths having fought at different times for the rebel forces, the pro-government militia and the government army. In a patrimonial polity, where 'clientelism is a major means through which inter-generational transfers of knowledge and assets are achieved, young people are always on the lookout for new sources of patronage' (Richards 1996: 24).

While for some this crisis is one of 'lumpen' youth, to use Abdullah's term, Richards and Peters argue that in Sierra Leone it was an expression of generational conflict (see also Carey 2006: 98). Their analysis is the only one in which the young people's motivation for joining the RUF forces was neither pragmatic (they had nothing better to do) nor incidental. In their view the RUF attracted young fighters because they operated on principles of meritocracy rather than gerontocracy. In support of their argument Richards and Peters contend that although the RUF did abduct young people, including young children, once the children and youth understood the RUF's politics they chose to stay with the rebels. On the other hand reports by former child soldiers in Sierra Leone suggest that the choice to stay with the rebels was far from freely made; the initiation of fighters into the militias through brutal acts of violence including amputation and rape and the murder of attempted deserters made child soldiers fear the consequences of leaving.

So long as neo-patrimonial rulers could dispense rewards to juniors, their control over resources might be tolerated. Once the state started to lose the ability to meet its obligations seniors exacted increased labour obligations from juniors (young men) without adequate compensation. Whether juniors had increased expectations over previous generations or whether the rewards themselves had diminished because of the crisis of the neo-patrimonial state, or most likely a combination of the two, the result of perceived increased depredations was resentment of old men by young men.

William Murphy agrees that rebel forces in Liberia and Sierra Leone should be understood as patrimonial institutions in which child soldiers are located in 'a social organisation of domination and reciprocity based on violence structured through patronage ties with military commanders' (Murphy 2003: 61, 65–6; see also Reno 1995). In most situations children would not be considered to have the social agency that could enable them to enter into patron–client relations with themselves as clients. Children or children's labour would usually be considered as objects used within patronage networks rather than participants or bargainers in these networks: a client might give a child (or their labour) to a patron and in return the client would get other goods from the patron (Murphy, 2003: 74). If Murphy is right that in this conflict and social context children had sufficient agency to become clients in patronage networks where rebel leaders were patrons, this should not be understood to mean that child soldiers were in a relationship of equal reciprocity with their commanders. Patrons depend on clients for support, but because patron–client relations are highly unequal this dependence is not the same as the clients' dependence on their patrons. A useful analogy might be that a lord is dependent on the labour of his serfs but he still wields power over them and controls the land that they labour on (Murphy 2003: 78).

The increase in the availability of lightweight weapons or small arms has also been offered as an explanation for the expansion in children's recruitment into armed forces (Singer 2006: 46–8; Honwana 2006: 31). This may be a factor, but it is worth recalling that many of the most brutal atrocities of recent civil wars have been carried out with cutlasses and machetes, easily available in subsistence farming societies.

Is war different when children are soldiers?

In the previous section I showed that children and youth join rebel and government armies to escape poverty and secure protection and to advance their own and their generation's control over economic resources. In the following section I discuss how the extensive recruitment (forced and voluntary) of children and youth into armies has affected how war is prosecuted by looking at the extent of sexual violence and the terrorist methods that have come to be associated with these armies of the young.

Gender and sexual violence

The impact of war on girls is not of course limited to the increased threat and actuality of sexual violence. Girls also join armed forces for political and economic reasons, just as boys do. Girls usually take on ancillary or support roles in the army camps. The exception to this general rule is when girls fight with nationalist movements that are aligned with progressive ideologies of gender equality (West 2000). When girls join national liberation struggles they sometimes do so because of the promise of being able to 'do as if you were a boy' (McKay and Mazurana 2004: 91; West 2000). Girls most commonly cite escape from domestic exploitation and abuse as their motive for joining armed forces, and rarely give religion or ethnicity as a motivating factor (McKay and Mazurana 2004: 87–8).

When girls are abducted into fighting forces the likelihood that they will be raped is very high, and almost all girls associated with fighting forces in any way – regardless of whether or not they volunteered – report widespread sexual violence (McKay and Mazurana 2004: 58–61). Over half of all women who came into contact with the boys in the RUF in Sierra Leone were raped or sexually assaulted. One RUF operation in Sierra Leone was called 'Operation Fine Girl'; its aim was to find and abduct pretty girls, especially virgins (Singer 2006: 104; Operation Fine Girl at: www.witness. org). Frequently, the evidence of a girl's rape is that she now has a child, and the shame of this makes it almost impossible for her to return home or to be reintegrated into her community if she does return (McKay and

Mazurana 2004: 45; Shepler 2005a: 237–47). A Human Rights Watch report concluded that in Sierra Leone rape was so widespread that it is no longer stigmatized (2003). This claim is not consistent with McKay and Mazurana's findings. They argue that 'the significant issue of stigma is being glossed over; indeed, this same HRW report found that many girls felt intense personal shame and anger' (McKay and Mazurana 2004: 45). Shepler found that 'in many cases it is easier for a boy to be accepted after amputating the hands of villagers than it is for a girl to be accepted after being the victim of rape' (Shepler 2002: 9–10). The shame attached to rape is in many cases extended to the child conceived through rape (McKay and Mazurana 2004: 56).

Girls who are raped are referred to as 'combat wives' by the other girls themselves as well as by most NGOs. Although this term is a euphemism for repeated rape, often of very young girls, by the same man, it is also true that some girls come to think of themselves as the wife of the man or boy who raped them – especially if they have a child with them. When the conflict ends some girls want to have these 'bush marriages' made legitimate through the usual rites of passage associated with marriage in their community (bride price, asking for the father's permission, etc.). A child protection worker with the NCDDR in Sierra Leone in an interview with the researchers on the Where are the Girls Project commented that 'the child protection agencies . . . the approach they used was wrong in the first place . . . in trying to get these girls out. The girls were abducted, yes. This is a terrible crime, yes. They were raped, yes. They have been impregnated, yes. But over the years this may have . . . provided a certain amount of security for them. This man has protected them. This man has provided for them. So a bond has started to exist between the woman and the man . . . We're all women, we all want some amount of security, and we all want a man who can take care of us' (McKay and Mazurana 2004: 6). What it meant to be a 'wife' in the Sierra Leone conflict is further complicated by the fact that wives of commanders, who ranged in age from nine to nineteen, 'held considerable power and influence within RUF compounds' (McKay and Mazurana 2004: 93).

In Mozambique during the civil war girls were abducted and taken to the rebel military camps just as boys were, but whereas the boys were taught to kill, girls were raped repeatedly and continually. This 'fact was so commonly understood that many young women took their listeners' knowledge for granted and avoided mentioning the specifics in their retrospective accounts: "RENAMO soldiers kidnapped us, and took all our cattle. We were taken to the military camp . . . I suffered a lot while I was there. I am not going to tell you everything that happened to me in the military camp because it was very ugly"' (Honwana 2006: 83).

Sexual violence against girls and women has always been used as a tactic of war (Brownmiller 1977). It is impossible to say if the sexual violence in these 'new wars' is more brutal and perpetrated against younger girls because so many of the soldiers were boys (rather than men). Certainly, boys were encouraged – even ordered – by their commanders to rape and assault girls. In the Sierra Leone conflict rape and sexual assault of girls was seen by soldiers – boys and men – as a right of war, another kind of prize that went together with stealing money and diamonds, and another tactic with which to terrorize the civilian population.

Young terrorists

Children are 'among the most vicious combatants in the war' (Singer 2006: 106). Alex Vines describes, in an account that bears comparison with the treatment of children in the RUF camps in Sierra Leone ten years later and with accounts from former child soldiers in the Lord's Resistance Army (LRA) in Uganda, how 'Renamo's child combatants appear undisciplined and sometimes to be on drugs. They too seem to have been put through psychological trauma and deprivation, such as being hung upside down from trees until their individualism is broken, and encouraged and rewarded for killing. Some commentators believe that massacres in southern Mozambique are committed by these child combatants, who have been programmed to feel little fear or revulsion for such actions, and thereby carry out these attacks with greater enthusiasm and brutality than adults would' (Vines 1991: 95–6; see also Nordstrom 1997). They are then subjected to a brutal socialization – 'children made beasts', in Hilary Anderson's words (1992: 59–60).

Alicia Honwana interviewed a former child soldier in Mozambique when he was twenty. He was kidnapped by the rightist rebel forces, RENAMO, when he was about ten years old. His father and sister were also kidnapped, but they were separated when they reached the RENAMO village. The boy was ordered to join a group of young boys and start military training. A few weeks later after a secret meeting with his father they tried to run away together but were caught. The boy was ordered to kill his father and he did so. After this first killing he 'grew into a fierce RENAMO combatant and was active for more than seven years. He does not remember how many people he tortured, how many he killed, how many villages he burned, and how many food convoys and shops he looted' (Honwana 2006: 49). In virtually every account by former child soldiers this is the narrative that is told: 'I was kidnapped; I was made to kill someone I loved (a friend or close family); after this I committed countless atrocities'. Invariably the stories end: 'I had no choice' (Honwana 2006: 50).

Paul Richards and Krijin Peters have both argued for the essential rationality of the amputations, viewing them as violent actions that compensated for the RUF's lack of ammunition and guns. Richards argues that all war is barbaric and the RUF's attacks are no more barbaric than the death and injury caused by more technologically sophisticated weapons. They also claim that amputations were a warning to the peasantry not to vote or provide government forces with food. Carey extends this level of symbolic action to argue that the amputations carried out on the village block for pounding grain, which often also involved sexual violence, were symbolic attacks on fertility and reproduction (2006: 114). Leach offers a similar analysis. These 'tactics' of public executions, beatings, rape and amputation can be understood, she argues, 'as part of the relationships among social practices, ecology, and fertility. Forced to break the strongest laws governing social and ecological order, people invite devastating effects on their future fertility and prosperity, and they become locked into subordinate relationships to those who can claim the power to cleanse or protect them' (2000: 590).

Furley contrasts this brutal violence with the behaviours of those children who 'tagged along' with the NRA. Abbink also distinguishes the NRA, together with the Eritrean People's Liberation Front (EPLF) in Eritrea, the Tigrayan People's Liberation Front (TPLF) in Tigray-Ethiopia, and the Partido Africano para a Independência da Guiné e Cabo Verde (PAIGC) in Guinea-Bissau from later armed insurgencies in Somalia, DRC and Sudan that lack any ideological content. These armed movements 'seem to have turned into predatory looting machines that seek not only material booty and destruction but also humiliation through torture and mutilation, terror through the arbitrary killing of innocent individuals, and sexual gratification, as is evident from the large-scale abuse of women and girls in the civilian population' (Furley 2005: 12). This contrast between the behaviour of the young in ideologically motivated or political wars, and their behaviour in economic wars or predatory wars of 'greed not grievance' suggests that there is nothing inevitable about youth behaving brutally in conflict. It rather suggests that how youth behave in war will depend on the discipline of their commanders and what has motivated them to fight.

Working with war-affected children

Despite the seeming intractability of many of the conflicts at the beginning of the twenty-first century, at some point, even if it turns out to be temporary, the continuation of war becomes untenable or peace becomes a more viable strategy for warring groups to pursue their ends. Even while conflicts are ongoing some children escape, or are released to NGOs for demobilization. This section looks at some strategies for working with war-affected children to heal the trauma of war and make it less likely that they will return to the army.

Social ecology

The Psychosocial Working Group, a group of academic partners and humanitarian agencies working with war-affected children using models of psychosocial health, has devised a conceptual framework on psychosocial wellbeing and psychosocial interventions (Boothby et al. 2006: 7). Their model is based on five principles: attention to context, attention to meaning, active engagement, a focus on social, cultural and human resources (rather than on deficits), and resilience.

In attending to context, the psychosocial model maintains that it is important to understand the possibilities for individual wellbeing within the social context in which the individual is situated. This context includes the meanings that are available to an individual to interpret traumatic experiences. Children can draw on many resources to maintain or restore psychosocial wellbeing; this model identifies three core resources: human capacity (physical and mental health, skills and knowledge of people in a community), social ecology (relations in families, peer groups, social institutions), and culture and values. The aim of the Psychosocial Working Group framework is to provide a model that 'recognizes the centrality of those who have themselves been affected by conflict in coping with its impact'. They argue that those who want to work with war-affected children would best see themselves 'as facilitators, offering . . . [their] own resources and perspectives but ultimately empowering people to choose their own way forward' (Boothby et al. 2006: 11–12).

Spiritual healing

If the social ecology model is about how outside agencies might respond to war-affected children in ways that promote their mental health, spiritual healing rituals may be seen as an insider response to the same issue. Throughout sub-Saharan Africa children who have returned to their villages at the end of conflict (or having escaped from the military during a conflict) have been purified in local rituals of spiritual cleansing or healing. These rituals vary from place to place but have core elements in common. They all recognize the returning child as socially polluted by their exposure to and involvement in unsanctioned acts of violence. For the children to be cleansed they will have to appeal to their ancestors for forgiveness, usually through a ritual involving singing, herbal remedies, prayer and offerings to the ancestral spirits. The use of these rituals to heal the trauma of war has been documented in Northern Uganda (Last 2000b), Mozambique, and Angola (Honwana 2006: 104–34). They are more common in rural than in urban areas (Honwana 2006: 109). The father of a young boy who was abducted into RENAMO and escaped after several months described to Alicia Honwana the cleansing ritual a healer performed for his son:

> We took him to the bush about two kilometers away from our house. There we built a small hut covered with dry grass in which we put him, still dressed in the dirty clothes he came back with from the RENAMO camp. Inside the hut he was undressed. Then we set fire to the hut and Paulo [the boy] was helped out by an adult relative. The hut, the clothes, and everything else that he had brought from the camp we burned in the fire. Paulo then had to inhale the smoke of some herbal remedies and was bathed with water treated with medicine to cleanse his body internally and externally. Finally, we made him drink some medicine and gave him *ku thlavela* [vaccination] to give him strength and protect him.
>
> (Honwana 2006: 111)

Amadu Sesay describes a strikingly similar cleansing ceremony of a fifteen-year-old boy soldier in Sierra Leone. The elders in his family

> took the boy to the bush where a hut had been built using grass for the boy's cleansing ceremony. On entering the hut, Amadu was asked to undress himself that is, to take off the clothes he used to put on while with the RUF. The hut and the clothes were then set alight while an adult relative helped the boy out quickly. The burning of the hut and the clothes and everything else that the boy brought from the war symbolically represents his sudden break from an evil past. Immediately thereafter, a chicken was sacrificed to the spirits of the dead and the blood smeared around the ritual place.
>
> (Sesay 2003: 188)

The psychosocial model is not necessarily in opposition to local models of spiritual healing; it might encourage or suggest the use of Western models of talk-based therapy, but there would be no reason for them to be antagonistic or sceptical about the efficacy of religious healing rituals. Both approaches recognize the emotional trauma of war at some level. War-affected children also need practical support to leave the military and to reintegrate in their communities. This kind of support can be given through programmes of disarmament, demobilization and reintegration.

Disarmament, Demobilization and Reintegration

In the mid 1990s in its first attempt to resolve the conflict in Sierra Leone the UN made US $34 million available for disarming, demobilizing and reintegrating soldiers; less than US $1 million of this was for child soldiers. The settlement failed and most of the child ex-combatants rejoined the military factions (Singer 2006: 184). The rationale of Disarmament, Demobilization and Reintegration (DDR) programmes is that they will prevent further conflict by effectively reintegrating former soldiers into civilian society. Ignoring the needs of child soldiers makes it more likely that they will be susceptible to being recruited back into the armed forces if the conflict resumes, as happened in 1994 in Sierra Leone. In East Timor the UN simply sent child soldiers back to their villages; the same lack of attention to disarming, demobilizing and reintegrating child soldiers happened in Afghanistan, Liberia and Kosovo.

The purpose of DDR programmes is to restore security. They tend to marginalize ex-combatants – girls and young children – who are not seen as a security threat. In Sierra Leone only 506 girls compared with 6,052 boys went through a DDR programme (McKay 2006: 99). In Angola only one girl was recognized as eligible for DDR, and in the Democratic Republic of Congo only 23 girls as compared to 1,718 boys were demobilized by four international NGOs. This is despite girls being recruited or abducted as much as boys were in that conflict (McKay 2006: 99).

The second peace treaty in Sierra Leone, the 1999 Lomé Accords, was the first peace treaty to recognize the existence of child soldiers and to make specific provision for their demobilization and reintegration (Sesay 2003: 183). Since the recruitment of child soldiers is illegal, parties to the conflict are likely to deny their existence and therefore the necessity of any special provision for them (Singer 2006: 184–5). Given the well-established fact that children make up a significant percentage of fighting forces in contemporary wars, the Lomé Accords could serve as a model for other peace settlements.

Reintegration requires more than giving up weapons and relinquishing an identity as a soldier. For children and youth the main strategies that have been adopted for securing their reintegration into their communities and decreasing the chances that they will re-join the armed forces are family-tracing, education, and training or work. Education and work/training are important for re-establishing the routines of normal life. However, given that many children and youth join the military to escape poverty and to increase their opportunities, education and training or work have to be seen to provide concrete benefits. This can be fraught with difficulties in post-conflict situations. In Sierra Leone, for example, people who did not fight in the war, especially those who were attacked by rebels or soldiers, felt very resentful at the end of the war when demobilized soldiers were being given money, tools and seeds as part of their DDR package.

Child prisoners of war

International law (see chapter 2) gives children legal protection in conflict. It is now a war crime to use under-eighteens in combat (they can be used in ancillary roles). The spirit of this legislation is clearly intended to view under-eighteens as victims caught up in conflict rather than as protagonists. Despite this, the USA is holding at least twenty-two under-eighteens prisoner in Guantanamo Bay. One of these boys, who was fifteen when he was captured in Afghanistan by the US army, has been held in Guantanamo Bay for six years and is about to be tried for war crimes (Shephard 2008a; 2008b).

Summary

There is a growing literature on the impact of war on children (Peterson and Read 2002). Most of this literature has been produced by international non-governmental and quasi-governmental agencies. There is also a smaller body of ethnographic literature on specific conflicts (Rosen 2005; Honwana 2006) and on child soldiers (Singer 2006; Boyden and de Berry 2004; Briggs 2005). Broadly speaking, the NGO studies want to show the innocence and passivity of child soldiers whereas ethnographies of war-affected children complicate this picture through investigating how local conceptions of childhood and youth, including those of children themselves, explain the involvement of children in fighting forces. In this chapter I have drawn on this ethnographic material to understand children's (gendered) involvement in war as a crisis of social reproduction intimately connected to the globalization of capitalism and of organized crime and the loss of state power and legitimacy at the end of the Cold War. I have suggested that the abduction of children by fighting forces, contrary to the claims of much of the academic literature, cannot be explained through cultural models that legitimate child soldiering. Rather, I have argued that war itself is a crisis of social reproduction which children are caught up in because of their specific modalities as children in a particular cultural context. In Sierra Leone, for example, the rebel forces were producing in the bush a parallel society, a kind of shadow of village life. The ethnographic accounts of the war show that the rebel camps were organized like villages with a sexual and generational division of labour, families, schools, churches and mosques. Children were as necessary to bush life as they were to village life. Girls were forcibly pushed into a familiar role in social reproduction through abduction, sexual violence and particularly forced marriage and child-bearing. Rebels engaged in the most brutal, sadistic violence so as to maintain the boundaries between bush 'village' life and real village life. Nor is this peculiar to Sierra Leone. It is apparently a characteristic of insurgent wars fought over a long duration that the rebel forces come increasingly to resemble normal life in the rebel territory but that the boundaries between these rebel settlements and ordinary settlements are then policed with increasing ferocity.

Recommended further reading

Bay, E. G. and D. L. Donham (eds.). 2006. *States of Violence: Politics, Youth and Memory in Contemporary Africa*. Charlottesville and London: University of Virginia Press.
A seminal contribution to the literature on violence in Africa.

Boyden, J. and J. de Berry (eds.). 2004. *Children and Youth on the Front Line: Ethnography, Armed Conflict and Displacement*. Oxford: Berghahn Books.
An important collection of papers unified by their attention to the impact of war on cultures of childhood, with a useful set of chapters on using participatory methods to research children's experiences of war.

Ferme, M. C. 2001. *The Underneath of Things: Violence, History, and the Everyday in Sierra Leone*. Berkeley: University of California Press.
A compelling ethnography of Sierra Leone that illuminates the contexts in which youth and children were pulled into militias and the army.

Honwana, A. 2006. *Child Soldiers in Africa*. Philadelphia: University of Pennsylvania Press.

Essential reading for understanding the impact of war on childhood in contemporary Africa and how children become soldiers.

Singer, P. 2006. *Children at War*. Berkeley: University of California Press.
A very useful study that brings together the research and policy on children at war.

8

Rescuing children and children's rights

Introduction

In this book I have explored how childhood is being reshaped by global processes and structures. Global norms about who children are and what childhood should be are circulating through international law, global media and transnational NGOs. These new global norms are about more than protecting children from harm or acting in their 'best interests'. Global norms of childhood use criteria derived from liberal ethics to establish what 'harms' and 'best interests' are. At the heart of liberal ethics is a concept of the human as a subject who is universally a free, autonomous, rational, choosing individual. International children's rights law, news reporting on children and how NGOs frame their work with children are each inscribed with these same ethical premises that the child is a universal subject who should everywhere be enabled to be a free, autonomous, choosing and rational individual. The normative model of contemporary childhood is then not simply about what it means to be a child, it is essentially about what it means to be human.

These global norms of childhood should be thought of as ethical codes or models; they do not map onto most, perhaps any, children's experiences of the world. The universal subject that is at the heart of liberal theory does not and cannot exist because it presupposes that all humans share the same potential experience of the world. This could only be true if the social world were not shot through with inequalities. Most of this book is about the children and childhoods that do not conform to global norms. It has shown how global and local inequalities make conformity to global norms impossible. I have shown how, when new liberal concepts of childhood were first being developed, in the nineteenth century, some groups of children were purposefully excluded from them; the boundaries between those children who were entitled to protected childhoods and those who were not were drawn by race, gender and class. Well into the twentieth century the racialized exclusion of black children from the supposedly universal rights of childhood was not only prevalent, but in many countries – the USA until 1965, Australia until 1964, South Africa until 1994 – a matter of government law and policy.

This book has also been concerned with the tension between how governments attempt to establish global norms and how they, and child-saving institutions, act when this fails. Chapters on international law and representation (chapters 1 and 2) showed how law, media and NGOs evaluate children's lives by a universal legal standard. It is these structures and agents that also continually activate discourses about childhood as a space of innocence and freedom. Some of these practices, say international law, can seem rather distant and abstract. In chapter 4 on the family I showed how, in seemingly insignificant practices like registering births and marriages or an appointment with the paediatrician, governments use law and public policy to set the limits on what constitutes a proper family and good parenting. In these ways domestic law and policy give concrete form to the abstract and general principles in a legal instrument like the UN Convention on the Rights of the Child. The chapter also explored what happens to children when families cannot continue to support them or contain them.

The family and the school are the two institutions whose role it is to simultaneously protect children and socialize them into particular ways of being human. In school children do not only learn bodies of knowledge, they also learn how to behave and think in particular ways. The aim of the modern school is to inculcate in the child the kinds of habits and sensibilities that are congruent with liberal ethics: a sense of individuality, competitiveness, independence, rationality, and freedom.

In the family and the school children are still in the spaces and places where they belong. The chapters in question also looked at how children are governed when they leave these spaces – whether because they have to or because they want to – by considering children on the street, orphans, and children working. In the last two chapters I discussed those sites which are seen as entirely opposed to the protected and free spaces of childhood: politics and war.

A central concern of this book then has been to trace how different effects of globalization are impacting on children's lives across the world in very contradictory ways. On the one hand some global processes – international law and transnational NGOs – are trying to establish childhood as a protected space for the inculcation of liberal ethics, whilst on the other processes such as international war, organized crime, global economic inequality are pulling and pushing children into very unprotected and illiberal spaces. This chapter argues that to understand how and why globalization can act on children's lives in such contradictory ways it is necessary to understand the role of children and young people in processes of social reproduction in a global capitalist economy.

What is social reproduction?

Social reproduction is about 'how we live' (Mitchell et al. 2003: 416). It is a concept that captures the idea that life needs to be reproduced, not only physically but also socially, and requires an answer to the question: what do we need to reproduce and sustain life? It is about how we get access to food, water, shelter and medicines. Equally it is about how people make and sustain social networks, cultural practices, moral dispositions and a sense of self (Mitchell et al. 2003; Katz 2001a; Katz 2001b).

Social reproduction is the work of reproducing society collectively and individually. How this is done is deeply affected by how work is organized. In societies where most people are subsistence farmers – and this is still how about one half of the world feed themselves – they can directly provide for many of their everyday needs: for food, shelter, water and health care. When people cease to have direct control over their food security (through their access to or ownership of land, seeds and cattle) and become dependent on the market for their access to food and housing, processes of social reproduction are made more vulnerable. Imagine, for example, a farmer who moves to the city and becomes a labourer. She can still feed herself and her family, perhaps even better than she could before, so long as she earns a wage and can afford to buy food. If she loses her job or the price of food increases but her wages do not, then her family's food security is at risk. The global food crisis that many people in the world are currently experiencing is not a scarcity of food; it is a scarcity of food at an affordable price. It is capitalism that separates people from control of land, seeds and cattle which makes them vulnerable to hunger when food prices rise.

Capitalism separates producers from the means of production (Marx 1976; Cammack 2003) so that it is impossible for them to meet their needs except by buying things in the marketplace. In order to get cash to buy the goods that they need they will either have to sell their goods at the market or sell their labour. How does capital decide what wage to pay the individual worker and what costs does the individual worker have to meet with that wage? The worker has to get a wage that is at least sufficient to meet the costs of keeping her alive and provide enough food for her to have the energy to continue working. This is the barest wage that capital can pay to labour. Political economists have long realized that capital will have to pay workers more than this because of the problem of under-consumption of goods. Imagine all workers only get paid a wage that is sufficient to meet their individual needs for the barest reproduction of life and that their job is to produce, let's say, mobile phones. Mobile phones are obviously not essential to life (despite what some people might think!) so, if all workers are only paid enough to meet their bare living costs, who will buy the mobile phones? Capitalists then cannot only concern themselves with the production of goods or services, they also have to think about who can buy these goods and services. Imagine another scenario: workers that are paid enough for their bare needs plus sufficient wages to buy things they do not need. This may seem to solve the problem – people are now simultaneously workers and consumers: there are goods on the market and people have enough money to buy them. This is how capitalists like to imagine the human subject – as an individual freely making choices in a free market unencumbered by social ties; but the worker is not unencumbered because she has social ties, which may include children. So the worker needs a wage that is not only sufficient for her and for the consumption of goods in the market but that can also meet the costs of raising her children. In the 1960s trade unionists argued that a man's wage should be sufficient to cover the costs of his dependants – his wife and children – i.e. that a man's wage should be a family wage. Feminists argued that this was sexist and presumed that women should not be allowed to earn a 'family wage'– and of course they are right, but how then are the wages of people with children determined: who meets the costs of raising children? If the determinant of a wage is that it should be set at a rate that is independent of the worker (equal pay for equal work), then who meets the costs of the social reproduction of children?

This question cannot be answered in the abstract; it will be different depending on the context in which it is asked and the particular balance of power between capital, organized labour and the state and the generational and gendered division of labour. I ask it in order to draw attention to the fact that the costs of raising children have to be met by somebody, somewhere. Children have to have food, water, housing and health care, and they have to learn skills and knowledge either in school, at work, or within their social field. After the Second World War governments in Europe and North America accepted that these costs, the costs of social reproduction, should be borne at least at a minimal level by the state (Marshall 1950; Katz 2001a and 2001b: 709; Hindess 2004: 138). In the Soviet Union it was a basic legitimating principle of state power that it was the state's responsibility to provide housing, health care, food, child care and education. As is well known, the provision of welfare to the general population in the Soviet Bloc ended with the collapse of the Soviet Union; in Europe and the USA there has been a gradual retreat from the welfare state (already very limited in the USA) since the resurgence of liberalism in the 1970s.

In any case the point is that capital always tries to repudiate these costs – putting them onto the worker's family, onto the state, onto the immigrant worker's country of origin – rather than let them eat into the profits of capital. One of the ironies of this is that it is capital of course that organizes the production of the things which are necessary for social reproduction. Capital buys land, builds housing for rent, organizes food production and distribution, and builds the infrastructure necessary for cities to have water and electricity. It creates a market in the basic necessities of human life as if what people need to sustain life is equivalent to any other kind of commodity. In most of the world, certainly in the urban and industrial centres, families have to bear the costs of social reproduction by earning sufficient wages that will allow them to buy housing, food and health care.

Liberal political theory contends not only that it is legitimate for capital to refuse to bear the costs of social reproduction but even that it is ethical for it to do so. This is so because the freely choosing individual is at the centre of liberal theory. All the adages and clichés of liberalism – you made your bed, now lie on it; cut your cloth according to your means; God helps those who help themselves – evoke the belief that the freely choosing individual, having made her choice, must bear its costs. If these choices mean that families cannot support their children, then for liberal theory, unless there are seriously mitigating circumstances, they should not have chosen to have children. Liberal theory does not countenance either structural inequality (this is why equality before the law is so central to this theory) or social interdependencies. It would create what liberals call a moral hazard to reward people for making wrong or unsustainable choices.

Since capital refuses to bear the costs of social reproduction, they must be met by families. In the advanced capitalist countries the state takes on some of these costs, but in most of the world it is not the state that accepts the responsibility for social reproduction but workers themselves and their families (Hindess 2004: 138). The physical care of children is done within the family, usually by women and other children. If the gendered division of labour is impacted by, say, the emigration of women workers to other countries (often to care for other people's children) then men may take over this care (Salazar Parreñas 2005), but, regardless of who does it, the cost of it will be borne by the family. Migration is a growing strategy by which the poor try to find the financial resources to support their families, even though it more often than not involves leaving them behind. In Britain we have the seemingly illogical situation of the government paying for child care so that mothers can go out to work even if that work involves the care of other people's children. Urban agriculture is another strategy through which the poor family in the urban and industrial centres tries to meet the costs of social reproduction (Freeman 1991; Tripp 1994). People grow food so that they do not need to buy it and this lessens their dependence on waged labour and on the caprices of commodity markets.

For some families some of these strategies will be successful; for some families the money that migrants send home will ensure their basic security and sometimes it will do much more than that. For most they will not be. People have migrated to urban centres around the world in unprecedented numbers. For the first time in history there are now more people living in cities than in the countryside (UNFPA 2007). This has many impacts and one of them is that it changes the conditions of social reproduction. Thousands of people are living in cities without land, or safe homes, without jobs and without recourse to any support from government. In most of the world's largest cities a majority of the population are unregistered, living in illegal settlements, with no access to safe water, unsafely hooked up to electricity grids, and in very fragile houses built from discarded or very cheap materials. One third of all city dwellers live in urban settlements like this – slums or shantytowns. In sub-Saharan Africa nearly three out of every four city dwellers, and in South Asia one in every two households, live in slums (UN Habitat 2006). The state is unwilling to pay to improve their homes or support their families; in fact, when it decides to do something about slum dwellers, this mostly involves demolishing their homes and dispersing them. International bodies including the IMF and the World Bank have exacerbated the situation by insisting that states privatize their assets, withdraw subsidies on staple foods that many governments put in place in urban areas to lessen the likelihood of food riots, and create markets in education and health care. These measures have unravelled the limited support that the state provided for the urban population (the wages they can earn barely cover the living costs of one adult, let alone their children: Davis 2006).

Each and all of these crises of social reproduction inevitably impact on children's lives and shape ideas about what childhood can or should be. Children who live in squatter settlements, slums, shantytowns or favelas are living in overcrowded conditions, and as they get older it is not difficult to imagine that these children will find that they have more space and opportunities on the street than they do at home. Where adult family members cannot earn a wage to support their children and in contexts where in any case children who are not at work are also not in school but more likely on the street, their parents may expect their children to be with them at work and to contribute to the family income (see chapter 5). Children whose parents have died of AIDS-related illnesses may be taken in by other family members or they may, as is increasingly the case in Africa, establish their own households, with the eldest children acting as heads of households (Audemard and Vignikin 2006; Robson et al. 2006). Youth whose aspirations are in no way met by the opportunities normally available to them may join rebel forces, gangs or paramilitary organizations (Comaroff and Comaroff 2000: 306–9).

Rescuing children

What does government do in response to these crises of social reproduction and their impact on children and childhood? To answer this question I use an analytical framework that Michel Foucault (1991) outlined in his later work and that has since been developed by Foucauldian scholars to explain what contemporary governments do and how they legitimate their actions (Burchell 1996; Dean 1991; Gordon 1991; Inda 2005; Larner and Walters 2004). This framework is called governmentality – a word that Foucault coined to capture how understanding governments requires an understanding of how they think, of their 'mentality'.

Governmentality is a particularly useful device for analysing contemporary government because it attends to the constitution of identity, and to the multidimensional sites of power and its incoherent and often fragmentary operation, in ways that can be empirically investigated. Governmentality has been applied to the analysis of globalization only very recently (Larner and Walters 2004). It is a very useful tool for analysing global government precisely because global government is dispersed and fragmented. In relation to childhood it is of particular interest because of the claim that the goal of contemporary government is the increase in the welfare and health of the population.

The government of childhood is almost entirely orientated around the trope of child-saving: the care of the child, the identification and realization of the child's best interests, the healthy and normal emotional, physical, intellectual and psychic development of the child. Given this congruence between the techniques of child-saving and Foucault's claim that government targets the health and welfare of populations, governmentality seems a particularly felicitous device through which to analyse the government of childhood (Chen 2005).

Government can be analysed using the governmentality framework by investigating how it operates in three interrelated dimensions: reasons, technics (or techniques) and subjects. Nikolas Rose (1999a) has said that government cannot be its own rationale. The development of democratic politics and the corresponding loss of the credibility of the ancient 'divine right to rule' mean that rulers have to justify their rule. They do this, according to the theory of governmentality, through reasons or rationalities of government. Principal amongst these rationalities is that government says it governs to improve the health and welfare of the population. Reasons of government construct knowledge about populations – for example, how to identify an insane or criminal person or, most relevant to our purposes, how to identify bad childhoods and children.

The advice of all kinds of professional experts – bureaucrats, academics, social workers, teachers, doctors – is essential in establishing what the reasons of government should be. It is through the activities of experts that government can claim to know what it is that it governs and what it has to do to govern effectively. Reasons of government are fundamentally orientated towards the identification of problems.

Reasons of government depend on the construction of knowledge about the populations that it governs. Governmentality theorists bracket together all the different ways in which governments construct knowledge as technologies or technics of government. These technics organize populations by reference to knowledge about what is normal and what is abnormal or pathological and what government needs to do to control and shape populations. This is done in numerous ways.

The design of spaces, the architecture of buildings and the arrangement of objects (including bodies) within space is an important technique of government. Schools are a good example of how technics of government manage populations, in this case the population of school children. Technologies of government also include the methods of examining, calculating and enumerating the problems that government has the goal of addressing. Here, in relation to children, we might include school assessment tests and other school exams, and routine paediatric care (such as weighing and measuring babies and children). The professional vocabularies of experts play their role in normalizing some conduct and practices and pathologizing others. Material inscriptions are also a significant technic of government. These are 'all the mundane tools – surveys, reports, statistical methodologies, pamphlets, manuals, architectural plans, written reports, drawings, pictures, numbers, bureaucratic rules and guidelines, charts, graphs, statistics, and so forth – that represent events and phenomena as information, data, and knowledge. These humble technical devices make objects "visible" ' (Inda 2005: 9).

If the central reason of government is the production of problems, its central technique is the production of programmes that aim to resolve these problems. Of central importance to how modern government resolves problems is getting the people who are part of the problem to feel that they want to behave differently. So government does not just limit itself to technical and measurable interventions – although this is an important part of how it operates; it also wants to intervene psychically to get people to feel differently. Modern government aims to do this with all populations – child and adult alike – but because children are already thought of as people in need of moral instruction it is particularly through children that a lot of this psychic work of government gets done.

Rescuing street children

So governmentality theorists think that government operates like this: it identifies problems and makes them visible as discrete objects that can be the target of specific interventions which are bound up with getting people to behave in particular ways. This may seem rather abstract, so let me illustrate it with a news item that I read today. The headline is: 'Police bring in evening curfew to keep town's under 16-s off streets' (*The Guardian*, 9 July 2008). The problem that the local authority has identified in this town is anti-social behaviour. Already existing techniques of government including the Anti-Social Behaviour Act 2003 and an unrelenting discourse in the media about unruly youth had constituted children and parents as a discrete object that could become the target of a specific intervention. The intervention they chose was the setting of a summer curfew. The intent of the curfew is that it enforces particular kinds of behaviour on children and their parents. Not only does it enforce the removal of children from the streets in the evening (after 9 p.m. for under-fifteens and after 8 p.m. for under-tens), it also insists that parents have to make sure that their children comply with the curfew. If parents do not do so they may be visited by social services and issued with Parenting Orders which can compel parents to attend counselling or guidance sessions. The council's 'anti-social behaviour coordinator' said: 'While the vast majority of parents are extremely responsible, we need to encourage all parents to take responsibility for their children so that the community is a safer place for everyone' (*The Guardian*, 9 July 2008: 14).

In this example we can see not only the use of a technical or rule-bound intervention (no children out in public after 9 p.m.), but also the insistence that the objects targeted (children and their parents) have to agree with the intervention and if they do not they need to learn how to agree through psychological techniques (counselling and guidance).

In the case of juvenile curfews the target group, the object of intervention, is simply 'children' rather than a particular kind of child. In an abstract way curfews target all children without discrimination. (In practice juvenile curfews impact on black and working-class children more than they do on middle-class and white children, but the point is that there is nothing in the wording of curfew ordinances that insists on this.) Most child-saving or child-rescue campaigns do not work like this – they do not target all children of a particular age group. What they do is take a particular set of behaviours and group them together into an object that can be the target of intervention. 'Street children' are a good example of this. To identify the problem or the target of intervention, 'the street child', the governmental agency (whether a part of the government or a non-governmental organization) first has to have a reference point for identifying a street child and distinguishing him or her from other children in public space. The reason of government in this case is the rescue of children from potentially or actually harmful situations. This is identified by activities like being on the street after a certain time, sleeping or eating on the street, taking drugs, having sex, stealing, being untidy and dirty. These diverse activities – some risky and some harmless – are, as it were, congealed by governmentality into an object: the street child. Once government has identified its object it can then act on it through a range of material and psychic interventions. These include the forced removal of children from the street and their incarceration in penal and rehabilitation institutions, or their enrolment onto education and training programmes – the latter intended to encourage and facilitate a change of behaviour and of feeling in the 'street child'. All of these programmes address the 'street child' as an individual who can choose a different lifestyle; the role that structural problems like poverty and a general crisis in social reproduction play in making it necessary and possible for large numbers of children to leave their homes and live on the street is ignored in favour of attempts to reform the child's sensibilities.

Rescuing child soldiers

Campaigns to rescue child soldiers work in a similar way to those aimed at rescuing street children. As we saw in chapter 7, children join with rebel and government armed forces for many different reasons including poverty, being orphaned, a desire for retribution, being abducted, for protection. Some of these children are very young and probably do think of themselves as children; others are older – most children in militaries are in their late teens. These 'children' will be regarded as adults in their local context. Most of the girls and younger boys in rebel armies do not fight – they are more likely to act as scouts, spies, decoys, couriers, guards, cooks and cleaners. All of these multiple reasons and activities are congealed through governmental technics into the object 'child soldiers'; the child soldier, like the street child, is seen, especially by charitable organizations, as both culpable and innocent. They have done bad things, in the case of child soldiers probably terrible things, but they did it without full knowledge or understanding because they are children and therefore fundamentally innocent. The intervention involves separating the problem from its context (the street child from the street; the child soldier from his guns) and rehabilitating him for normal life by getting him to think of himself as a child again and to restore his lost innocence. In order for the children to rehabilitate themselves, the aim of these programmes is to return them to normal life, usually by insisting that they give up their guns and in return get a support package – usually money, seeds and tools, and often enrolment onto education and training programmes. One of the peculiar effects of these programmes is that in order to benefit from them children have to describe themselves as 'child soldiers' (Shepler 2005a; 2005b; 2005c). This means that in post-conflict situations children who fought in the war, often committing the most brutal acts of violence against their compatriots, are seen to be rewarded with money, tools and training whilst other children who do not need to be demobilized are not. In any event, the child soldier interventions, like those for street children, target the individual child ignoring the structural crises that caused the war or made the child join the military.

Rescuing children in failing families

In the examples I gave above street children (see also chapter 4) and child soldiers (see also chapter 7) are made into objects amenable to intervention. I stressed that child-saving tends towards individual solutions that bracket off the effects on children's decisions of structural inequalities and crises in social reproduction. This preference for individual solutions is also evident in the way in which the state governs parents who do not parent as government considers adequate or appropriate.

Child-rescue programmes generally include both material and psychic/

emotional interventions. This is not the case when the object of concern is the parent. In this case interventions are almost entirely concerned with changing the parents' attitudes and sensibilities. The strong presumption is that when families fail to care for their children this is because they have the wrong attitude towards parenting. Since this involves an interference by the government (for example social workers) or other public actors (like charities) in the private sphere of the family, it has to have a strong reason that can allow it to claim that it can legitimately override family privacy. The reason that government agencies cite is the best interests of the child – they claim therefore that how the parent rears their child is not simply different to dominant norms but that it is harmful to the child (Boeck and Honwana 2005).

Establishing a kind of common sense about what is good or bad parenting is achieved through all kinds of technics. These technics include documentaries, films, advice columns, parenting magazines, and the advice of paediatricians, teachers and other child care professionals. If, knowing what the norms are, the parents still refuse to comply they may find themselves subject to both coercive and encouraging measures. If the family is drawing welfare benefits or living in social housing then the government may use these technologies to force the parents to comply. In Britain, for example, local authorities have the power to issue parenting contracts to the parents of unruly children. If the parents break the contract they can be ordered by the court to attend parenting classes and pay fines. Parents can also be fined if their child breaches the terms of an Individual Support Order. These were introduced in 2001 as part of the Anti-Social Behaviour Act. They are aimed at children between the ages of ten and fourteen, and can compel a child to attend psychological counselling and drugs counselling. Parents whose children truant may be fined for failing to get their child or children to school; if their child continues to truant, the parents can be jailed.

Rescuing children: the impact on children's lives

This book has talked about children's experiences of war, politics, homelessness and work. The scale of these experiences shows very clearly that the UN Convention on the Rights of the Child has had very little impact on reshaping children's lives. The proliferation of child-saving organizations is testimony to the extent to which over a century of child-saving has not succeeded in getting the majority of the world's children a safe, protected childhood that is focused on play and learning.

In fact the multiple crises in social reproduction that are generated by the rapaciousness and inequalities of global capitalism seem to have intensified children's economic, political and physical insecurity. The end of the Cold War triggered not so much a new world order as a new world *disorder*. Economic and political insecurity has expanded the numbers of migrants, whether they are moving across national borders or from rural to urban areas within national borders. A disproportionate number of displaced persons are women and children. The global feminization of the international labour market means that it is now mostly women that emigrate. The absence of women in migrant-sending countries like the Philippines is changing family relations and often compromising children's emotional wellbeing. Campaigns to increase school attendance have not reduced child labour – which suggests that children are now busier than they were before; where the number of children working has fallen, the numbers in school have not always increased. There are more children who are neither in school nor in work; many of these 'idle' children are working at home looking after younger siblings and doing household chores, often so that adults can go out to work. Raced, gendered and classed inequalities continue to impact on children's life chances.

The rights of cultures and the rights of children

Child-saving: an ethical imperative?

Child-saving, the identification of populations of children as problems whom specific programmes of intervention are designed to rescue and remove from risk, through reform or other measures, is widely accepted as a benevolent and appropriate response to some children's lives. The children's vulnerability, dependency and lack of capacity demand that somebody 'do something' to protect them and make them safe. If the protection of children is not forthcoming from local adult populations or institutions, then it is the moral duty of other adults and institutions to intervene since adults, all adults, have a moral duty to act in (any) child's best interests. For advocates of global child-saving, the idea of childhood that is inscribed into the CRC and is in the process of being globalized (see chapter 2) constitutes a moral imperative for adults to act in an attempt to secure some progress towards the realization of this model in children's lives. In this view, it is not that the liberal model of childhood is different from other models but that it is better than them. The changes in ideas about how children should live (what their relations with adults and with other children should be, what they should do with their time, where they should be) are changes that have improved the quality of children's lives and represent both progress and the realization of children's human rights. It is, in this view, objectively better for children to have private space rather than to have to share with other children and adults; it is better for children to go to school rather than work; it is better for children to play with their peers than to look after their younger siblings.

In this view, rescuing children is a moral imperative that can never be trumped by culture. Children's needs are not culturally shaped, they are universal and can be scientifically, objectively determined. No one, they might insist, could argue that children should be fighting in wars, living on the street, left to cope if their parents die. No one could argue that children are not more vulnerable than adults and that they do not need to be protected from harm on behalf of their vulnerability and dependency on others.

Child-saving: a neo-imperial intervention?

Against this view of universal harms or risks is the standpoint of cultural relativists, who argue that cultural practices are morally incommensurable. That is to say that what one culture regards as an essential part of childhood – say, starting work – another culture might consider as antithetical to childhood, and no judgement can be made about which culture is right and which is wrong (Freeman 1997: 129–48). In the view of cultural relativists, it is an effect of power that a good childhood is the childhood which has become accepted as the dominant norm in the advanced capitalist countries and to a great extent amongst the global bourgeoisie. It is not, in other words, that a liberal childhood is objectively better for children than models that preceded it or still coexist with it, but merely that it has the support of the global powers. In the view of cultural relativists, child-saving is a thinly disguised neo-imperialism that mistakes the particular cultural practices predominant in Europe and North America for universal norms only because they have the power to disseminate those norms through their influence over international law-making (Boyden 1990; Harris-Short 2003), their control of the International Financial Institutions, their influence over global education discourses, and ultimately their capacity for military intervention.

Child-saving: ethically defensible but impractical?

A third view of child-saving is that, whilst it may be ethically defensible to say that liberal childhood and its technics – for example, to exclude children from work and include them in school – are better for children than other kinds of childhood, in practice most societies in Africa, Asia and Latin America do not have the level of economic development necessary for them to become a local norm. In this view, which I call pragmatic relativism, it is really a moot point whether it is better for children to go to school than to work because neither their parents nor the state are in a position to meet the costs of, say, universal primary schooling.

Pragmatic relativism is one of the weakest criticisms to be levelled at child-saving; for whilst it positions itself in relation to an anti-imperialist and anti-interventionist stance (Pupavac 2001) it is a view which upholds global inequality. There are many possible responses to the self-evident fact that some countries do not have the level of capital accumulation or state capacity to make it viable for children to stop working. However, unless children working can be defended on ethical grounds, and such a defence is possible so long as harmful kinds of work are excluded, then it cannot be defended on pragmatic grounds. Indeed, if it cannot be defended on ethical grounds and yet the conditions are not in place to make it possible for children to work, then this would seem to demand more, not less, efforts at child-saving, and an examination of the legitimacy of global inequalities.

Rights-based approaches to rescuing children

The rights-based approach to child-saving is in part an attempt to address the criticisms –and specifically the charge of neo-imperialism – made by cultural relativists against global child-saving organizations. It does this by claiming to act as the advocate of children themselves rather than acting as the paternalistic adjudicator of children's best interests. There is also an acknowledgement here, perhaps, that paternalistic adjudication has led in the past to what are now recognized as entirely wrong 'child-saving' measures, such as Barnardo's sponsorship of the emigration of 'orphans' to Canada in the nineteenth century or the removal of mixed-parentage aboriginal children from their parents in Australia (see chapter 3). This approach fits well with the implicit criticism of child-saving made by the new sociology of childhood that children are generally not recognized as capable, independent and self-realizing actors but only as a set of potentials. The argument of the new sociology of childhood is that the focus of child-saving, whether in the field of psychology, pedagogy or political economy, is not the intrinsic merit of the child's life but only what kind of adult the child will develop into and how he or she can be shaped to develop into the right kind of adult. Child rights agencies address this issue by attending to the 'voice' of the child, involving children in participatory research methods designed to elicit their view of their current lifeworld or some part of it (Hart 1992; Johnson et al. 1998; Ansell 2005: 225–56). It is for this reason that rights-based child-saving agencies place so much emphasis on the UNCRC as a participatory rights instrument despite the fact that participation is a very minor key in the Convention, which is predominately an instrument of child protection and provision organized around the fuzzy concept of best interests.

In fact, the claim that contemporary child-saving is merely ventriloquizing the child's voice in order to articulate their claims to rights is not very convincing. It is not convincing firstly because there are no representative mechanisms through which children can articulate their claims. Children's parliaments sound like they might be representative institutions such as parliaments are in a democracy. This is not the case for children's parliaments because individuals are elected to them from some other non-representative body: typically this would be a conference for children organized by NGOs. Secondly, the rights that children are entitled to according to the UNCRC are not rights in the historical meaning of the word but conditions necessary for the constitution of particular kinds of childhood.

Rights do not adhere to humans by virtue of our common humanity but are won in political struggle and defended by persons with capacity. In other words, rights imply both the capacity to defend them and the possession of legal personhood (Chandler 2001; Ruddick 2003; 2006). Rights are not bequeathed by the powerful in a fit of beneficence. When legal instruments are enacted that are based on the assumption that those with power want to make a better world for those without power purely motivated by an excess of good will, these legal instruments are either ineffective as tools for the upholding of rights or they have the effect of extending rather than limiting the scope of power. The latter is the case with international legislation for children: it has, in the name of the best interests of the child, given the most powerful countries in the international system of states yet another mechanism for intervening in the governing of less powerful countries (Pupavac 2001).

If the Convention on the Rights of the Child is put to one side and instead participatory research methods are used to uncover the child's voice or empower the child's actions, this still does not resolve the difficulties with any claim that child-saving agencies are animated by children. This is simply because participatory research methods are necessarily limited in the scale of the population who can participate. The question then arises: who participates and how are they selected for inclusion in research projects? By what measure do these participants claim to be representative of the larger population whom their efforts will impact on? To this objection might be added the problem that, since child-saving agencies are charitable organizations, their fields of action are limited by charity law. If, for example, children in a participatory research project thought that the most effective means of pressing their case was to organize politically, the charitable NGO could not publicly support that or provide funds to enable it to happen. Similarly, if NGOs receive grants for specific activities, they are constrained by the contract between themselves and the donor to spend the money in the way specified in this contract so that once again, if the child participants decided that some other course of action would be more beneficial, the NGO could not support it without getting their contract with the donor changed.

Child rights approaches to child-saving also act as another reason and technic of government that produce and inscribe a liberal model of childhood in children's lives on a global scale. The iconic figure of the child as the privileged site of innocence and vulnerability marshals a sentimental and uncritical response to governmental interventions carried out in the name of the child. In this respect, the child is a powerful mobilizing figure in defence of the legitimacy of the global powers and of global capitalism. The claim implicit in the liberal model of childhood is that the expansion of capitalism has made childhood a happier, more secure, less risky period of life than it has been under any other political–economic system. Capitalism works in children's best interests, so the argument goes, because, contrary to the claim of cultural relativists, liberal childhood (and therefore the system that makes it possible) is progressive. For the first time in history children are recognized as a population with inherent rights whose delivery the duty-holder has a moral and legal responsibility to ensure. Children's rights regimes are the caring face of capitalism. The international institutions of global capitalism are involved in attempting to implement liberal childhood across the globe through such devices as encouraging Corporate Social Responsibility, monitoring the extent of children's economic activity, and setting goals for the elimination of childhood poverty. All of these activities have very little practical impact, but what they do is act as rhetorical devices for legitimating global capitalism at the same time as extending the exercise of power by global states and the international system over weak, marginal and developing states.

Conclusion

The claim of cultural relativists that child-saving is neo-imperialist is irrefutable in some respects. In particular, it is undeniable that the ability to extend a particular model of childhood is clearly a function not of its intrinsic merits but of its ontology. However, the cultural relativist model can itself come very close to reproducing a racialized and colonial world-view in which 'their' children have different vulnerabilities to 'our' children and in which the terror of living with violence, the pain of living with loss, the insecurity of living in poverty is underplayed. Most child-saving interventions do not have to be imposed over the objections of parents who practise other cultural models of childhood. There is very little, if any, evidence that parents in sub-Saharan Africa or South Asia have, for example, any principled objection to their children attending school (Nieuwenhuys 1994; Katz 2004), and although there is some evidence that in many cultures work is considered to be an essential and ethically desirable part of childhood, work that exposes children to bodily or emotional harm is no more likely to be desired for or by children than it is for or by adults. The heart of the disagreement between different cultures about what constitutes a childhood probably rests more on the ontological question of what it means to be human – and therefore how children should be raised – than on ethical objections to international charities supplying food, medicines, clothing or shelter to families in poor neighbourhoods, or dealing with disasters and emergencies. Of course, some of these activities and in particular those that form child populations into objects of child-saving (child soldiers, child workers, street children, orphans) also depend on and inscribe a particular way of being a child. Despite the ethical problems with a cultural relativist stance on child-saving it is still an important corrective to liberal universalism in its insistence on the importance of imagining that there are different ways to be human, some of which may be incommensurable to one another but may not be more or less harmful for children than one another.

The current programme of child-saving does not accept the possibility of culturally incommensurable models of childhood that are equally ethically defensible. Contemporary global child-saving is explicitly about globalizing a model of childhood that is underpinned by a liberal political philosophy. This much is evident from how it conceives of a good childhood and indeed of an ethical life. Even in Europe, from where the UNCRC began, there is considerable disagreement about the ethics of liberal individualism and of the constitution of the self as a rational, autonomous, self-disciplined, independent being. Whatever else can be said about liberal ethics it should be clear that it does not offer the only or the best way to be human. There are other ways to be an ethical person – a fact that is attested to by people's everyday practices of friendship, family, religious life and, indeed, caring for children.

Is it possible to find a way to navigate the complexities of our responsibilities towards children in a globalized world other than a blithe belief either that we know what is in children's best interests because those interests are the same everywhere, or that cultures of childhood are so incommensurable that what children need for their political, economic, social and corporeal security differs radically from one context to another? If children's vulnerabilities make a moral claim on adults, how can this claim be responded to without either resorting to a nineteenth-century moral philanthropy, embracing the liberal model of childhood (and with it liberal ways of being in the world), or retreating into localism? I think there is another way to think about our responsibilities towards children in a global context. The central argument of this book has been that the liberal model of childhood is tied to the globalization of capitalism and its neo-liberal subjects. It is in that claim, I think, that one of the possible responses to our contemporary responsibilities towards children can be found. In particular, I suggest that it has to be made explicit that the multiple insecurities of children in the contemporary world are being driven by global capitalism and its constant production of crises in social reproduction that displace and unsettle children and their families. The problem of children's insecurities, in other words, lies not with individual children and their families, but with the structural inequalities that mark their lives. Of course, individual children and their families respond to these crises with more or less resilience and more or less resourcefulness, but this should not be taken to mean that all children need is to be trained in resilience and resourcefulness. Secondly, it is important to recognize that children's rights, child-saving or however else the connections between children's vulnerabilities and adults' responsibilities are made are fundamentally ways of thinking about what it means to be in the world; what it means to be human (Aitken 2001a; 2001b). The liberal model of childhood needs to be treated sceptically and critiqued not only, as most have done, with reference to its cultural specificity and its modernity or with reference to the limits to the possibility of its production but by thinking about what it implies for how to be human, and the deep connections between this particular way of being human and late capitalism.

Recommended further reading

Inda, J. X. (ed.). 2005. *Anthropologies of Modernity: Foucault, Governmentality and Life Politics*. Malden, MA: Blackwell.
An excellent example of how Foucault's concept of governmentality can be applied to contemporary culture and politics.

Katz, C. 2004. *Growing up Global: Economic Restructuring and Children's Everyday Lives*. Minneapolis, MN: University of Minnesota Press.
A ground-breaking ethnography of the comparative impact of globalization on the lives of young people in a Sudanese village and a New York neighbourhood.

Larner, W. and W. Walters (eds.). 2004. *Global Governmentality: Governing International Spaces*. London and New York: Routledge.
The first study to apply governmentality theory to international politics.

Mitchell, K., S. A. Marston and C. Katz. 2003. *Life's Work: Geographies of Social Reproduction*. Malden, MA and Oxford: Blackwell.
Required reading for understanding the significance of the concept of social reproduction in the contemporary global economy.

Bibliography

Abbink, J. 2005. Being young in Africa: the politics of despair and renewal. In: J. Abbink and I. Van Kessel (eds.), *Vanguard or Vandals: Youth, Politics and Conflict in Africa*. Leiden: Brill, pp. 1–34.

Aboud, F. E. 1988. *Children and Prejudice*. New York: Blackwell.

Abrahamian, E. 1989. *Radical Islam: The Iranian Mojahedin*. London: I. B. Tauris.

Ahluwalia, S. 2001. Controlling births, policing sexualities: a history of birth control in Colonial India, 1877–1946. Unpublished PhD thesis, University of Cincinnati.

Aitken, S. C. 2001a. *The Geographies of Young People: The Morally Contested Spaces of Identity*. London and New York: Routledge.

2001b. Global crises of childhood: rights, justice and the unchildlike child. *Area* 33 (2), pp. 119–27.

Alanen, L. 1994. Gender and generation: feminism and 'the child question'. In: Qvortrup et al. (eds.), *Childhood Matters: Social Theory, Practice and Politics*. Aldershot: Avebury, pp. 27–42.

2001. Explorations in generational analysis. In: L. Alanen and B. Mayall (eds.), *Conceptualising Child–Adult Relations*. London: Routledge, pp. 11–22.

Ali, S. 2003. *Mixed-Race, Post-Race: Gender, New Ethnicities, and Cultural Practices*. Oxford and New York: Berg.

Amato, P. A. and A. Booth. 1997. *A Generation at Risk: Growing up in an Era of Family Upheaval*. Cambridge, MA: Harvard University Press.

Amoko, A. O. 2001. The problem with English literature: canonicity, citizenship, and the idea of Africa. *Research in African Literatures* 32 (4), pp. 19–43.

Anderson, H. 1992. *Mozambique: A War against the People*. London: Macmillan.

Angel, W. D. (ed.). 1995. *The International Law of Youth Rights*. The Hague: Martinus Nijhoff Publishers.

Ansell, N. 2005. *Children, Youth and Development*. London: Routledge.

Apple, M. W. 2008. Evolution versus creationism in education. *Educational Policy* 22 (2), pp. 327–35.

Aptekar, L. 1994. Street children in the developing world: a review of their condition. *Cross-Cultural Research* 28 (3), pp. 195–225.

Archard, D. 2004. *Children, Rights and Childhood*. London: Routledge.

Aries, P. 1973 [1960]. *Centuries of Childhood*. Harmondsworth: Penguin.

Arnson, C. J. 2006.The political economy of war: situating the debate. In: C. J. Arnson and I. W. Zartman (eds.), *Rethinking the Economics of War*. Washington, DC: Woodrow Wilson Center Press, and Baltimore: Johns Hopkins University Press, pp. 1–22.

Asad, T. 1993. *Genealogies of Religion: Discipline and Reasons of Power in Christianity and Islam*. Baltimore, MD: Johns Hopkins University Press.

Audemard, C. and K. Vignikin. 2006. *Orphans and Vulnerable Children in Sub-Saharan Africa*. Ceped. Available at: http://ceped.cirad.fr/cdrom/orphe-lins_sida_2006/en/index.html, accessed 16 July 2007.

Barthes, R. 1981. *Camera Lucida*. Translated by R. Howard. New York: Hill & Wang.

Basu, K. and P. H. Van. 1998. The economics of child labor. *American Economic Review* 88 (3), pp. 412–27.

Bay, E. G. and D. L. Donham (eds.). 2006. *States of Violence: Politics, Youth and Memory in Contemporary Africa*. Charlottesville and London: University of Virginia Press.

Bayart, J.-F. 1993. *The State in Africa: The Politics of the Belly*. London: Verso.

1999. The social capital of the felonious state or the ruses of political intelligence. In: J. F. Bayart, S. Ellis and B. Hibou, *The Criminalization of the State in Africa*. Oxford: James Currey, pp. 32–48.

Beazley, H. 2000. Home Sweet Home? Street children's sites of belonging. In: S. Holloway and G. Valentine (eds.), *Children's Geographies: Living, Playing, Learning and Transforming Everyday Worlds*. London: Routledge, pp. 194–210.

Becker, G. S. 1964. *Human Capital: A Theoretical and Empirical Analysis, with Special Reference to Education*. New York: Columbia University Press.

1991. *A Treatise on the Family*. Cambridge, MA and London: Harvard University Press.

Bennet, T. W. n.d. *Using Children in Armed Conflict: A Legitimate African Tradition? Criminalising the Recruitment of Child Soldiers*. Available at: http://www.essex.ac.uk/armedcon/Issues/Texts/Soldiers002.htm, last accessed 22 July 2008.

Berdal, M. and D. M. Malone (eds.). 2000. *Greed and Grievance: Economic Agendas in Civil Wars*. Boulder, CO: Lynne Rienner.

Bernstein, B. 1971. *Class, Codes and Control: Theoretical Studies Towards a Sociology of Language*. London: Routledge and Kegan Paul.

Bettie, J. 2003. *Women without Class: Girls, Race and Identity*. Berkeley: University of California Press.

Biggeri, M. et al. 2003. The puzzle of 'idle' children: neither in school nor performing economic activity: evidence from six countries. Working paper, UCW Project: Faculty of Economics, University of Rome. Available at: www.ucw-project.org/pdf/publications/standard_idlechildren_3nov2003.pdf.

Blaut, J., G. McCleary and A. Blaut. 1970. Environmental mapping in young children. *Environment and Behaviour* 2 (3), pp. 335–49.

Blaut, J. and D. Stea. 1971. Studies of geographic learning. *Annals of the Association of American Geographers* 61, pp. 387–93.

Bledsoe, C. 1990. No success without struggle: social mobility and hardship for foster children in Sierra Leone. *Man* 25 (1), pp. 70–88.

Boeck, de F. and A. Honwana. 2005. Introduction: children and youth in Africa. In: A. Howman and F. de Boeck (eds.), *Makers and Breakers: Children and Youth in Postcolonial Africa*. London: James Currey, pp. 1–18.

Boldt, G. M. 1996. Sexist and heterosexist responses to gender bending in an elementary classroom. *Curriculum Inquiry* 26 (2), pp. 113–31.

2002. Towards a reconceptualization of gender and power in an elementary classroom. *Current Issues in Comparative Education* 5 (1), pp. 7–23.

Boltanski, L. 1999. *Distant Suffering: Politics, Morality and the Media*. Cambridge: Cambridge University Press.

Boothby, N., A. Strang and M. Wessells. 2006. *A World Turned Upside Down: Social Ecological Approaches to Children in War Zones*. Bloomfield, CT: Kumarian Press.

Bourdieu, P. 1990. *The Logic of Practice*. Translated by R. Nice. Cambridge: Polity Press.

Boyden, J. 1990. Childhood and the policy makers: a comparative perspective on the globalization of childhood. In: A. James and A. Prout (eds.), *Constructing and Reconstructing Childhood*. London: Falmer, pp. 190–229.

Boyden, J. and J. de Berry (eds.). 2004. *Children and Youth on the Front Line: Ethnography, Armed Conflict and Displacement*. Oxford: Berghahn Books.

Boyden, J., B. Ling and W. Myers. 1998. *What Works for Working Children*. Stockholm: Rädda Barnen/UNICEF.

Brannen, J. and M. O'Brien (eds.). 1996. *Children in Families: Research and Policy*. London: The Falmer Press.

Breen, C. 2003. The role of NGOs in the formulation of and compliance with the optional protocol to the Convention on the Rights of the Child on involvement of children in armed conflict. *Human Rights Quarterly* 25 (2), pp. 453–81.

Bremmer, R. 1971. *Children and Youth in America: A Documentary History*. Cambridge, MA: Harvard University Press.

Brett, R. and I. Specht. 2004. *Young Soldiers: Why they Choose to Fight*. Boulder, CO: Lynne Rienner.

Briggs, J. and I. Yeboah. 2001. Sub-Saharan Africa and the contemporary sub-Saharan city. *Area* 33 (1), pp. 18–26.

Briggs, L. 2006. Making 'American' families: transnational adoption and U.S. Latin America policy. In: A. L. Stoler (ed.), *Haunted by Empire*. Durham and London: Duke University Press, pp. 344–65.

Brocklehurst, H. 2006. *Who's Afraid of Children: Children, Conflict and International Relations*. Aldershot: Ashgate.

Brown, S., D. Cohon and R. Wheeler. 2002. African American extended families and kinship care: how relevant is the foster care model for kinship care? *Children and Youth Services Review* 24 (1–2), pp. 53–77.

Brownmiller, S. 1977. *Against our Will: Men, Women and Rape*. Harmondsworth: Penguin.

Brunsma, D. L. 2005. Interracial families and the racial identification of mixed-race children: evidence from the Early Years Longitudinal Survey. *Social Forces* 84 (2), pp. 1131–57.

Bundy, C. 1987. Street sociology and pavement politics: aspects of youth and student resistance in Cape Town. *Journal of Southern African Studies* 13 (3), pp. 303–30.

Burchell, G. 1996. Liberal government and techniques of the self. In: A. Barry, T. Osborne and N. Rose (eds.), *Foucault and Political Reason: Liberalism, Neo-Liberalism and the Rationalities of Government*. Chicago: University of Chicago Press, pp. 19–36.

Burgess, T. 2005. Introduction to youth and citizenship in East Africa. *Africa Today* 51 (3), pp. 7–24.

Burman, E. 1994. Innocents abroad: Western fantasies of childhood and the iconography of disaster. *Disasters* 18 (3), pp. 238–53.

Burr, R. 2006. *Vietnam's Children in a Changing World*. New Brunswick, NJ: Rutgers University Press.

Burr, R. and H. Montgomery. 2003. Family, kinship and beyond. In: J. Maybin and M. Woodhead (eds.), *Childhoods in Context*. Chichester: John Wiley & Sons, pp. 39–80.

Butler, J. 1990. *Gender Trouble: Feminism and the Subversion of Identity*. New York and London: Routledge.

1997. *The Psychic Life of Power: Theories in Subjection*. Stanford: Stanford University Press.

Cammack, P. 2003. The governance of global capitalism: a new materialist perspective. *Historical Materialism* 11 (2), pp. 37–59.

Cantwell, N. 1992. The origins, development and significance of the UNCRC. In: S. Detrick (ed.), *The UNCRC: A Guide to the Travaux Préparatoires*. Dordrecht: Martinus Nijhoff, pp. 19–30.

Cardoza, T. 2002. 'These unfortunate children': sons and daughters of the regiment in Revolutionary and Napoleonic France. In: J. Marten (ed.), *Children and War: A Historical Anthology*. New York: New York University Press, pp. 205–15.

Carey, E. 2005. *Plaza of Sacrifices: Gender, Power, and Terror in 1968 Mexico*. Albuquerque, NM: University of New Mexico Press.

Carey, M. 2006. Survival is political: history, violence and the contemporary power struggle in Sierra Leone. In: E. G. Bay and D. L. Donham (eds.), *States of Violence: Politics, Youth and Memory in Contemporary Africa* Charlottesville and London: University of Virginia Press, pp. 97–126.

Carton, B. 2000. *Blood from Your Children: The Colonial Origins of Generational Conflict in South Africa*. Charlottesville: University of Virginia Press.

Cartwright, L. 2005. Images of 'waiting children': spectatorship and pity in the representation of the global social orphan in the 1990s. In: T. A.Volkman (ed.), *Cultures of Transnational Adoption*. Durham and London: Duke University Press, pp. 185–212.

Castells, M. 1997. *The Information Age: Economy, Society, and Culture* ii. *The Power of Identity*. Oxford and Malden, MA: Blackwell.

Chan, A., J. Rosen and J. Unger. 1980. Students and class warfare. *The China Quarterly* 83, pp. 397–446.

Chandler, D. 2001. Universal ethics and elite politics: the limits of normative human rights theory. *The International Journal of Human Rights* 5 (4), pp. 72–89.

Chang, K. A. and L. H. M. Ling. 2000. Globalization and its intimate other: Filipina workers in Hong Kong. In: M. H. Marchand and A. S. Runyan (eds.), *Gender and Global Restructuring: Sightings, Sites and Resistances.* London and New York: Routledge, pp. 27–43.

Charnley, H. 2000. Children separated from their families in the Mozambique war. In: C. Panter-Brick and M. Smith (eds.), *Abandoned Children*. Cambridge: Cambridge University Press, pp. 111–30.

Chatterjee, N. and N. E. Riley. 2001. Planning an Indian modernity: the gendered politics of fertility control. *Signs* 26 (3), pp. 811–45.

Chawla, L. (ed.). 2002. *Growing up in an Urbanising World*. London: UNESCO and Earthscan, Ltd.

Chen, G. Z. 1997. Youth curfews and the trilogy of parent, child and state relations. *New York Law Review* 72 (131), pp. 131–74.

Chen, X. 2003. Cultivating children as you would valuable plants: the gardening governmentality of child saving, Toronto, Canada, 1880s–1920s. *Journal of Historical Sociology* 16 (4), pp. 460–86.

2005. *Tending the Gardens of Citizenship: Child Saving in Toronto, 1880s–1920s.* Toronto: University of Toronto Press.

Chevannes, B. 2001. *Learning to Be a Man: Culture, Socialization and Gender Identity in Five Caribbean Communities*. Barbados: The University of the West Indies Press, and Chicago: University of Chicago Press.

Chikane, F. 1986. The effects of the unrest on Township children. In: S. Burman and P. Reynolds (eds.), *Growing up in a Divided Society: The Contexts of Childhood in South Africa*. Johannesburg: Ravan Press, pp. 333–44.

Chirwa, W. C. 1993. Child and youth labour on the Nyasaland plantations, 1890s–1953. *Journal of Southern African Studies* 19 (4), pp. 662–80.

Chouliaraki, L. 2006. *The Spectatorship of Suffering*. London: Sage.

Ciscel, D. H. et al. 2003. Ghosts in the global machine: new immigrants and the redefinition of work. *Journal of Economic Issues* 37 (2), pp. 333–42.

Clapham, C. 1988. *Transformation and Continuity in Revolutionary Ethiopia*. Cambridge: Cambridge University Press.

Clapham, C. 1998. Introduction. In: C. Clapham (ed.), *African Guerrillas*. Oxford: James Currey.

Clark, A., D. Hocevar and M. H. Dembo. 1980. The role of cognitive development in children's explanations and preferences for skin color. *Developmental Psychology* 16, pp. 332–9.

Clement, P. F. 1997. *Growing Pains: Children in the Industrial Age, 1850–1890*. New York: Macmillan.

Cohen, C. P. 2006. The role of the United States in the drafting of the Convention on the Rights of the Child. *Emory International Law Review* 20 (185), pp. 185–92.

Cohen, C. P., S. N. Hart and S. M. Kosloske. 1996. Monitoring the United Nations Convention on the Rights of the Child: the challenge of information management. *Human Rights Quarterly* 18 (2), pp. 4389–471.

Cohen, S. 2001. *States of Denial: Knowing About Atrocities and Suffering*. Cambridge: Polity Press.

Cole, J. and D. Durham. 2007. Introduction: age, regeneration and the intimate politics of globalization. In: J. Cole and D. Durham (eds.), *Generations and Globalization: Youth, Age and Family in the New World Economy*. Bloomington and Indianapolis: Indiana University Press, pp. 1–28.

Collier, P. 2000. Doing well out of war: an economic perspective. In: M. Berdal and D. M. Malone (eds.), *Greed and Grievance: Economic Agendas in Civil Wars*. Boulder, CO: Lynne Rienner, pp. 91–112.

Collier, P. and A. Hoeffler. 1998. On economic causes of civil war. Available at: http://www.worldbank.org/research/conflict/papers.htm, last accessed 5 July 2007.

1999. Justice-seeking and loot-seeking in civil war. Available at: http://www.worldbank.org/research/conflict/papers/justice.htm, last accessed 5 July 2007.

2000. Greed and grievance in civil war. Policy research working paper 2355. Washington, DC: World Bank.

Collins, D. C. A. and R. A. Kearns. 2001. Under curfew and under siege? Legal geographies of young people. *Geoforum* 32 (3), pp. 389–403.

Comaroff, J. and J. L. Comaroff. 1999. Occult economies and the violence of abstraction: notes from the South African postcolony. *American Ethnologist* 26 (20), pp. 279–303.

2000. Millennial capitalism: first thoughts on a second coming. *Public Culture* 12 (2), pp. 291–343.

Connolly, P. 1998. *Racism, Gender Identities and Young Children: Social Relations in a Multi-ethnic, Inner-City Primary School.* New York and London: Routledge.

Cook, S. 2001. *After the Iron Rice Bowl: extending the safety net in China.* IDS discussion paper 377. Surrey: Institute of Development Studies.

Coole, D. 2000. Cartographic convulsions: public and private reconsidered. *Political Theory* 28 (3), pp. 337–54.

Corsaro, W. 2005 [1997]. *The Sociology of Childhood.* Thousand Oaks, California: Pine Forge Press.

Croll, E. 2000. *Endangered Daughters: Discrimination and Development in Asia.* London and New York: Routledge.

Cross, M. and L. Chisholm. 1990. The roots of segregated schooling in twentieth-century South Africa. In: M. Nkomo (ed.), *Pedagogy of Domination.* Trenton, NJ: Africa World Press, pp. 43–74.

Cunningham, H. 1995. *Children and Childhood in Western Society Since 1500.* New York: Longman.

Dalla Costa, M. and G. F. Dalla Costa (eds.). 1995. *Paying the Price: Women and the Politics of International Economic Strategy.* London: Zed Books.

Davis, M. 1990. *City of Quartz.* London: Verso.

2006. *Planet of Slums.* London and New York: Verso.

de Block, E. and D. Buckingham. 2007. *Global Children, Global Media.* Basingstoke: Palgrave Macmillan.

de Mause, L. (ed.). 1988. *The History of Childhood: The Untold Story of Child Abuse.* New York: Peter Bedrick Books.

de Schweinitz, R. L. 2004. If they could change the world: children, childhood and African-American civil rights politics. Unpublished PhD thesis, University of Michigan.

Dean, M. 1991. *Governmentality: Power and Rule in Modern Society.* London: Sage.

Diamant, N. J. 2000. *Revolutionizing the Family: Politics, Love and Divorce in Urban and Rural China, 1949–1968.* Berkeley: University of California Press.

Dickinson, E. R. 1996. *The Politics of Child Welfare from the Empire to the Federal Republic.* Cambridge, MA: Harvard University Press.

Diseko, N. J. 1991. The origins and development of the South African Student's Movement (SASM): 1968–1976. *Journal of Southern African Studies* 18 (1), pp. 40–62.

Dlamini, S. N. 2005. *Youth and Identity Politics in South Africa, 1990–1994.* Toronto: University of Toronto Press.

Dolby, N. E. 2001. *Constructing Race: Identity and Popular Culture in South Africa.* Albany: State University of New York Press.

Donham, D. L. 2006. Staring at suffering: violence as subject. In: E. G. Bay and D. L. Donham (eds.), *States of Violence.* Charlottesville and London: University of Virginia Press, pp. 16–34.

Donzelot, J. 1980. *The Policing of Families.* Translated by R. Hurley. London: Hutchinson.

1991. Pleasure in work. In: G. Burchell et al. (eds.), *The Foucault Effect: Studies in Governmentality*. Chicago: University of Chicago Press, pp. 251–80.

Dorow, S. 2006. *Transnational Adoption: A Cultural Economy of Race, Gender and Kinship*. New York and London: New York University Press.

Driskell, D. 2002. *Creating Better Cities with Children and Youth*. London: UNESCO and Earthscan, Ltd.

Durham, D. 2000. Introduction: youth and the social imagination in Africa. *Anthropological Quarterly* 73 (3), pp. 113–44.

Dywer, P. 2004. Creeping conditionality in the UK: from welfare rights to conditional entitlements. *Canadian Journal of Sociology/Cahiers canadiens de sociologie* 29 (2), pp. 265–87.

Edmonds, E. V. 2007. *Child Labor*. Cambridge, MA: National Bureau of Economic Research.

Ehrenreich, B. and A. Hochschild. 2002. Introduction. In: B. Ehrenreich and A. Hochschild (eds.), *Global Woman: Nannies, Maids, and Sex Workers in the New Economy*. New York: Metropolitan/Owl Books, pp. 1–14.

Ekerwald, H. 2001. The modernist manifesto of Alva and Gunnar Myrdal: modernization of Sweden in the thirties and the question of sterilization. *International Journal of Politics, Culture & Society* 14 (3), pp. 539–62.

Emerson, P. M. and A. P. Souza. 2003. Is there a child labor trap? Intergenerational persistence of child labor in Brazil. *Economic Development and Cultural Change* 51 (2), pp. 375–98.

Ennew, J. 1995. Outside childhood: street children's rights. In: B. Franklin (ed.), *The Handbook of Children's Rights: Comparative Policy and Practice*. London: Routledge, pp. 308–403.

Fass, P. 2003. *The Encyclopedia of Children and Childhood: In History and Society*. New York: Macmillan Reference.

Ferme, M. C. 2001. *The Underneath of Things: Violence, History, and the Everyday in Sierra Leone*. Berkeley: University of California Press.

Fisher-Thompson, D. 1993. Adult toy purchase for children: Factors affecting sex-typed toy selection. *Journal of Applied Developmental Psychology* 14 (3), pp. 385–406.

Fonseca, C. 2002. The politics of adoption: child rights in the Brazilian setting. *Law and Policy* 24 (3), pp. 199–227.

2005. Patterns of shared parenthood among the Brazilian poor. In: T. A. Volkman, *Cultures of Transnational Adoption*. Durham and London: Duke University Press, pp. 142–61.

Fottrell, D. (ed.). 2000. *Revisiting Children's Rights: 10 Years of the UN Convention on the Rights of the Child*. The Hague and Boston, MA: Kluwer Law International.

Foucault, M. 1979. *Discipline and Punish: The Birth of the Prison*. Translated by A. Sheridan. New York: Vintage Books.

1988. Sexuality, morality and the law. In: L. D. Kritzman (ed.), *Politics,*

Philosophy, Culture: Interviews and Other Writings. Translated by A. Sheridan. New York: Routledge, pp. 271–85.

1990 [1978]. *The History of Sexuality* I. *The Will to Knowledge.* Translated by R. Hurley. London: Penguin.

1991. Governmentality. In: G. Burchell et al. (eds.), *The Foucault Effect: Studies in Governmentality.* Chicago: University of Chicago Press, pp. 87–104.

Fox, L. K. 1967. *East African Childhood: Three Versions.* Nairobi and New York: Oxford University Press.

Freeman, D. 1991. *A City of Farmers: Informal Urban Agriculture in the Open Spaces of Nairobi, Kenya.* Montreal and London: McGill-Queen's University Press.

Freeman, M. 1997. *The Moral Status of Children: Essays on the Rights of the Child.* The Hague: Martinus Nijhoff Publishers.

Freyre, G. 1963 [1933]. *The Masters and the Slaves: A Study of the Formation of Brazilian Society.* Translated by S. Putnam. London: Weidenfeld & Nicholson.

Fuchs, R. G. 1984. *Abandoned Children: Foundlings and Child Welfare in Nineteenth-Century France.* Albany: State University of New York Press.

Fukuyama, F. 1992. *The End of History and the Last Man.* New York: Free Press.

Furley, O. 1995. Child soldiers in Africa. In: O. Furley (ed.), *Conflict in Africa.* London: I. B. Tauris, pp. 28–45.

Galindo-Rueda, F. and A. Vignoles. 2005. The declining relative importance of ability in predicting educational attainment. *Journal of Human Resources* 40 (2), pp. 335–53.

Galperin, A. 2002. Child victims of war in Africa. In: A. de Waal and N. Argenti (eds.), *Young Africa: Realising the Rights of Children and Youth.* Asmara: Africa World Press, pp. 105–22.

Gathii, J. T. 2003. The structural power of strong pharmaceutical patent protection in U.S. foreign policy. *Journal of Gender, Race and Justice* 7 (2), pp. 267–301.

Geffray, C. 1990. *La cause des armes au Mozambique: anthropologie d'une guerre civile.* Paris: Éditions Karthala.

Gold, T. B. 1991. Youth and the state. *The China Quarterly* 127, pp. 594–612.

Goldberg, D. T. 2001. *The Racial State.* Malden, MA: Blackwell.

Goodman, M. E. 1952. *Race Awareness in Young Children.* Cambridge, MA: Addison-Wesley Press.

Gordon, C. 1991. Governmental rationality: an introduction. In: G. Burchell et al. (eds.), *The Foucault Effect: Studies in Governmentality.* Chicago: University of Chicago Press, pp. 1–52.

Gottlieb, A. 2004. *The Afterlife is Where we Come from: The Culture of Infancy in West Africa.* Chicago: University of Chicago Press.

Goulding, M. 1999. The United Nations and conflict in Africa since the Cold War. *African Affairs* 98, pp. 155–66.

Green, A. 1997. *Education, Globalization and the Nation State*. Basingstoke: Macmillan.

Grier, B. C. 2006. *Invisible Hands: Child Labor and the State in Colonial Zimbabwe*. Portsmouth, NH: Heinemann.

Guarcello, L. et al. 2006. *Child Labour in the Latin American and Caribbean Region: A Gender Based Analysis* (Understanding Children's Work Project). Geneva: ILO. Available at: http://www.ucw-project.org/pdf/publications/gender_publication.pdf.

Guy, D. J. 2002. The child-saving movement in Brazil: ideology in the late nineteenth and early twentieth centuries. In: T. Hecht (ed.), *Minor Omissions: Children in Latin American History and Society*. Madison: The University of Wisconsin Press, pp. 139–64.

Hansen, K. T. 1990. Labor migration and urban child labor during the colonial period in Zambia. In: B. Fetter (ed.), *Demography from Scanty Evidence: Central Africa in the Colonial Period*. Boulder and London: Lynne Rienner, pp. 219–34.

Hanson, K. and A. Vandaele. 2003. Working children and international labour law: a critical analysis. *The International Journal of Children's Rights* 11, pp. 73–146.

Harris-Short, S. 2003. International human rights law: imperialist, inept and ineffective? Cultural relativism and the UN Convention on the Rights of the Child. *Human Rights Quarterly* 25 (1), pp. 130–80.

Hart, R. 1979. *Children's Experience of Place*. New York: Irvington.

1992. *Children's Participation: From Tokenism to Citizenship*. UNICEF Innocenti essays 4. Florence: UNICEF/International Child Development Centre.

Hawes, J. 1997. *Children between the Wars: American Childhood, 1920–1940*. New York: Twayne Publishers.

Hawes, J. and N. R. Hiner. 1985. *American Childhood: A Research Guide and Historical Handbook*. Westport, CT: Greenwood Publishing Group.

Hecht, T. 1998. *At Home in the Street: Street Children of Northeast Brazil*. Cambridge and New York: Cambridge University Press.

(ed.). 2002. *Minor Omissions: Children in Latin American History and Society*. Madison: University of Wisconsin Press.

Held, D. 2006. *Models of Democracy*. Cambridge: Polity Press.

Henderson, A. T. and N. Berla. 1994. *A New Generation of Evidence: The Family is Critical to Student Achievement*. Washington, DC: National Committee for Citizens in Education.

Hendrick, H. 1997. *Children, Childhood and English Society*. Cambridge: Cambridge University Press.

Hewitt, R. and K. Wells. n.d. *On the Margins: A Qualitative Study of White Camden Households at Risk of Exclusion from Education and Employment*. London: Centre for Urban and Community Research, and London Borough of Camden.

Heywood, C. 1988. *Childhood in Nineteenth-Century France: Work, Health and Education among the classes populaires*. Cambridge: Cambridge University Press.

2001. *A History of Childhood: Children and Childhood in the West from Medieval to Modern Times*. Cambridge: Polity Press.

Hibou, B. 1999. The social capital of the state as an agent of deception: or the ruses of economic intelligence. In: J. F. Bayart, S. Ellis and B. Hibou, *The Criminalization of the State in Africa*. Oxford: James Currey, pp. 69–113.

Hill, S. A. 2002. Teaching and doing gender in African American families. *Sex Roles* 47 (11–12), pp. 493–506.

Hindess, B. 2004. Neo-liberal citizenship. *Citizenship Studies* 6 (2), pp. 127–43.

Hochschild, A. 2002. Love and gold. In: B. Ehrenreich and A. Hochschild (eds.), *Global Woman: Nannies, Maids, and Sex Workers in the New Economy*. New York: Metropolitan/Owl Books, pp. 15–30.

Hoffman, D. 2003. Like beasts in the bush: synonyms of childhood and youth in Sierra Leone. *Postcolonial Studies* 6 (3), pp. 295–308.

2006. Disagreement: dissent politics and the war in Sierra Leone. *Africa Today* 52 (3), pp. 3–22.

Holland, P. 1992. *What is a Child? Popular Images of Childhood*. London: Virago Press Ltd.

2004a. Little Ali and other rescued children. In: D. Miller (ed.), *Tell me Lies: Propaganda and Media Distortion in the Attack on Iraq*. London: Pluto Press, pp. 185–94.

2004b. *Picturing Childhood: The Myth of the Child in Popular Imagery*. London: I. B. Tauris.

Holloway, S. and G. Valentine. 2000. Children's geographies and the new social studies of childhood. In: S. Holloway and G. Valentine (eds.), *Children's Geographies: Playing, Living, Learning*. London: Routledge, pp. 1–26.

Honwana, A. 2006. *Child Soldiers in Africa*. Philadelphia: University of Pennsylvania Press.

Hood-Williams, J. 1990. Patriarchy for children: on the stability of power relations in children's lives. In: L. Chisholm, P. Buchner, H.-H. Kruger and P. Brown (eds.), *Childhood, Youth, and Social Change: A Comparative Perspective*. London: Falmer, pp. 155–71.

Howman, A. and F. de Boeck (eds.). 2005. *Makers and Breakers: Children and Youth in Postcolonial Africa*. London: James Currey.

Hsiung, P.-C. 2005. *A Tender Voyage: Children and Childhood in Late Imperial China*. Stanford: Stanford University Press.

Human Rights Watch. 2000. *Fingers to the Bone: United States Failure to Protect Child Farmworkers*. New York: Human Rights Watch.

2003. 'We'll kill you if you cry': sexual violence in the Sierra Leone conflict. HRW report 15, 1 (A), January 2003. Available at: http://www.hrw.org/sites/default/files/reports/sierleon0103.pdf.

Hunter, I. 1994. *Rethinking the School*. St Leonards, Australia: Allen and Unwin.

1996. Assembling the school. In: A. Barry, T. Osborne and N. Rose (eds.), *Foucault and Political Reason*. London: UCL Press, pp. 143–66.

Huntington, S. 1993. The clash of civilizations? *Foreign Affairs* 72 (3), pp. 22–49.

Ickes, W. 1993. Traditional gender roles: do they make, and then break our relationships? *Journal of Social Issues* 49, pp. 71–85.

Iliffe, J. 1995. *Africans: The History of a Continent*. Cambridge: Cambridge University Press.

Inda, J. X. (ed.). 2005. *Anthropologies of Modernity: Foucault, Governmentality and Life Politics*. Malden, MA: Blackwell.

International Labour Organization (ILO). 2006. *The End of Child Labour: Within Reach*. Geneva: ILO. Available at: http://www.ilo.org/public/english/standards/relm/ilc/ilc95/pdf/rep-i-b.pdf.

Jackson, R. H. 1991. *Quasi-States: Sovereignty, International Relations and the Third World*. Cambridge: Cambridge University Press.

Jackson, S. 1982. *Childhood and Sexuality*. Oxford: Blackwell.

James, A. and A. James. 2004. *Constructing Childhood: Theory, Policy and Social Practice*. London: Macmillan.

James, A., C. Jenks and A. Prout. 1998. *Theorizing Childhood*. Cambridge: Polity Press.

Jenks, C. (ed.). 1982. *The Sociology of Childhood: Essential Readings*. Aldershot: Gregg Revivals.

1996. *Childhood*. New York: Routledge.

Johnson, K. 2005. Chaobao: the plight of Chinese adoptive parents in the era of the one-child policy. In: T. A. Volkman, *Cultures of Transnational Adoption*. Durham and London: Duke University Press, pp. 117–41.

Johnson, V. et al. (eds.). 1998. *Stepping Forward: Children and Young People's Experience in the Development Process*. London: Intermediate Technology Publications.

Jones, O. 2000. Melting geography: purity, disorder, childhood and space. In: S. Holloway and G. Valentine (eds.), *Children's Geographies: Playing, Living, Learning*. London: Routledge, pp. 29–47.

Jones, S. 1993. *Assaulting Childhood: Children's Experiences of Migrancy and Hostel Life in South Africa*. Johannesburg: Witwatersrand University Press.

Kagan, R. 2008. *The Return of History and the End of Dreams*. New York: Alfred Knopf/Random House.

Kaldor, M. 2001. *New and Old Wars: Organized Violence in a Global Era*. Stanford: Stanford University Press.

Kalyvas, S. N. 2001. 'New' and 'old' civil wars: a valid distinction? *World Politics* 54 (1), pp. 99–118.

Kandeh, J. 2005. The criminalization of the RUF insurgency in Sierra Leone.

In: C. J. Arnson and I. W. Zartman (eds.), *Rethinking the Economics of War*. Washington, DC: Woodrow Wilson Center Press, and Baltimore: Johns Hopkins University Press, pp. 84–106.

Kaplan, R. 1994. The coming anarchy. *The Atlantic Monthly* 273 (2), February 1994, pp. 44–76.

Katz, C. 2001a. Vagabond capitalism and the necessity of social reproduction. *Antipode* 33 (4), pp. 709–28.

2001b. The state goes home: local hypervigilance of children and the global retreat from social reproduction. *Social Justice* 28 (3), pp. 47–56.

2002. Stuck in place: children and the globalization of social reproduction. In: R. J. Johnston, P. J. Taylor and M. Watts (eds.), *Geographies of Global Change: Remapping the World*. Malden, MA: Blackwell, pp. 248–60.

2004. *Growing up Global: Economic Restructuring and Children's Everyday Lives*. Minneapolis, MN: University of Minnesota Press.

Katz, M. 1986. Child-saving. *History of Education Quarterly* 26 (3), pp. 413–24.

Katz, P. A. 1976. The acquisition of racial attitudes in children. In: P. A. Katz (ed.), *Towards the Elimination of Racism*. New York: Pergamon, pp. 125–53.

1987. Developmental and social processes in ethnic attitudes and self-identification. In: J. S. Phinney and M. J. Rotheram (eds.), *Children's Ethnic Socialization: Pluralism and Development*. Beverly Hills: Sage Publications in cooperation with the Society for Research in Child Development, pp. 92–100.

Keddie, N. 2003. *Modern Iran: Roots and Results of Revolution*. New Haven and London: Yale University Press.

Keen, D. 1998. The economic functions of civil wars. Adelphi paper 320. London: International Institute for Strategic Studies.

2000. Incentives and disincentives for violence. In: M. Berdal and D. M. Malone (eds.), *Greed and Grievance: Economic Agendas in Civil Wars*. Boulder, CO: Lynne Rienner, pp. 19–42.

Kett, J. F. 1977. *Rites of Passage: Adolescence in America 1790 to the Present*. New York: Basic Books.

Kilbride, P. L. et al. 2000. *Street Children in Kenya: Voices of Children in Search of a Childhood*. Westport, CT and London: Bergin and Garvey.

Kimmel, M. S. 2004. *The Gendered Society*. New York: Oxford University Press.

King, W. 2005. *African American Childhoods: Historical Perspectives from Slavery to Civil Rights*. New York: Palgrave Macmillan.

Klausen, S. M. 2004. *Race, Maternity, and the Politics of Birth Control in South Africa, 1910–39*. Basingstoke: Palgrave Macmillan.

Kleinman, A. and J. Kleinman. 1996. The appeal of experience; the dismay of images: cultural appropriations of suffering in our times. In: A. Kleinman, V. Das and M. Lock (eds.), *Social Suffering*. Berkeley: University of California Press, pp. 1–23.

Kluger, R. 2004. *Simple Justice: The History of Brown v. Board of Education and Black America's Struggle for Equality*. New York: Alfred A. Knopf.

Koven, S. 1997. Dr. Barnardo's 'artistic fictions': photography, sexuality, and the ragged child in Victorian London. *Radical History Review* 69, pp. 6–45.

Kress, G. and T. van Leeuwen. 1996. *Reading Images: The Grammar of Visual Design*. London: Routledge.

Kress, G. et al. 2005. *English in Urban Classrooms*. London and New York: Routledge.

Krosner, K. 2006. Women forced into sterilisation protest to UN. *British Medical Journal* 333 (7565), p. 410.

Kruger, D. 2007. Coffee production effects on child labor and schooling in rural Brazil. *Journal of Development Economics* 82 (2), pp. 448–63.

Kurlansky, M. 2005. *1968: The Year that Rocked the World*. London: Jonathan Cape.

Kuznesof, E. A. 2005. The house, the street, the global society: Latin American families and childhood in the twenty-first century. *Journal of Social History* 38 (4), pp. 859–72.

Kyei, T. E. 2001. *Our Days Dwindle: Memories of My Childhood Days in Asante*. Portsmouth, NH: Heinemann.

Laming, Lord. 2003. *The Victoria Climbie Inquiry: Report of an Inquiry by Lord Laming*. Norwich: HMSO. Available at: http://www.victoria-climbie-inquiry.org.uk/finreport/report.pdf.

Langohr, V. 2001. Educational 'subcontracting' and the spread of religious nationalism: Hindu and Muslim nationalist schools in colonial India. *Comparative Studies of South Asia, Africa, and the Middle East* 21 (1–2), pp. 42–9.

2005. Colonial education systems and the spread of local religious movements: the cases of British Egypt and Punjab. *Comparative Studies in Society and History* 47 (1), pp. 161–89.

Larner, W. and W. Walters (eds.). 2004. *Global Governmentality: Governing International Spaces*. London and New York: Routledge.

Lasch, C. 1977. *Haven in a Heartless World: The Family Besieged*. New York: Basic Books.

Last, M. 2000a. Children and the experience of violence: contrasting cultures of punishment in Northern Nigeria. *Africa* 70 (3), pp. 359–93.

2000b. Healing the social wounds of war. *Medicine, Conflict and Survival* 16 (4), pp. 370–82.

Leach, M. 2000. New shapes to shift: war, parks and the hunting person in modern West Africa. *Journal of the Royal Anthropological Institute* 6 (4), pp. 577–95.

Leaper, C., K. J. Anderson and P. Sanders. 1998. Moderators of gender effects on parents' talk to their children: A meta-analysis. *Developmental Psychology* 34 (1), pp. 3–27.

Lee, N. 2001. *Childhood and Society: Growing up in an Age of Uncertainty.* Buckingham: Open University Press.

Leeder, E. J. 2004. *The Family in Global Perspective: A Gendered Journey.* Thousand Oaks, CA and London: Sage Publications.

Lefebvre, H. 1991. *Critique of Everyday Life.* Translated by J. London. New York: Verso.

Lester, B. J. 1996. Is it too late for juvenile curfews: QUTB logic and the constitution. *Hofstra Law Review* 25, pp. 665–701.

Leung, J. C. B. 1994. Dismantling the 'Iron Rice Bowl': welfare reforms in the People's Republic of China. *Journal of Social Policy* 23 (3), pp. 341–61.

Levine, M. and A. Levine. 1992. *Helping Children: A Social History.* New York and Oxford: Oxford University Press.

Lewis, A. E. 2003. *Race in the Schoolyard: Negotiating the Color Line in Classrooms and Communities.* New Brunswick, NJ: Rutgers University Press.

Liebel, M. 2004. *A Will of Their Own: Cross Cultural Perspectives on Working Children.* London and New York: Zed Books.

Lugalla, J. and C. Kibassa. 2003. *Urban Life and Street Children's Health.* Münster and London: Lit.

Luiz de Moura, S. 2002. The social construction of street children: configuration and implications. *British Journal of Social Work* 32, pp. 353–67.

Lutz, C. A. and J. L. Collins. 1993. *Reading National Geographic.* Chicago: University of Chicago Press.

Lynch, K. 1997. *Growing up in Cities.* Cambridge, MA: MIT Press.

Lyon, C. 2007. Interrogating the concentration on the UNCRC instead of the ECHR in the development of children's rights in England? *Children and Society* 21 (2), pp. 147–53.

Macaulay, T. 1920. Minute by the Honourable T. B. Macaulay, dated the 2nd February 1835. Bureau of Education. Selections from Educational Records, Part (1781-1839). Edited by H. Sharp. Calcutta: Superintendent, Government Printing. Reprint Delhi: National Archives of India, 1965, pp. 107–17. Available at: http://www.columbia.edu/itc/mealac/pritchett/00generallinks/macaulay/txt_minute_education_1835.html, last accessed 27 June 2007.

Maccoby, E. E. and C. N. Jacklin. 1974. *The Psychology of Sex Differences.* Stanford: Stanford University Press.

MacFarquhar, R. and M. Schoenhals. 2006. *Mao's Last Revolution.* Cambridge, MA: Harvard University Press.

Machel, G. 2001. *The Impact of War on Children: A Review of Progress since the 1996 Report on the Impact of Armed Conflict on Children.* London: Hurst and Company.

Macleod, D. I. 1998. *The Age of the Child: Children in America, 1890–1920.* New York: Twayne Publishers.

Maitra, P. and R. Ray. 2002. The joint estimation of child participation in schooling and employment: comparative evidence from three continents. *Oxford Development Studies* 30 (1), pp. 41–62.

Manne, R. 2001. *In Denial: The Stolen Generations and the Right*. Melbourne, Victoria: Schwartz Publishing.

Mannheim, K. 1972 [1928]. The problem of generations. In: Karl Mannheim, *Essays on the Sociology of Knowledge*. London: Routledge and Kegan Paul, pp. 276–320.

Marks, M. 2001. *Young Warriors: Youth Politics, Identity and Violence in South Africa*. Johannesburg: Witwatersrand University Press.

Marquez, P. C. 1999. *The Street is My Home: Youth and Violence in Caracas*. Stanford: Stanford University Press.

Marshall, T. H. 1950. *Citizenship and Social Class and Other Essays*. Cambridge: Cambridge University Press.

Martin, K. 2005. William wants a doll. Can he have one? Feminists, child care advisors, and gender-neutral child rearing. *Gender & Society* 19 (4), pp. 456–79.

Marx, K. 1976 [1867]. *Capital: A Critique of Political Economy* i. Chapter 26: The secret of primitive accumulation. Translated by B. Fowkes. Harmondsworth: Penguin.

Matthews, H., M. Limb and M. Taylor. 2000. The street as thirdspace. In: S. Holloway and G. Valentine (eds.), *Children's Geographies: Playing, Living, Learning*. London: Routledge, pp. 63–79.

Mayall, B. 1994. *Children's Childhoods Observed and Experienced*. London: Falmer.

—— 2002. *Towards a Sociology for Childhood: Thinking from Children's Lives*. Maidenhead: Open University Press.

McDowell, L. 2000. Learning to serve? Employment aspirations and attitudes of young working class men in an era of labour market restructuring. *Gender, Place and Culture* 7 (4), pp. 389–416.

—— 2002. Transitions to work: masculine identities, youth inequality and labour market change. *Gender, Place and Culture* 9 (1), pp. 39–59.

McGrew, A. (ed.). 1997. *The Transformation of Democracy?* Cambridge: Polity Press.

McHale, S. et al. 2003. The family contexts of gender development in childhood and adolescence. *Social Development* 12 (1), pp. 125–48.

McKay, S. 2006. The inversion of girlhood: girl combatants during and after armed conflict. In: N. Boothby, A. Strang and M. Wessells (eds.), *A World Turned Upside Down: The Social Ecologies of Children in Armed Conflict*. Bloomfield, CT: Kumarian Press, pp. 89–109.

McKay, S. and D. Mazurana. 2004. *Where Are the Girls? Girls in Fighting Forces in Northern Uganda, Sierra Leone and Mozambique: Their Lives during and after War*. Montreal: International Centre for Human Rights and Democratic Development.

McRobbie, A. and J. Garber. 1976. Girls and subcultures. In: S. Hall and T. Jefferson (eds.), *Resistance through Rituals: Youth Subcultures in Postwar Britain*. London: Hutchinson, pp. 209–22.

Mears, D. P. et al. 2007. Public opinion and the foundation of the juvenile court. *Criminology* 45 (1), pp. 223–57.

Merrick, T. W. 2002. Population and poverty: new views on an old controversy. *International Family Planning Perspectives* 28 (1), pp. 41–6.

Metz, C. 1975. The imaginary signifier. *Screen* 16 (3), pp. 14–76.

Mintz, S. 1986. *Sweetness and Power: The Place of Sugar in Modern History*. New York and London: Penguin.

2004. *Huck's Raft: A History of American Childhood*. Cambridge, MA: Harvard University Press.

Mitchell, K., S. A. Marston and C. Katz. 2003. *Life's Work: Geographies of Social Reproduction*. Maldon, MA and Oxford: Blackwell. Originally published in *Antipode* 35 (3), pp. 415–41.

Mitchell, T. 1988. *Colonising Egypt*. Berkeley: University of California Press.

Moeller, S. D. 1999. *Compassion Fatigue: How the Media Sell Disease, Famine, War and Death*. New York and London: Routledge.

Monbiot, G. 2005. The victims of the tsunami pay the price of war on Iraq: US and British aid is dwarfed by the billions both spend on slaughter. *The Guardian*, 4 January 2005.

Morris, S. 2008. Police bring in evening curfew to keep town's under-16s off streets. *The Guardian*, 9 July 2008.

Moses, A. D. 2004. *Genocide and Settler Society: Frontier Violence and Stolen Indigenous Children in Australian History*. New York and Oxford: Berghahn Books.

Mulvey, L. 1975. Visual pleasure and narrative cinema. *Screen* 16 (3), pp. 6–18.

Murdoch, L. 2006. *Imagined Orphans: Poor Families, Child Welfare, and Contested Citizenship in London*. New Brunswick, NJ and London: Rutgers University Press.

Murphy, W. P. 1980. Secret knowledge as property and power in Kpelle society: elder versus youth. *Africa* 50 (2), pp. 193–207.

2003. Military patrimonialism and child soldier clientelism in the Liberian and Sierra Leonean civil wars. *African Studies Review* 46 (2), pp. 61–87.

Myers, W. 1989. Urban working children: a comparison of four surveys from South America. *International Labour Review* 128, pp. 321–35.

Nayak, A. 2003. Boyz to men: masculinities, schooling and labour transitions in de-industrial times. *Educational Review* 55 (2), pp. 147–59.

Newson, J. and E. Newson. 1968. *Four Years Old in an Urban Community*. London: Allen and Unwin.

Nieuwenhuys, O. 1994. *Children's Lifeworlds: Gender, Welfare and Labour in the Developing World*. London: Routledge.

1999. The paradox of the competent child and the global childhood agenda. In: R. Fardon et al. (eds.), *Modernity on a Shoestring*. Leiden and London: EIDOS, pp. 33–48.

Nolte, I. 2004. Identity and violence: the politics of youth in Ijebu-Remo, Nigeria. *Journal of Modern African Studies* 42 (1), pp. 61–89.

Nordstrom, C. 1997. *A Different Kind of War Story*. Philadelphia: University of Pennsylvania Press.

2007. *Global Outlaws: Crime, Money and Power in the Contemporary World*. Berkeley: University of California Press.

O'Neil, M. L. 2002. Youth curfews in the United States: the creation of public spheres for some young people. *Journal of Youth Studies* 5 (1), pp. 49–67.

Ortiz, A. T. and L. Briggs. 2003. The culture of poverty, crack babies, and welfare cheats: the making of the 'healthy white baby crisis'. *Social Text* 76, 21 (3), pp. 39–57.

Pascoe, P. 1996. Miscegenation law, court cases, and ideologies of 'race' in twentieth-century America. *The Journal of American History* 83 (1), pp. 44–69.

Pateman, C. 1987. Feminist critiques of the public/private dichotomy. In: A. Phillips (ed.), *Feminism and Equality*. Oxford: Blackwell, pp. 103–26.

Patterson, J. T. 2002. *Brown v. Board of Education: A Civil Rights Milestone and Its Troubled Legacy*. New York: Oxford University Press.

Penna, S. 2005. The Children Act 2004: child protection and social surveillance. *Journal of Social Welfare and Family Law* 27 (2), pp. 143–57.

Peters, K. and P. Richards. 1998. 'Why we fight': voices of youth combatants in Sierra Leone. *Africa* 68 (2), pp. 183–210.

Peterson, A. L. and K. A. Read. 2002. Victims, heroes, enemies: children in Central American wars. In: T. Hecht (ed.), *Minor Omissions: Children in Latin American History and Society*. Wisconsin: University of Wisconsin Press, pp. 6–18.

Platt, A. 1969. *The Child Savers: The Invention of Delinquency*. Chicago: University of Chicago Press.

Pollock, L. 1983. *Forgotten Children: Parent–Child Relations from 1500 to 1900*. Cambridge: Cambridge University Press.

Poncz, E. 2007. China's proposed International Adoption Law: the likely impact on single U.S. citizens seeking to adopt from China and the available alternatives. 48 *Harvard International Law Journal Online* 74. Available at: http://www.harvardilj.org/online/112?sn=0&PHPSESSID=a59875 bccbdabacc2bca07cbf0568315.

Prout, A. (ed.). 2000. *The Body, Childhood and Society*. Basingstoke: Macmillan.

Prout, A. and A. James. 1990. *Constructing and Reconstructing Childhood: Contemporary Issues in the Sociology of Childhood*. London: Falmer.

Pupavac, V. 2001. Misanthropy without borders: the international children's rights regime. *Disasters* 25 (2), pp. 95–112.

Quinn, O. W. 1954. The transmission of racial attitudes among white southerners. *Social Forces* 33, pp. 41–7.

Qvortrup, J. et al. (eds.). 1994. *Childhood Matters: Social Theory, Practice and Politics*. Aldershot: Avebury.

Rabwoni, O. 2002. Reflections on youth and militarism in contemporary Africa. In: A. de Waal and N. Argenti (eds.), *Young Africa: Realising the Rights of Children and Youth*. Asmara: Africa World Press, pp. 155–70.

Ramanathan, V. 2002. What does 'literate in English' mean? Divergent literacy practices for vernacular vs. English-medium students in India. *The Canadian Modern Language Review* 59 (1), pp. 125–51.

Reinier, J. S. 1996. *From Virtue to Character: American Childhood, 1775–1850*. New York: Twayne Publishers.

Reno, W. 1995. Reinvention of an African Patrimonial State: Charles Taylor's Liberia. *Third World Quarterly* 16, pp. 109–20.

    1998. *Warlord Politics and African States*. Boulder, CO: Lynne Rienner.

    2000. Shadow states and the political economy of civil wars. In: M. Berdal and D. M. Malone (eds.), *Greed and Grievance: Economic Agendas in Civil Wars*. Boulder, CO: Lynne Rienner, pp. 43–68.

Rheingold, H. L. and K. V. Cook. 1975. The contents of boys' and girls' rooms as an index of parents' behavior. *Child Development* 46, pp. 459–63.

Richards, P. 1996. *Fighting for the Rainforest: War, Youth and Resources in Sierra Leone*. London: James Currey.

Ritterhouse, J. 2006. *Growing up Jim Crow: How Black and White Southern Children Learned Race*. Chapel Hill: University of North Carolina Press.

Robson, E. et al. 2006. Young caregivers in the context of the HIV/AIDS pandemic in sub-Saharan Africa. *Population, Space and Place* 12 (2), pp. 93–111.

Rose, N. 1996. *Inventing Ourselves: Psychology, Power and Personhood*. Cambridge: Cambridge University Press.

    1999a. *Governing the Soul: The Shaping of the Private Self*. 2nd edn. London: Routledge.

    1999b. *Powers of Freedom*. Cambridge: Cambridge University Press.

Rosen, D. M. 2005. *Armies of the Young: Child Soldiers in War and Terrorism*. New Brunswick, NJ: Rutgers University Press.

Ruddick, S. 2003. The politics of aging: globalization and the restructuring of youth and childhood. *Antipode* 35 (2), pp. 334–63.

    2006. Keynote. Contested Bodies of Childhood and Youth conference, University of Durham, 17–18 July 2006.

Rueschemeyer, D. and P. B. Evans. 1996. The state and economic transformation: toward an analysis of the conditions underlying effective transformation. In: P. B. Evans, D. Rueschemeyer and T. Skocpol (eds.), *Bringing the State back in*. Cambridge: Cambridge University Press, pp. 44–77.

Saari, J. L. 1990. *Legacies of Childhood: Growing up Chinese in a Time of Crisis, 1890–1920*. Cambridge, MA: Harvard University Press.

Saito, N. and Y. Imai. 2004. In search of the public and the private: philosophy of education in post-war Japan. *Comparative Education* 40 (4), pp. 583–94.

Salazar Parreñas, R. 2005. *Children of Global Migration: Transnational Families and Gendered Woes*. Stanford: Stanford University Press.

Sallee, S. 2004. *The Whiteness of Child Labor Reform in the New South*. Athens, GA and London: The University of Georgia Press.

Saulle, M. R. and F. Kojanec. 1995. *The Rights of the Child: International Instruments*. New York: Transnational Publishers.

Schildkrout, E. 1981. The employment of children in Kano (Nigeria). In: G. Rogers and G. Standing (eds.). *Child Work, Poverty and Underdevelopment*. Geneva: ILO, pp. 81–112.

— 2002 [1978]. Age and gender in Hausa society: socio-economic roles of children in urban Kano. Reprinted in *Childhood* 9 (3), pp. 344–68.

Schoen, J. 1997. Fighting for child health: race, birth control, and the state in the Jim Crow South. *Social Politics* 4 (1), pp. 90–113.

Schultz, T. W. 1971. *Investment in Human Capital: The Role of Education and of Research*. New York: Free Press, and London: Collier-Macmillan.

Seiter, E. 1995. *Sold Separately: Children and Parents in Consumer Culture*. New Brunswick, NJ: Rutgers University Press.

Sesay, A. 2003. *Civil Wars, Child Soldiers and Post Conflict Peace Building in West Africa*. Ibadan, Nigeria: College Press & Publishers.

Shaw, M. 1997. Globalization and post-military democracy. In: A. McGrew (ed.), *The Transformation of Democracy?* Cambridge: Polity Press, pp. 26–48.

Shephard, M. 2008a. This week, a 16-year-old boy was seen crying for his mother under interrogation in Guantanamo. How did he get there? *The Guardian*, 19 July 2008.

— 2008b. *Guantanamo's Child: The Untold Story of Omar Khadr*. Mississauga, Ontario: Wiley.

Shepler, S. 2002. Les filles-soldats: trajectories d'aprés guerre en Sierra Leone. *Politique Africaine* 88, pp. 49–62.

— 2005a. Conflicted childhoods: fighting over child soldiers in Sierra Leone. Unpublished Ph.D. thesis, University of California.

— 2005b. Globalizing child soldiers in Sierra Leone. In: S. Maria and E. Soep (eds.), *Youthscapes: The Popular, the National, the Global*. Philadelphia: University of Pennsylvania Press, pp. 119–33.

— 2005c. The rites of the child: global discourses of youth and reintegrating child soldiers in Sierra Leone. *Journal of Human Rights* 4 (2), pp. 197–211.

Sheppard, A. 2000. Child soldiers: is the optional protocol evidence of a 'straight-18' consensus? *The International Journal of Children's Rights* 8, pp. 37–70.

Singer, P. 2006. *Children at War*. Berkeley: University of California Press.

Smillie, I., L. Gberie and R. Hazelton. 2000. *The Heart of the Matter: Sierra Leone, Diamonds and Human Security*. Ottawa: Partnership Africa Canada.

Sondhi-Garg, P. 2004. *Street Children: Lives of Valor and Vulnerability*. New Delhi: Reference Press.

Sontag, S. 2003. *Regarding the Pain of Others*. New York: Farrar, Straus & Giroux.

Srivastava, S. 1998. *Constructing Post-Colonial India: National Character and the Doon School*. London and New York: Routledge.

Stallybrass, P. and A. White. 1986. *The Politics and Poetics of Transgression*. Ithaca, NY: Cornell University Press.

Starrett, G. 1998. *Putting Islam to Work: Education, Politics and Religious Transformation in Egypt*. Berkeley: University of California Press.

Stearns, P. N. 2006. *Childhood in World History*. New York: Routledge.

Stephens, S. 1995. Introduction. In: S. Stephens (ed.), *Children and the Politics of Culture*. Princeton: Princeton University Press.

Stoler, A. 1995. *Race and the Education of Desire: Foucault's History of Sexuality, and the Colonial Order of Things*. Durham, NC and London: Duke University Press.

Straker, G. 1992. *Faces in the Revolution: The Psychological Effects of Violence on Township Youth in South Africa*. Cape Town: David Philip.

Strange, S. 1986. *Casino Capitalism*. Oxford: Blackwell.

Street, B. V. 1995. *Social Literacies: Critical Approaches to Literacy in Development, Ethnography, and Education*. London and New York: Longman.

(ed.). 2001. *Literacy and Development: Ethnographic Perspectives*. London and New York: Routledge.

Swai, B. 1979. The labor shortage in the 1930s: Kilimanjaro and the subsequent employment of child labor. *Utafiti* 4, pp. 111–32.

Sweetland, S. R. 1996. Human capital theory: foundations of a field of inquiry. *Review of Educational Research* 66 (3), pp. 341–59.

Tajfel, H. 1981. *Human Groups and Social Categories*. Cambridge: Cambridge University Press.

The Guardian. 2004. Special report: Indian Ocean Tsunami disaster. Available at: www.guardian.co.uk/gall/0,8542,1380089,00.html and www.guardian.co.uk/gall/0,8542,1379875,00.html, last accessed 27 March 2007.

Thobejane, M. 2001. Foreword. In: M. Marks, *Young Warriors: Youth Politics, Identity and Violence in South Africa*. Johannesburg: Witwatersrand University Press.

Thomson, D. and I. White. 1993. Kinder der Traumzeit: es war einmal in Australien. In: M. van de Loo and M. Reinhart (eds.), *Kinder: Ethnologische Forschungen in fünf Kontinenten*. Munich: Trickster, pp. 366–81.

Thorne, B. 1993. *Gender Play: Girls and Boys in School*. New Brunswick, NJ: Rutgers University Press.

Tizard, B. and A. Phoenix. 1993. *Black, White or Mixed Race: Race and Racism in the Lives of Young People of Mixed Parentage*. London: Routledge.

Tripp, A. M. 1994. Deindustrialization and the growth of women's economic associations and networks in urban Tanzania. In: S. Rowbotham and S. Mitter (eds.), *Dignity and Daily Bread: New Forms of Economic Organization Among Poor Women in the Third World and the First*. London: Routledge, pp. 142–60.

Troyna, B. and R. Hatcher. 1992. *Racism in Children's Lives: A Study of Mainly White Primary Schools*. London: Routledge.

Turner, V. 1967. *The Forest of Symbols: Aspects of Ndembu Ritual*. Ithaca, NY: Cornell University Press.

Twine, F. W. 1996. Brown-skinned white girls: class, culture and the construction of white identity in suburban communities. *Gender, Place & Culture: A Journal of Feminist Geography* 3 (2), pp. 205–25.

2004. A white side of black Britain: the concept of racial literacy. *Ethnic & Racial Studies* 27 (6), pp. 878–907.

Uhlmann, A. J. 2006. *Family, Gender and Kinship in Australia: The Social and Cultural Logic of Practice and Subjectivity*. Aldershot and Burlington, VT: Ashgate.

UNAIDS. 2006. *2006 Report on the Global AIDS Epidemic*. Geneva, Switzerland: UNAIDS.

UNFPA. 2007. *State of the World's Population: Unleashing the Potential for Urban Growth*. Available at: http://www.unfpa.org/swp/2007/english/introduction.html.

UN-Habitat. 2006. *State of the World's Cities 2006/7: The Millennium Development Goals and Urban Sustainability*. London: Earthscan.

UNICEF. 1998. Intercountry adoption. *Innocenti Digest* 4. Available at: http://www.unicef-irc.org/publications/pdf/digest4e.pdf.

2006. *Excluded and Invisible Children*. State of the World Children's report.

Valentine, G. 2004. *Public Space and the Culture of Childhood*. Aldershot: Ashgate.

Van Ausdale, D. and J. Feagin. 2001. *The First R: How Children Learn Race and Racism*. Lanham, MD: Rowman & Littlefield Publishers.

Van Bueren, G. 1998. *International Law on the Rights of the Child*. The Hague: Kluwer Law International.

van Krieken, R. 1999. The 'stolen generations' and cultural genocide: the forced removal of Australian indigenous children from their families and its implications for the sociology of childhood. *Childhood* 6 (3), pp. 297–331.

Vann, R. T. 1982. The youth of centuries of childhood. *History and Theory* 21 (2), pp. 279–97.

Varzi, R. 2006. *Warring Souls: Youth, Media, and Martyrdom in Post-Revolution Iran*. Durham and London: Duke University Press.

Vines, A. 1991. *Renamo Terrorism in Mozambique*. Oxford: James Currey.
Viswanathan, G. 1990. *Masks of Conquest: Literary Studies and British Rule in India*. London: Faber.
Volkman, T. A. 2005. Introduction: new geographies of kinship. In: T. A. Volkman (ed.), *Cultures of Transnational Adoption*. Durham and London: Duke University Press, pp. 1–22.
Voutira, E. and A. Brouskou. 2000. 'Borrowed children' in the Greek Civil War. In: C. Panter-Brick and M. Smith (eds.), *Abandoned Children*. Cambridge: Cambridge University Press, pp. 92–110.
Waksler, F. (ed.). 1991. *Studying the Social Worlds of Children: Sociological Readings*. London: Falmer.
Ward, C. 1978. *The Child in the City*. New York: Pantheon Books.
Wee, V. 1995. Population policy in Singapore. In: S. Stephens (ed.). *Children and the Politics of Culture*. Princeton: Princeton University Press, pp. 184–217.
Weili, Ye with Ma Xiaodong. 2005. *Growing up in the People's Republic*. Basingstoke: Palgrave Macmillan.
Wells, K. 1999. International and domestic sources of state stability and regime collapse: merchant capital in Ethiopia, 1974–1995. Unpublished PhD thesis, London School of Economics.
——— 2005. Strange practices: children's discourses on transgressive unknowns in urban public space. *Childhood* 12 (4), pp. 495–506.
——— 2007. Narratives of liberation and narratives of innocent suffering: the rhetorical uses of images of Iraqi children in the British press. *Journal of Visual Communication* 6 (1), pp. 55–71.
——— 2008a. Giving to receive: gifts, donations and international child sponsorship. Unpublished paper presented to the International Childhood and Youth Research Network Child and Youth Research in the 21st Century: a critical appraisal conference, 28–29 May, Nicosia, Cyprus.
——— 2008b. Diversity without difference: modelling 'the real' in the social aesthetic of a London multicultural school. *Visual Studies* (22) 3, pp. 270–82.
Wen, Chihua. 1995. *The Red Mirror: Children of China's Cultural Revolution*. Boulder, CO: Westview Press.
Werner, E. W. 1998. *Reluctant Witnesses: Children's Voices from the Civil War Era*. Boulder, CO and Oxford: Westview Press.
West, C. and D. H. Zimmerman. 1987. Doing gender. *Gender and Society* 1 (2), pp. 125–51.
West, H. 2000. Girls with guns: narrating the experience of war of FRELIMO's 'Female Detachment'. *Anthropological Quarterly* 73 (4), pp. 180–94.
White, L. and D. Brinkerhoff. 1981. The sexual division of labor: evidence from childhood. *Social Forces* 60 (1), pp. 170–81.
White, O. 1999. *Children of the French Empire: Miscegenation and Colonial Society in French West Africa 1895–1960*. Oxford: Clarendon Press.

Willis, P. 1977. *Learning to Labour: How Working Class Kids Get Working Class Jobs.* Farnborough: Saxon House.

Woodhead, M. 1999. Reconstructing developmental psychology, some first steps. *Children and Society* 13 (1), pp. 3–19.

Wyness, M., L. Harrison and I. Buchanan. 2004. Childhood, politics and ambiguity: towards an agenda for children's political inclusion. *Sociology* 38 (1), pp. 81–99.

Zack-Williams, A. B. 1995. *Tributors, Supporters and Merchant Capital: Mining and Underdevelopment in Sierra Leone.* Aldershot: Avebury.

2001. Child soldiers in the civil war in Sierra Leone. *Review of African Political Economy* 28 (87), pp. 73–82.

Zelitzer, V. A. 1985. *Pricing the Priceless Child: The Changing Social Value of Children.* New York: Basic Books.

Index